Penguin Books
A SPY'S REVENGE

Richard Hall was born in Melbourne in 1938. Educated in Sydney, he worked as a journalist in newspapers, radio and magazines. In 1968 he joined the staff of Gough Whitlam, leader of the Opposition, and stayed through his ascent to Prime Minister in 1972.

Since leaving politics in 1973, Hall has worked as an author and freelance journalist and broadcaster. *The Secret State* (1978) was the first critical historical treatment of the Australian Security and Intelligence Organisation. Other published works include history, biography and crime. His most recent book, *Disorganised Crime* (1986) is a critical study which among other topics deals with some of the abuses and myths of police intelligence.

Hall is currently working on a study of Russian espionage in Australia in the 1940s.

Hall covered the Wright trial for the *Guardian, Time Australia* and Irish Radio.

Annitzl

Ma.G.83

A SPY'S REVENGE

RICHARD V. HALL

Penguin Books

Penguin Books Ltd,
Harmondsworth, Middlesex, England
Viking Penguin Inc.,
40 West 23rd Street, New York, NY 10010, USA
Penguin Books Australia Ltd,
487 Maroondah Highway, PO Box 257
Ringwood, Victoria, 3134, Australia
Penguin Books Canada Ltd,
2801 John Street, Markham, Ontario, Canada L3R 1B4
Penguin Books (NZ) Limited,
182–190 Wairau Road, Auckland 10, New Zealand

First published by Penguin Books Australia 1987
Reprinted 1987
Published in Penguin Books in Great Britain 1987

Copyright © Richard V. Hall, 1987

All Rights Reserved. Without limiting the rights under copyright reserved
above, no part of this publication may be reproduced, stored in or introduced
into a retrieval system, or transmitted, in any form or by any means
(electronic, mechanical, photocopying, recording or otherwise), without
the prior written permission of both the copyright owner and the above
publisher of this book.

Typeset in Clearface Regular by Leader Composition Pty Ltd
Made and printed in Great Britain by Richard Clay Ltd, Bungay, Suffolk

CIP

Hall, Richard, 1937–
A spy's revenge.

ISBN 0 14 010 387 2

1. Wright, Peter, 1916–   . 2. Spies – Great
Britain. 3. Secret service – Great Britain. 4
Intelligence service – Great Britain. 5. Espionage,
British. I. Title.

327.1′2′0941

Contents

Tory's appeal to close
chapter on treacheries

Continued from page one

Sir Robert said that the Prime Minister decided not to make my statement.

Mr Turnbull showed the Judge, Mr Justice Powell, a large pile of books, newspaper articles, transcripts of television programmes, and reports by the S...

.etting the cat
out of the bag

of the most interesting figures to emerge the British spy trial ustralia is the stylish yer representing MI5 alcolm Turnbull, 32, is the handsome rk-haired solicitor who attempting—to the astration of the British overnment—to prevent ban on a book by Mr right which contends at a former Secret service boss, Sir Roger Hollis, was a Russian spy.

Mr Turnbull is seen each night fussing around his client on the television news, is well known to Fleet Street.

During his period as a Rhodes scholar at Oxford University, the ambitious young Turnbull wrote for a national paper in our parish.

So what kind of chap is 7, this promising young the Aussie who is now making a fool of our mast '45 'casts after Mrs through the book case' He criticised the Gov ng, the Cab. Wal

SCOURGE...Turni senior Civil Servant, Robert Armstrong, figure who is attemi to protect our Govern ment's interests.

We can disclose that Turnbull is known among his friends to have explosive tempe nicknamed by "The Stranger

"Why is he asked.

"He once writes girlfriend's secrets Sydney o rely on la ... xts actors.

Mr Justice Bow for he Australian decline in a mor

Sir Robert as someone who might be called a double ill insider.

At the end of Sir Robert's testimony in open court—he will be questioned in secret t session t the rema issue wh

Civil servants
backed by
rmstrong over
bby 'abuse'

Carvel,
Correspondent

binet secretary, Si mstrong

last raised. It was not in a personal "

unattributable given to lobby esting that Mr was unfit to be

wright raised to be p

Mr S thanking Sir Robert confirmation that the did in fact take place.

"I must confess thou I was saddened to receiv mation of the ro ants find

MI5 trial delay
rejected

 jev all official hat it was ction against the terial which ncerned. ly in the book The charge MI5 officials ng to p y of con cher was today Villiams iii Wales hursday when he tter said to hav velations to Mr Wright the to last Pincher, the Jo ... cted in box for case. therks, with Sir as writt williams d

candidate taken no

PM silent
after
spy trial
hostility

Channel 4 dramatises tr.

A DRAMATISATION of the Sydney trial is to be screened on Channel 4 tomorrow night. writes Peter Eiddick. Unlike the nightly accounts of last year's Ponting trial, which for Channel 4's Sydney o rely on artists' sketches and the reading of ar transcripts, Court Report ist actors.

played by the aur, and Sir emselves. level of persona. That is a confirmation of part of a sad decline ir integrity and moral prac of the civil service." Sedgemore said that Sir

Robert Armstrong by Phili played Lloyd George in the B Robertson, who plays an MI5 latest James Bond movie, an Turnbull, the defence counsel.

The programme is being rec London reproduction of the Sy room this week, using offici The final submissions will be tomorrow.

MI5 Mr Pinche approached, Sir "I wish it had been

The question why iction was taken an afidavit was couched it was was a legal Sir Michael.

Sir Robert's apolo

leaked documents Guardian about the Government intended to publicity surroundin arrival of oruico missile

"The Government's was consistent but the is not in practice the every case," Sir Robert It was up to the neral to take a deci davit which rticular

Government move to halt
spy book meets setback

Continued from page one

ing to use the court to change the basis on which the trial it self—before the New South Wales Supreme Court—should be conducted.

They did so after Mr Simo in what he described as 'fallback position,' said 'Government would no longer argue that information in cluded in the Wright book but already made public elsewhere would be damaging.

The government he said, now argued that only those al

nce agencies. Mr Turnbull since 1978 the CIA's view committee manuscripts of

Double standard
over spy books

by Heine publisher, and the CIA did to its former em same principles to this the US would think ployees, the Wright book. Sir Robert any the less of MI5. Sir Robert right to express view on the replied: "I can't say

The intelligent way to control MI

more power- often a reduction in – the activ- ties of the security services. But, they have always

The Maxwell Fyfe rules have survived to this day because the essentials of what made sense in 1952 have remained sensible. could deny that

security agencies h more important.

Last year Mrs onstrated the need management of persuaded Sir A Director

Peter Wright
v.
The Rest 1

Peter Wright, the old boffin, crossing Queens Square, outside the Supreme Court in Sydney.
Photo: Colin Townsend

The old man is crossing the square, walking slowly, slightly hunched, his eyes fixed on the distance, a gaggle of TV cameramen, sound operators and reporters dancing attendance. On the steps of the court, the building behind him, pedestrians stop to watch. The old man is wearing a dark suit, a very conservative cut of the kind rarely seen these days. Firmly planted on his head is a big khaki felt wide-brimmed hat, which he has told people is a bushman's hat. It isn't. The title is a new-fangled ad-man's creation. People who work on country properties call themselves stockmen. Also, no stockman would have to keep the hat on, a leather thong of the kind worn by Mexican cowboys in the old westerns. It would be a breach of form comparable to wearing tennis shorts on a horse.

There is, to the observer watching the cavalcade progressing across Queen's Square, as the space is called, something rather stagey about it. There is quite a bit of the ham in Peter Wright, the old man, who has left his modest home to sally out against the forces of the British Establishment, and of course, at another remove, the Russian intelligence service. Sometimes it is possible to believe that the Establishment is the main target. Wright has a way of bringing a tone of emphatic contempt to the way he pronounces the word.

He reaches the other side of the square and leaning slightly on his brass-handled stick, the head of which contains a phial for whisky,

Peter Wright carefully descends the stairs into a pedestrian subway. His wife, Lois, is at his side, her hair in braids, neatly dressed, supporting him as she has done loyally all their married life. Wright had come to Court 8D, in the building behind, where he and his publisher are locked in the legal struggle with the UK government. He has written a book, *Spycatcher*, about some, not all, of his twenty years in MI5, Britain's Security Service. It is more than a memoir, it is a pulpit for his analyses, theories, on the Russian threat to the West, the articulation of the beliefs of a persevering group within Britain's MI5 and MI6. The UK government seeks to block the publication in Australia and claims that the book will breach the confidentiality owed by Wright to his former employer. Their case has nothing to do with an oath, although again and again this myth was published throughout the trial. As it happens, Wright swore no oath of secrecy, no one did in the Service. The test will be the application of the legal doctrine of confidentiality to Wright's position, but the interpretation of this concept is far from simple.

How Mr Justice Powell of the Supreme Court of New South Wales, who is presiding, will interpret confidentiality is only part of the question. The Judge will have to deal with the propositions of the defence that even if the UK government establishes confidentiality, there are a whole cluster of countervailing arguments: that the material is in the public domain anyhow, that it is in the public interest, that it should be published, and that the inconsistency of the UK government on the handling of such books undermines its case.

How Peter Wright, the patriot's patriot, came to the confrontation is a long story with a curious and very large cast of characters: spies, scientists, defectors (both Soviet and British), prime ministers, journalists, authors, publishers, lawyers, judges, civil servants, a lord, TV producers and a number of dead men.

Wright's early life was conventional enough, born in 1916, the son of Maurice Wright, an early pioneer with the Marconi company, a firm founded upon the brilliance of Guglielmo Marconi before World War One and which attained a dominant position in England and much of the world between the wars. Its founder was able to combine being a senator in Rome, nominated by Mussolini, with a thriving business supplying the British Admiralty.

His father was able to send Peter first to the local grammar school at Chelmsford, near the Marconi factory, and later to Bishop's Stortford, a minor public school in Essex, north of London. Bishop's Stortford College 'was founded in 1868, chiefly by non-conformists in the East of England and was at that time intended mainly for the education of non-conformists. It was reconstituted in 1904 and now educates members of all Protestant denominations, Anglican and others. It is administered by the governors of the Incorporated Bishop's Stortford College Association, the governing council consisting of fifteen members, several of whom are old Stortfordians.' The continuity of the school's view of itself is demonstrated by the fact that that description from the *Public Schools Directory* of Wright's time has altered only to include 'members of all Christian denominations' and to decrease the number of governors by one. The school lacks the cachet of the more ancient public schools or the social status of the more gilded. Its claim to being remembered by other public school boys is swimming: every year, then and now, Bishop's Stortford produced enough good swimmers to be in the top three or four of the public schools competition. In Wright's time, as now, it was laid down that every boy must be able to swim. In the early 1930s school fees were 120 pounds for the year. The school's academic record was steady. Interestingly enough, one of the old boys is Sir Dick Goldsmith White, who was the head of MI5 when Wright joined and later the head of MI6, the only man to have held both offices. The only other prominent old boy mentioned in the general histories was Edward Crankshaw, an historian who specialised in Central European and Russian history.

Wright's immediate choice on leaving school was not the academy nor, at first, science. He worked on a farm in Scotland and still has big, farmer's hands. In 1937 he enrolled in the School of Rural Economy at Oxford. The school was attached to St Peter's Hall, as it then was, and had a bias to the practical. Its student numbers were small, about twenty to thirty in each year of the three year course. The students had little to do with the more visible side of Oxford; indeed, talking to a range of Oxford men from the thirties, it is common to find surprise that such a school existed. Wright left in 1940, without taking a degree, and joined the Admiralty Research Station at Teddington, the principal Royal Navy scientific

5

laboratory.

His first real career, that of a boffin, had begun. This word 'boffin' is vital to understanding the personality of Peter Wright, the framework within which he thinks, and even the sources of his dislike of the Establishment. 'Boffin' has almost passed from usage now, gone like other World War Two slang words like 'wacko' and 'gremlin'. It seems to have originated in RAF slang and applied to a small group of scientists working, before the war, on the very considerable innovation of radar. By 1945 it had widened, according to *The Times*, to include backroom scientists in general. It first turns up in a novel in 1948 in Neville Shute's *No Highway*. A boffin is by definition the backroom boy who gets things done while big people fuss about out front. Being a British scientist, he was used to doing things with pretty inadequate laboratory equipment. Boffins mightn't have won the war by themselves, but remember that in the Battle of Britain, without radar, the fighter pilots might well have lost. The true boffin has to be a bit of a rebel, his bright ideas are often not given the recognition they deserve. Although perhaps they won't admit it, they can be pretty savage in-fighters: the history of British scientific innovation in World War Two is a record of bitter committee meetings.

The quintessential book on the boffin (although it doesn't mention the word) is *The Small Back Room* by Nigel Balchin, published during the war, 1943. The hero is a brilliant scientist working in a small irregular organisation on war research, under a very clever, if doddering, professor. Doing the job is what counts, not degrees. The organisation's expert on fuses is an army corporal who has been co-opted and works equally with the scientists. Outside, the organisation is threatened by jealous scientific bureaucrats; it becomes clear that the worst enemies are fellow scientists. The politicians, as seen through the off-stage presence of the cabinet minister in charge, are a bit foolish, the minister can't understand what is really happening in research, so he is easily bamboozled. In the end the bad scientists win. *The Small Back Room* was immensely popular. John Betjeman described Balchin as 'one of our dozen readable living writers of genius.' The boffin-type hero – touchy, proud, without any flash university degrees and a doer rather than a talker, has continued in English popular fiction.

Hammond Innes had the same kind of hero in the late forties and fifties; Neville Shute's engineers are of the same kind; in the sixties Desmond Bagley carried on the tradition of adventurous Englishmen overseas. Today Dick Francis in his racing thrillers with the intelligent, well-bred steeple jockey, weary of the big nouveau riche owners and the stupidity of the Jockey Club stewards continues the breed. All of them are prepared to be quite savage about the people at the top, as bitter about the Establishment as any leftie. They don't like the Old School Tie, because they know it's been used to do down their kind of people, even if they did go to a good grammar school or minor public school. They also worry about money – but not in a greedy, ostentatious way or in the grasping, nasty trade-unionists' style, but they worry about it. They want their fair share, what is due to them.

When Wright says, as he does with a deprecatory grin, 'I'm just a boffin,' he's affirming that outsider role, what can you expect of the powers-that-be? they won't understand. When, in 1940 the young Wright walked out before taking his degree and started work at Teddington, he became a protege of Frederick Brundrett, who had been with the scientific side of the Admiralty since 1919: it was Brundrett who later introduced him to MI5.

Wright's main work was with magnetic mines. One of the triumphs of the group he worked with was to devise the magnetic mines which in 1943 when laid by midget submarines, crippled the German battleship *Tirpitz* in a Norwegian fjord. They also worked on anti-magnetic mine measures at Dunkirk.

He remained a temporary civil servant throughout those years and stayed on in the end. In 1946 Wright took part in a competitive exam for a permanent place (as he recalled in court forty years later, he came top with 290 out of 300) and then was given a post as Principal Scientific Officer. Wright is always very precise about titles, as he is about money. Interestingly enough, the man who would later turn his skill against trade unionists was a union representative and indeed chaired the Admiralty Research Laboratory branch of his union. Wright's career seemed assured, no thought of return to the School of Rural Economy. The line stretched on through Chief Scientific Officer, perhaps even Chief of the Royal Naval Scientific Service, a knighthood (Brundrett was to get one in 1950), honoured

***Years later Wright was to recall that 'Brundrett told me that
he had told Sillitoe that he did not need an eminent scientist
with a FRS to assist the Service with scientific matters. He
said you need a young man with a good war who is a problem solver, as opposed to an analytical theorist.'***

retirement with a good pension, a cottage in the country and
possibly even a few directorships. Instead he would end up with a
pension of 600 pounds a month, living in a ricketty cottage in far
distant Tasmania and facing absolute ruin if he were to lose a very
expensive case against his old employers, the UK government.

It was his patron, Sir Frederick, who diverted Wright's path and,
paradoxically it was to be the first outside head of MI5 who began
using the outsider Wright. Sir Percy Sillitoe was a policeman put in
to head the Service in 1946 by the Labour Prime Minister, Clement
Attlee who, remembering MI5's historic dislike of Labour, wanted
his own man in there. Sillitoe now sought new advice in the scientific
area. Certainly no bleeding heart liberal, Sillitoe nevertheless
became very bitter about the way he was treated as an outsider by
the old line MI5 officers. In 1950 he had asked Brundrett to
establish a committee to advise on scientific matters and the Royal
Navy scientist recommended Wright as a member of the committee.
Years later Wright was to recall that 'Brundrett told me that he had
told Sillitoe that he did not need an eminent scientist with a FRS to
assist the Service with scientific matters. He said you need a young
man with a good war who is a problem solver, as opposed to an
analytical theorist.'

If you had wanted a neat definition of a boffin, you couldn't have
done better. The committee was given a brief to include MI6 as well.
As Wright recollected: 'The basic problem was that there was no
application or understanding of science other than what the Post
Office provided. There was also a pretty elementary chemical
laboratory for detecting secret writing and secret inks. It was almost
a schoolboy operation.' However, despite the establishment of the
committee, things were still done on the cheap. Wright continued
his full-time work with the RNSS, which had meanwhile seconded
him to a laboratory at his father's old firm, Marconi, to work on a
special radar system for detecting submarine snorkels. At night and
at weekends he worked on developing eavesdropping devices for

There was quite a bit about the difficulties over his pension rights in his statement to the court in Sydney and this has helped to fuel some crude misunderstanding of Wright's motives in the whole affair. On one argument he is simply motivated by a burning grievance about his pension. This is stupid.

MI5.

Then in 1952 the CIA gave him the opportunity to show his developing skill. At its newly-opened embassy building in Moscow, the US government had found a microphone hidden in the Great Seal of the United States attached to the wall in the ambassador's office. The device, code named SATYR, was taken to Washington. The scientists there were unable to explain how it worked. It was passed on to the UK and MI5 gave it to Wright who, after twelve weeks, cracked its secrets. It was a cavity microphone, not dependent upon batteries, and activated by microwave signals from outside. Having gained that prestigious victory, MI5 decided it needed more than a committee, it should get a full-time scientist. They couldn't pay enough to get a man from industry, and were not allowed to poach people from the rest of the civil service.

When Wright volunteered they unhappily described the rules, so Wright had to leave RNSS and spend some quarantine time at Marconi's in private industry before he could be re-employed by MI5. This meant that he had broken his civil service pension continuity. Wright told the court in Sydney: 'The MI5 people were adamant that these entitlements not be transferred over to MI5 where they said pensions were in line with those granted by the civil service but nonetheless entirely discretionary. They said I would not be disadvantaged however because they could make up any differences themselves. Subsequently the Service failed to honour the undertaking and my pension therefore reflects only my twenty-one years with the Service. It is therefore sixty per cent of what it ought to be.'

There was quite a bit about the difficulties over his pension rights in his statement to the court in Sydney and this has helped to fuel some crude misunderstanding of Wright's motives in the whole affair. On one argument he is simply motivated by a burning grievance about his pension. This is stupid. Wright's grievance is not about money for money's sake, he is like those boffins who want their fair share, nothing more, nothing less. A fair share, of course, defined in their terms. Living on a pension, the amount would rate as part of the fabric of his life as it would for any other pensioner, but to think that what he is doing is for money alone is to get it wrong.

Wright spent his cleansing year at Marconi and in July 1955 received a letter offering him a three-year period as Senior Principal Scientific Advisory Officer at 1700 pounds a year and the promise of a permanent appointment at the end of that time. By now the head of the Service was Dick Goldsmith White, that fellow old Stortfordian. Wright came into a Service whose leadership was deeply suspicious of MI6, the rival secret service where there was still a strong belief in the innocence of Kim Philby, who had been forced to resign from the Service because of his association with Guy Burgess, one of the two diplomats who had defected to the Soviets in 1951.

The original press tag for Guy Burgess and Donald Maclean when they went East in May 1951 was 'the missing diplomats'. That they had gone to Russia at a time when British troops were fighting Russian surrogates (the North Koreans and Chinese) was bad, but there was no public emphasis on any past espionage. The counter-intelligence services had no evidence that could have been used in court; no missing documents, observed meetings with Soviet contacts nor confessions of aquaintances. There was some evidence, it was claimed, but it was, in the Catch-22 way of the world of counter espionage, evidence which wasn't evidence because it couldn't be used in public. US codebreakers using old material, messages from the Soviet consulate in New York to Moscow, had extricated information on Soviet espionage in America in the mid-1940s. It was a very difficult operation.

Some recent writers give the impression that almost everything could be read, but this was not so. The decoders found scraps, and perhaps later another scrap, and then months later another one. Put together and helped by the Soviet habit of bureaucratically-pedantic descriptions of their agents, the scraps helped the decoders to some significant breakthroughs. Klaus Fuchs, a German refugee scientist, who was giving information on the atomic bomb, and members of the Rosenberg group, were all identified, even if not completely, as was a British diplomat stationed in Washington under the code name 'Homer', who proved to be Donald Maclean, then Second Secretary at the UK embassy.

Maclean, Guy Burgess, Kim Philby and a man called Anthony Blunt had all been at Cambridge together in the early thirties. They are now indissolubly linked by history as the Cambridge spies, sometimes the Cambridge comintern. They were, however, a diffuse group bound together ultimately only by a belief in Marxism, and from that a conviction that Soviet Russia represented the future, even if imperfect, and had to be defended.

Philby was something of a loner, Maclean was priggish. Only Blunt and Burgess were close personal friends. Burgess was the gregarious one of the group, while Blunt was in personality closer to Maclean. Acres of trees have been felled to provide paper for the analyses of those Cambridge converts, or traitors, as many in the media like to call them. The explanation is simple: they saw around them the failure of the old system and came to the new faith, Communism. They were told that the new faith and its geographical expression, the Soviet Union, was under threat directly from Fascists and indirectly from their cynical fathers and uncles, the English ruling class who wanted to use the Fascists and Nazis to destroy the Soviet Union. When they were asked to enlist in the defence of the Soviet homeland, they were not, in their sense, traitors. The word was an irrelevance. Of the four, three stayed loyal to their new faith. Burgess and Maclean died in Moscow and Philby still lives there, while Blunt, moved ambivalently sideways.

For someone who is living the life of a spy, discovery is always only a matter of time. Maclean, who went to the Foreign Office after leaving Cambridge served his cause, even at the cost of personal strain, for fifteen years. When he was warned that he was under threat of arrest he fled. From 1936 to 1951 was a long time for Moscow to have had an insight into the formation of UK foreign policy, but it was not information of an operational kind, like the valuable material another Russian spy, Richard Sorge, was able to send Moscow in 1941 (saying that Japan intended to strike south rather than into Siberia). Likewise, Maclean's access to nuclear material in Washington, because of the glamour of the topic then, has been over valued. Diplomatic secrets confirm prejudices, rather than win wars.

Guy Burgess, who fluttered on the fringes of security and secret services in the early years of the war, settled at the BBC for a time, before going to the Foreign Office to take a junior position in a junior minister's office. Burgess was one of those people who at university showed great promise, equalled only by a great capacity for friendship. The promise faded but the capacity for friendship survived with him. Burgess was outrageous, sober or drunk, but he was always funny, people said. His capacity to provide earth-shattering information from the Foreign Office could not have been large, although Burgess was good at picking up gossip, and secret services, like journalists, love gossip. Philby had served the cause as a journalist on the Franco side of the Spanish Civil War, and later in the war and after in MI6. There he was uniquely effective, among other things helping to destroy two covert action operations in Albania and the Ukraine. But 'helping' should be stressed, because the operations were doomed anyhow.

Then in 1949, Philby, was promoted to Washington to liaise with the CIA and the FBI and, briefed beforehand, became aware of the decoding operation. However Philby was not the first to tell the Russians about the cypher breakers. A spy in the American Armed Forces Agency, William Weisband, had sold information to the Russians in 1948. Philby, on arrival, could see how far the operation had moved on and was successfully identifying targets. The complicating factor was the arrival of Burgess, on a last chance to behave, posted to the embassy in Washington, where Philby was under diplomatic cover. In an attempt to keep him under control, Philby took in Burgess as a lodger, although Burgess was to be sent home in disgrace in April 1951. Philby, in his book *My Silent War*, later wrote of a decision being made to use Burgess to carry a warning to Maclean that the case against him was strengthening and to prepare for an escape. The intention seems to have been to take only Maclean, but Burgess went too. While things were damped down in public there was deep bitterness on the American side against Maclean for having betrayed atomic research and against Burgess for his remembered blatant anti-Americanism. It was proof of British incompetence, even though the FBI neglected to tell the British about their own spy, Weisband.

Blunt, the other member of the Cambridge group, had served in

The young Evelyn Waugh, roistering his way through Oxford in the mid-twenties, could hardly have expected his later works to have found an honoured place in convent libraries ... Neither would he have expected that his diary notes would feature in the files of MI5 and be used against one of his drinking companions at the Hypocrites Club, though that also has been his fate.

the Security Service, MI5, during the war and passed on much information, although one might doubt that what came from MI5 was of international importance. He also ran at least one other spy. At the end of the war Blunt extricated himself, becoming Director of the Courtauld Institute, the elite job for an art historian in the United Kingdom, as well as Surveyor of the Queen's Pictures and Drawings, a position of honour and prestige. He kept up social links with his old MI5 friends and with Guy Burgess. Blunt had in effect retired as a spy, however, for him, the defection of Burgess and Maclean broke the peace. Blunt, under the guise of helping MI5, was able to enter Burgess' flat after his defection to try and destroy anything incriminating, a task in which he was less than totally successful.

All these Cambridge men – Burgess, the navy officer's son; Maclean, son of a liberal cabinet minister; Philby, with an explorer father; and Blunt, from a clergyman's family with royal connections – were a long way from Peter Wright. Indeed if they had encountered a boffin in a corridor they probably wouldn't have given him the time of day, with the exception of Burgess, who would have been interested if he was good looking. Maclean, although married, was intermittently bisexual; Philby was firmly heterosexual but not monogamous; Blunt was homosexual, and Burgess voraciously so. All were heavy drinkers. Again, it was not the sober middle-class world of the boffin, working back at night and over the weekends on microphones.

Only a few months after Wright joined MI5, the government issued a white paper on Burgess and Maclean that was, to say the least, singularly misleading in understanding their role. Then, in November of the same year, the Foreign Secretary, Harold Macmillan, cleared Kim Philby whose guilt remained an article of faith for Wright's new colleagues. The question of the so-called Cambridge

13

group of spies was still very much alive, although few then could have predicted just how long the interest would survive. Dick Goldsmith White was transferred to be Chief of MI6 in 1956 and, on his recommendation, Roger Henry Hollis succeeded him.

The young Evelyn Waugh, roistering his way through Oxford in the mid-twenties, could hardly have expected his later works to have found an honoured place in convent libraries, his fate, as one unfairly and narrowly tagged a 'Catholic writer'. Neither would he have expected that his diary notes would feature in the files of MI5 and be used against one of his drinking companions at the Hypocrites Club, though that also has been his fate. Roger Hollis put up a performance at lunch in November 1924 which inspired Waugh to give him the eighteenth-century accolade of 'a good bottle man'. Hollis was the son of a bishop and his mother was the daughter of a canon, so there may have been an element of reaction in his Oxford life. One of his three brothers, Christopher Hollis, was an active Tory MP who campaigned effectively for the abolition of capital punishment, became a convert to Catholicism, and wrote rather well about cricket.

Communism at Oxford at the time was far from being a mass movement of the kind it became at Cambridge a decade later. Graham Greene records that he and Claude Cockburn joined the Oxford branch of the Communist Party hoping to obtain a free trip to the Soviet Union. However, 'our mercenary motive was seen through at once, by a very serious Australian Rhodes Scholar . . . ' A decade later, Cockburn did become a more serious Communist, and this was to be held against Hollis, who had known him in that flippant phase. It is thanks to the Rhodes Scholar, P. R. Stephensen, that we know how many students the Oxford Communist Party had as members: there were four. MI5, which had clearly infiltrated the Party, reported Stephensen and the others to the university authorities and the Rhodes Scholar was in danger of being sent down. This information from the MI5 reports is in the Australian Archives, passed on to the Australian counter-espionage body of the time, the Investigations Branch.

Hollis dropped out of Oxford without taking a degree and worked in London for a year to save his fare to China, arriving there early in the second quarter of 1927. He worked as a freelance journalist and when that proved precarious after a year, took a job with the British American Tobacco Company, which had a very large share of the large Chinese cigarette market. The company employed thousands of expatriates, not only in Shanghai but throughout China. Young men were not paid all that well and Hollis continued his freelance journalism. In late 1934 he showed signs of tuberculosis and by June 1936 his condition had worsened. He left China and spent some time in a sanatorium and married in 1937.

In 1938 through a series of acquaintances Hollis managed to get into MI5. Dick White, the old Stortfordian, who was later to take Hollis' side against Wright, pressed the then head of MI5, Sir Vernon Kell to employ Hollis. Kell would only have those who had been to a public school and were not homosexual or Catholic. (He may have kept the Catholics out, but he doesn't seem to have been totally successful with homosexuals.) Hollis' other reference in MI5 was Janet Sissmore (later Archer) who went to MI5 and is now regarded as contributing to the character Connie in Le Carre's Smiley books. Much has been made subsequently of Hollis trying to get into MI5, but those who see it as necessarily sinister haven't looked at the career alternatives in the late years of the Depression for a young man, from a good family, in his early thirties, with a bad medical record, no degree, and a capacity to handle Chinese. Hollis could hardly have got into the services, the police or commerce. What he needed was a desk job where introductions and family background counted, so MI5 and MI6 were ideal. The newcomer went into B Division, subsection F2A which watched for treasonable and subversive activities from the Communist Party of Great Britain.

Hollis was essentially an analyst, it seems, rather than an agent-runner. His spies inside the Party were manipulated as a quasi-independent operation by a bizarre figure, Maxwell Knight, thriller writer, naturalist and animal lover, who had his own pet bear and was one of the homosexuals who got through Kell's screen. Hollis, in what was probably pretty close to a vacuum, started to build a reputation as an intellectual authority on Communism. The Nazi-Soviet pact and Communist hostility to the war, up to the invasion of Russia in 1941, gave Hollis' section plenty of paper shuffling to do. Early in the war he became acting head of the subsection and was quickly confirmed and promoted to the status of assistant director.

He was seen as a protege of Dick White's, the man who had recommended his initial recruitment. As well as extra salary, his promotion put Hollis on various committees. One thing that emerges is that shyness and diffidence, his characteristic style, were actually helpful to him in committee work. After 1946, Hollis had no great rapport with Sillitoe. The new Director General was later to complain that when he asked for a list of Communist subversives from Hollis, all he got was a general paper on the state of the Communist Party.

However, it was in the role of an expert that Hollis was sent to Australia, in 1948, to put the case to the Labor government for the establishment of an MI5-type body in Australia. The Prime Minister, Ben Chifley, remained unconvinced, and it was only after a personal intervention from Attlee that he agreed. The Australian Security Intelligence Organisation as it was to be called, adopted the MI5 management structure, and established close liaison and training exchanges. Hollis carried out the liaison advisory role in his capacity as the newly promoted director of C branch, responsible for security in general, i.e. protective security. When Dick White became Director General in September 1953, he made his man, Hollis, Deputy Director General. Three years later, because MI6 had angered the Prime Minister, Sir Anthony Eden (by an operation against a visiting Russian warship which had cost the life of a frogman and damaged Eden's diplomatic plans), Dick Goldsmith White was transferred to head the Secret Service. On his recommendation, Hollis was promoted to Director General.

The MI5 which Wright had joined did not have a spectacularly successful decade in the fifties. In 1952, MI5 picked up a Foreign Office cypher man, William Marshall. He had been sighted by an alert surveillance man, or watcher, off-duty at the time, talking to a Russian diplomat. On his own initiative the watcher followed the Englishman home and further surveillance trapped him. The next piece of alertness by the watchers ended in a damaging failure. In March 1956, they picked up a young RAF officer, Anthony Wraight, who was seen visiting the Soviet embassy. But after being questioned he managed to flee to East Berlin. The next break for MI5 came from within the Czech embassy in Washington, where the Americans had a spy in place. Another Czech had carelessly mentioned in conversation enough to allow the spy to pass on the identification of an electronics engineer, Brian Linney, who was selling RAF missile secrets. He was convicted in 1958.

Certainly none of the new scientific advisers' devices were responsible for identifying spies in the United Kingdom. Overseas, MI5, whose charter covered the colonies, had a very active fifties. But that is another story, although Gough Whitlam in his evidence at the trial in Sydney lifted one edge of the curtain when he let slip that Wright's manuscript contained references to MI5 assassination plans in Cyprus.

It was 1961 before Wright got a major trial to which he made a contribution. This came with the breakup of the Portland ring. Harry Houghton and Ethel Gee, both clerks at the Admiralty Research Centre in Portland, were convicted as were Gordon Lonsdale, a deep cover Russian illegal, (an agent-runner who operates alone, unlike the 'legals', who operate under diplomatic cover) whose real name was Conon Molody, and two American undercover spies, fugitives from the Rosenberg ring in the United States, Morris and Lorna Cohen. The clue that led to their arrest had come from a write-in to the CIA from an anonymous spy in Polish Intelligence, later to become a defector, who gave a pointer to Houghton, and surveillance picked up the rest. Wright's devices played a part after Lonsdale and the Cohens were identified.

Houghton was no Cambridge ideologue. As a naval NCO in the UK embassy in Warsaw he had been compromised while doing black market deals and was recruited by the Poles. Miss Gee was simply his girlfriend. When the defector, Michal Goleniewski, came over in 1961, he gave the British enough information to pinpoint an MI6 officer, George Blake, who had worked in Berlin for some years. In operational espionage terms, Blake probably did more damage to individuals and networks than Philby, and certainly infinitely more than Burgess and would have rivalled in output Maclean's policy material. Blake confessed and claimed to have been converted to Marxism while a prisoner of war in North Korea, after being captured in 1950. This has been disputed and allegations have been made that his communism probably went back to his years in the Dutch Resistance, or even earlier when he was brought up in Egypt.

However one possibility has been overlooked. He was under

diplomatic cover in Seoul some time before the outbreak of the Korean War and many aspects of the Rhee regime were repulsive, perhaps enough so to turn Blake around. As well as blowing the cover of a number of individual agents Blake was able to inform on a very elaborate tunnel phone-tapping operation across the boundaries of West Berlin and into Soviet military communications.

The next case was that of William Vassall, a clerk in the Admiralty who, since his recruitment in 1954 while serving in the UK embassy in Moscow, had been passing on material. The lead to Vassall came from another defector, this time a KGB man, Yuri Nosenko. Although different postings within the Admiralty varied the quality of his material, Vassall would have been a very useful spy, particularly given the dominant Royal Navy role in NATO. Vassall was not ideological. He was, however, homosexual, and a great deal was made of that after his conviction in 1962. Some of the stuff written at the time was crudely homophobic and set a style for dealing with future disclosures.

MI5 or 'Security' as it tended to be called in the press, came under some criticism for not stopping Houghton's employment because he was a heavy drinker, a not altogether plausible view, given that if every heavy drinker were chased out of the armed services their numbers would be heavily reduced. Likewise it was suggested that Vassall as a homosexual should never have been employed.

The lesson for people in MI5 was that their only successes in years had come from the lucky dip of defectors from the other side. Further, both Goleniewski and Nosenko were walk-ins, not responding to any approach and in any case they had gone to the Americans. There had been attempts by MI5 throughout the fifties to suborn Russian satellite officers but they had failed.

There is some dispute as to just who was really responsible for the next breakthrough, the final firm identification of Philby. Some have attributed it to a defector Anatoliy Golitsin, who came out in Helsinki in December 1961. But it was January 1963 before MI6 sent someone to extract a confession from Philby, then living in Beirut, for a damage assessment, probably a deal. A few days later Philby vanished. In terms of timing, a more recent claim has more plausibility than Golitsin. Lord Rothschild was in Israel in June 1962 and spoke to a woman, Flora Solomon, who told him of an explicit approach by Philby to recruit her for the Comintern before the war. On his return to London, Lord Rothschild went to MI5, who had employed him during the war, and told them of this new evidence. Whatever the truth, Philby was gone and the United Kingdom and its allies were unpleasantly reminded of the Burgess-Maclean defection. While it can now hardly be doubted that Philby had been an active Russian agent, the significance of his defection was played down and the government was tight-lipped about his work before 1951. No one was told about the MI5 attempts to nail him in 1951 and 52, so publicly the Security Service did not come out well.

When Philby wrote *My Silent War* and published it in 1968 he left no doubt that he had been an ideological spy. That year also saw the publication of two books: *Philby: The Spy Who Betrayed A Generation* by three *Sunday Times* journalists Bruce Page, David Leitch, and Phillip Knightley; and *Philby: The Long Road to Moscow* by Patrick Seale and Maureen McConville. The books were more sophisticated than most of what had gone before, or much of what has come since, making a serious attempt to work out what actually motivated the Cambridge group of spies. There were scattered references in both books to Sir Anthony Blunt, holder of the sonorous title of Surveyor of the Queen's Pictures and Drawings. Blunt had overlapped with the group at Cambridge, and been in MI5 during the war, while a tenant at Bentinck Street. He had been a Marxist at Cambridge, but Seale and McConville noted 'for Blunt it was an extension of his affection for Burgess rather than a real commitment.' Blunt would have viewed those comments with mixed feelings and so did a number of old counter-espionage experts including Peter Wright, who knew a great deal about Anthony Blunt.

In June 1963, five years previously, Michael Straight had been offered, by President Kennedy, the post of Chairman of the newly-established National Arts Advisory Council. Straight came from a wealthy family and in the way of American politics, found that compatible with being a liberal Democrat. Twenty years later he published an autobiography *After Long Silence* and in it told how the night he was asked to chair the arts body he 'lay in darkness' anguishing over what the FBI could turn up when they investigated him. What it might discover was not, in hindsight, earth-shattering. Straight, educated in England, had become a Communist at Cambridge and after the death of a fellow student, John Cornforth, in the Spanish Civil War, had been approached by Blunt who told him that the best tribute he could pay to Cornforth's memory was to work for the Communist International. He, Straight, should return to the United States and become an insider on Wall Street. But Straight said he didn't like that, and a little later Blunt, on behalf of his masters, offered a compromise: Straight could go to the US as a secret Communist and serve the cause in some other way. But serve it he must, Stalin had personally decided. (Communications between Moscow and Cambridge were good that year, apparently.) Straight was introduced to a Russian in London before he went back to Washington; there he got an unpaid job in the State Department doing research on the German war economy. A Russian contact found him and, up to the Nazi-Soviet pact in 1939, Straight gave assessments to his control.

It wasn't a big deal, but if the FBI found out he would be in the same boat as Alger Hiss, so Straight went off to see Arthur C. Schlesinger, the White House resident intellectual, who agreed that he couldn't take the arts job and passed him on quickly to the FBI. Straight, whose book shows him as a nervy, pompous and priggish man, who doesn't seem to have grown up much since Cambridge, confessed all to the FBI. It took the Bureau six months to get around to telling MI5 and, when they did, one of its officers, Arthur Martin, happened to be in the United States. Straight and Martin came together in January 1964 for a fruitful meeting at the Mayflower Hotel in Washington. Martin was back in England within a few days. Straight had also come up with another Cambridge name to add to Blunt's, that of Leo Long.

Back in London the choice had to be made whether to prosecute or make a deal to find out just what had happened. Martin had also been told a story by Straight about a meeting with Guy Burgess and Anthony Blunt in London in 1949, when Straight had come over for the annual Apostles dinner, held in the distinctly unintellectual surroundings of the Royal Automobile Club.

Apart from the rest of the diners, Guy asked Straight, 'are you still with us?' Straight replied that he was not, but pressed, said he was not unfriendly. The 1930s story and the later account of the Royal Automobile Club, vague as it was, could hardly sustain a charge in court against Blunt (although in recent years Wright has obstinately claimed they could). Martin, while in sympathy with Wright on just about everything else, still defends the deal. 'The overriding need was to find out what he knew, what he told the Russians about MI5 and why the Russians allowed him to leave,' Martin says in *Conspiracy of Silence*, by Barrie Penrose and Simon Freeman, published late in 1985. Martin had interrogated Blunt in the polite follow-up interviews in 1951 in the wake of Burgess and Maclean's defection. It took until April after his return before Martin confronted Blunt in his flat at the Courtauld Institute in Portman Square. His notes were good enough years later to provide Penrose and Freeman with a couple of hundred words of description of Blunt's flat that day. Martin bowled first, saying that there was unequivocal evidence that Blunt had been a Russian agent; Blunt said there couldn't be because he hadn't been. Martin then said he had seen Straight. There was silence, and Martin made the offer of immunity from the Attorney General, a Conservative at that time. Blunt agreed to talk and the deal was on.

It was a secret limited to a very small number of people. The Queen's Secretary, Sir Michael Adeane, was told. As the years passed, however, the secret spread: each new Attorney General had to be told. In MI5 people talked, as more and more were put to work on follow-up leads from later Blunt interviews.

The immediate result of the deal was identification of another Cambridge Apostle, Leo Long, as a Soviet agent in the period he had spent in military intelligence during the war. Long was a working-class scholarship boy at Cambridge, who belonged to a Communist cell in Trinity, Blunt's old college. After Cambridge, Long had lost touch with Blunt, but in the war he found himself in the German section of the Directorate of Military Intelligence in London, largely dealing with information on the German army, derived from the code breakers at Bletchley. Blunt, now in MI5, reappeared and told Long the Russians weren't getting as much information as they should from an ally. Long agreed to pass information, which he did once a week for three years. It was at base ideological, although Long later said he had been too tired and overworked to talk much about politics. The information on the German order of battle was no doubt useful to the Russians, even when it dealt with units in the west. It would seem to be very similar to what the Russians were obtaining from the Lucy ring, a Swiss-based espionage group.

Ironically, there is a body of argument that says that MI6 itself was, after sanitising the Bletchley material to conceal its source, passing it on to the Lucy ring to help an ally without giving away the secret of how the information had been obtained. It is an unresolved question, with the odds probably against, but still an intriguing possibility. Long, after three years, got himself sent to Europe, breaking his connections with Blunt. He worked for the British Control Commission during the early stages of the occupation of Germany as a political adviser, but he said later that he had not passed on information. In 1946 Blunt recommended him to MI5 for a permanent job. Although interviewed by both MI5 and MI6, Long was unsuccessful and became a London businessman.

The unmasking of Blunt and Long, while secret, was the latest in a line of MI5 cases in which the Security Service could not claim the originating credit. Indeed it was now on a par with the mistrusted MI6 and the contemptible Foreign Office, in that it had had its spy during the war, and, arguably, came close to recruiting one afterwards. Apart from Straight, defectors had been crucial to their best cases and this dependence on defectors meant they had come to be listened to on subjects other than just names.

The act of defection is dramatic and its effect can be psychologically unbalancing, particularly if the defector is crudely handled. The simple truth is that defectors from Soviet intelligence agencies have a finite amount to deliver. They can name names, the names of their colleagues, and give descriptions of their colleagues, where they have changed their names for new postings. The content of training courses is important for a rival service to understand. Where the defectors have handled agents themselves they can give names and descriptions. Around headquarters they may have picked up some code names and descriptions attached to those code names which can provide clues to other agents. But finally, for them and for the interrogator the supply runs down and the temptation arises to change the defector into an expert of great insights, or to draw still lengthier hypotheses about names and possible penetration.

Status comes into it, where the defector becomes the pet of his handler. Jealousy thrives between rival agencies, the history of the treatment of defectors provides abundant examples. Finally, most defectors like to head for the United States. They know the rewards will be greater and, importantly, it is an easier country in which to get lost.

Anatoliy Golitsin, Commander of the British Empire, also known as Klimov, John Stone, Kago, Gollywog, A.E. Ladle, and Martel, presented himself at the home of the CIA resident in Helsinki in December 1961. Golitsin, in his mid-thirties, and Ukranian born, was a major in the KGB. After university and specialist intelligence training he had worked in the section responsible for counter-espionage against the US. He had also done some backup work on plans for the reorganisation of Soviet intelligence in the early fifties. He then served two years in Vienna, up to 1956, before returning to university for further training, this time in law, and came out to be an analyst in the NATO section of the First Chief Directorate of the KGB. Golitsin was a difficult man to handle, refusing to talk to anyone he didn't like – and he didn't like most people – as well as always demanding to talk to the top. The CIA arranged a meeting with Bobby Kennedy, then Attorney General, to flatter the defector. But in March 1963, angry at his treatment in America, he went off to live in England and MI5, using their particular form of flattery, made him an honorary Commander of the British Empire. In July, however, after the press had broken the news of the presence of the important defector (although misspelling his name), Golitsin went back to the United States. Short, fat, temperamental, without any of the artifices of courtesy, Golitsin was still able to build up a following of disciples in the Western counter-intelligence world. Not only did he have names, the common trade of defectors, but he had theories: he could interpret the 'methodology' of the KGB in a way that no one else could. Golitsin likes to use jargon and has adapted well to US sociological terms. As well as his analysis of KGB philosophy, Golitsin affirmed that there were moles, deepcover long-term agents, in all the western intelligence agencies.

The apotheosis of Golitsin's political analysis is his book *New Lies For Old*, published in 1984 in both the United States and the United Kingdom. Two of the four editors, who together wrote a joint

Probably the most diabolical of all was Czechoslovakia's 'democratisation' (Golitsin is keen on inverted commas). He refers throughout to the Dubcek 'progressives' as frauds.

foreword for the book, were Arthur Martin, the MI5 interrogator of Blunt, and Stephen de Mowbray, an ex-MI6 officer, who as Golitsin acknowledges 'did the lion's share of the editing'. Golitsin says that in 1959 the KGB took a new direction in the establishment of a new disinformation department, Division D. It was this division which from then on had masterminded a range of breathtaking disinformation exercises. Firstly they had managed to cover up a secret reconciliation between Tito and the Soviet Union and have maintained this deception ever since. Likewise the Soviet-Albanian split was a clever plot, as can be discerned from examining the wording of various communiques. Golitsin is great on textual analysis. Naturally enough, the Sino-Soviet split was not real but a product of 'bloc disinformation'. Rumanian independence in foreign policy is another piece of cleverness. Probably the most diabolical of all was Czechoslovakia's 'democratisation' (Golitsin is keen on inverted commas). He refers throughout to the Dubcek 'progressives' as frauds. Czechoslovak writers who demanded 'democratisation' were not acting spontaneously but in accordance with their Party role. It follows of course that Solidarity is another confidence trick. There is still more. The 'dissidents' in the Soviet Union are lying. According to Golitsin, Sakharov is not a genuine dissenter, he is part of a KGB plot: indeed, if you study his statements you can detect 'the future course of communist actions and their timing'. To understand it all we have to go back to those KGB decisions in 1959.

When his admirers in the CIA convened a conference of academics to listen to his theories, it was no wonder that non- or dis-believers in the Agency called it a 'flat earth conference'. But this man became a guru figure for the Chief of Counter Intelligence in the CIA, James Jesus Angleton, something of a guru figure himself, as well as for Peter Wright and his friends at MI5.

Angleton's discipleship was to have devastating effects on the CIA. Part of Golitsin's stock in trade was that there were moles everywhere, mole being the counter-espionage term for a deep-cover spy, whom it may have taken decades to manoeuvre into a key position. (Philby was a classic example, although he got there a little more quickly, taking only seven years.) He provided new names and more leads, a few of which were unmasked. Many more were wrong, simply deadends. But if he was given the files of CIA personnel he could tell from reading their profiles: Angleton obliged and Golitsin produced a list of suspects. As well as hunting out moles inside the Agency, Golitsin was pathologically jealous of all rival defectors, they were KGB plants. As Head of Counter Espionage, Angleton's job was to be suspicious. Relatively early in his career he'd been coolly deceived by Kim Philby who, while in Washington, worked with him and cultivated his friendship. Angleton was not going to be caught again. As well, his experience with Philby had turned him from being an admirer of England into something approaching an Anglophobe. A few years ago, when I lunched with him in Washington, Angleton was not prepared to give the British any credit for originality in cracking the German code in World War Two. They had only done it from the information supplied by the French and the Poles, he said. Angleton, plotting from his office where the curtains were never drawn, tore the CIA apart trying to find Golitsin's mole. *The Wilderness of Mirrors* by David C. Martin published in the United States in 1980, gives a well-informed account of the bizarre affair which ended only with the sacking of Angleton in 1974. Martin quotes an Agency Soviet specialist as saying, 'the effect of Golitsin was horrendous: the greatest disaster to western security that happened in twenty years.'

In M15, already an unhappy ship, the effect of Golitsin was also to be far reaching. Peter Wright had become a Golitsin follower, as keen as any of the CIA claque. *Spycatcher*, the book the UK government is trying to stop, is said to contain numerous citations of Golitsin. In particular Wright is said to support Golitsin's affirmation that Colonel Penkovsky, the best Soviet spy the West ever had was a diabolical KGB plant. Wright was ripe for Golitsin's documents. He had continued to develop his skills and techniques in eavesdropping and other devices, but none of his cases resulted in significant victories against the enemy. Two defeats in particular from his early years nagged him. In 1954 the Soviet embassy in Ottawa was destroyed by fire. The rebuilding provided an opportunity to place eight microphones in the building and Wright had

The Russians had, after all, invented the cavity microphone which had taken Wright almost three months to analyse, and it is at least an alternative proposition that they could have devised counter measures.

provided the technical know-how for the Royal Canadian Mounted Police. The Russians had sweepers in, and from then on the microphone transmitted only useless information. In Canberra, the Soviet embassy was closed down in 1954 after the defection of two diplomats until 1959 when it reopened. MI5 provided cavity microphones, a development of that same SATYR Russian microphone whose secrets Wright had cracked in 1952. It was installed before the Russians came back and to lull them was not activated for one year after the return. Its operation depended on a microwave activation to a room on the first floor of the Civic Hotel over the road. Surprise, surprise, nothing useful was heard. To Wright and those close to him, these two cases provided proof that the operations had been betrayed. Of course it was nothing of the kind. The Russians had, after all, invented the cavity microphone which had taken Wright almost three months to analyse, and it is at least an alternative proposition that they could have devised counter measures.

Wright proceeded up the promotion ladder in MI5; certainly he did not do badly under Hollis. By 1963 he was Deputy Chief Scientific Officer. But Wright wanted to be more than just a scientist, however much he retained the other traits of the boffin. The scientific section was only one part of one division. The action, promotion and spending money were in the counter espionage section. Wright manoeuvred to get there. Penrose and Freeman's book contains some sharply-worded memories from old colleagues: 'it was always number one with Peter Wright ... I think he impressed some of the senior people. They were mesmerised by a man who seemed to be able to use a slide rule,' and 'to be honest there was something bogus about him ...' and 'some people adored him, the ones who thought he was correct about Golitsin-Hollis.' The irony of it is in view of what came later, in that Hollis promoted Wright.

Some of the disinformation on Wright put out by the ubiquitous government sources in London has tried to present him as a not very important figure in MI5, a kind of minor technician, and some of the press have been gulled, for example the columnist in *Today* on 27 November 1986 described Wright as 'a not very senior operative.' The official record of employment tendered by the UK government in the case certainly shows otherwise. In 1963 Hollis promoted him to Senior Officer and later Assistant Director. He was 'initially responsible for the central study of the activities of hostile intelligence services: subsequently responsible for the study of past activities of hostile intelligence services. Also concerned with the investigation of the suspected penetration of the British intelligence community.'

Why had Hollis promoted him? The answer seems to lie in Hollis' character: a not unfamiliar type, a man who was diligent, but doesn't like creating waves. Hollis comes across as a man who, if not timid, avoids confrontation wherever possible, so perhaps it was rational to flatter Wright a bit to separate him from Martin. In 1963 he was under considerable pressure from the Profumo affair, an artificial storm created by a shrewd Labour MP who stirred up public prurience to create a security scandal on the grounds that a junior minister had slept with a whore who had also slept with a Russian naval attache. MI5, taking an interest in high level sex, as security services tend to do, had a rather murky role on the fringes of the affair. Although it escaped censure, for a time, it must have appeared to Hollis that trouble might come over its use as an agent of Stephen Ward, a semi-panderer, whose employment by the Security Service had given him delusions about a bigger role. It was not a year to be harsh with importunate people within the organisation and Hollis, anyhow, was probably attracted to the line of least resistance. So Wright moved into counter espionage. But even Hollis felt he had to take a stand in 1964 when he clashed with Martin over handling Blunt and the leads arising from the interrogation. In the argument, Hollis warned Martin against what he called Gestapo tactics. Martin resisted and the Director General summarily dismissed Martin, gaining the support of his senior officers – Martin's prickly personality and his devotion to Golitsin had not endeared him to all his colleagues. Martin was found a job in MI6. Wright had been at a few meetings, between Blunt and Martin, to help with taping for the record. For this reason, or perhaps to lure him away from Martin, Hollis let him take over.

In the same year, in the wake of the Philby defection, the dissident group had devised an explanation that Philby must have been warned about his impending interrogation, because of phrases he had allegedly used in the interview with the MI6 man, and because he defected. Only a very small number in MI5, MI6 and the government had known about these pending interviews so, for the dissidents, there must have been a leak from one of that list. The group, of whom Wright was one, went to see Goldsmith White at MI6, because they didn't trust Hollis to take them seriously enough.

Their first suspect was the Deputy Director General of MI5, Graham Mitchell. After pressure, apparently partially from White, Hollis agreed to an investigation of Mitchell. The grounds for suspicion of this MI5 veteran, as retailed again and again by members of the group to various journalists and researchers, seem very weak when read twenty years later. Watched through a one-way mirror Mitchell looked worried, there were marks in dust in one of his drawers which could be interpreted to mean he was taping meetings. (How did he press the button to start it, and what genius had devised the only tape recorder in the 1960s that didn't make a noise, or foul up frequently?) He also wore tinted glasses which was seen as a suspicious habit to enable him to avoid surveillance. Mitchell retired at the end of 1963, but those who believed in Golitsin's mole were unappeased. Suspicion shifted to Hollis, White was lobbied again.

Wright stepped into Martin's shoes as interrogator of Blunt and in doing so ruled off any chance of the whole affair being left as a kind of historical survey. Blunt had been in the Service, after all, a very long time ago, almost twenty years and so Hollis might reasonably have expected that the taping was for the record. This was a dangerous misconception of Wright the boffin, who took microphones apart to see how they worked, and in this case was prepared to take Blunt apart to see how the Cambridge spies worked. He interviewed Sir Anthony for hundreds of hours. During the interrogations Wright was, for the first few years, confident that he was being treated with honesty but, after later interviews, Wright nagged himself into doubting that. Blunt had only delivered up one spy, Long, whom Straight was going to hand over anyhow.

Wright applied himself methodically to the task. Reading his comments in interviews it is difficult to escape the conclusion that to him the shifting patterns of human relationships and friendships were connections that were as immutable as those of a chemistry equation.

What Wright did to wear him down was to produce names, photographs, records of interviews, old college magazines and newspapers to get more names for yet more interviews. The interrogator moved through the membership of the Communist cells: the Cambridge Socialist Society; the Apostles, a rather self-inflated society allowing young men to be intellectually priggish in the hope of impressing their elders, and getting some dalliance along the way. As well, Wright traced out all the webs of friendship built on school or, when crossing the lines, on ideology. The interrogator got names, people's past records, conversations and comments. The names Blunt gave Wright were not treated as history; to the investigator they were potential spies to be tracked down. The biographies and the names have been leaked since, in various books and in even more newspapers. The trial in Sydney stimulated a revival of biographies and recycled accounts. The cry in December of one widow was apposite, 'The whole thing stems from that wicked man Blunt who just spat out a list of names of people who went to college at Cambridge about the same time that he did.'

Of all the names there seemed to have been one or perhaps two who held positions where they might have dealt with highly classified information relating to defence or foreign affairs; it was hard to see what the others might have been able to do to serve a Marxist cause.

Wright applied himself methodically to the task. Reading his comments in interviews it is difficult to escape the conclusion that to him the shifting patterns of human relationships and friendships were connections that were as immutable as those of a chemistry equation. There is another unpleasant undercurrent which emerges very well in the chapter on Wright in *Conspiracy of Silence:* a capacity on the part of the interrogator to hear what he wants to hear, to use the word 'confession' with all its overtones of proven guilt, for exchanges which were not confessions at all. It was certainly very close to the kind of Gestapo tactics that Hollis had

29

feared from Martin when he sacked him. But Hollis was gone, in any case, by December 1965. Before he left, Hollis agreed to the formation of a joint MI5/MI6 committee, to be given the code name Fluency, which was to investigate penetration of both services. The membership was to be seven, three from each side, with a rotating chairman. Wright was to be the first chairman. Martin was one of the MI6 representatives as was his future collaborator on the Golitsin manuscript, Stephen de Mowbray, (In later years, they have sometimes been called the 'gang of three').

Other members at various times included Christopher Philpots, Geoffrey Hinton, and Terence Lecky, all of MI6, and Ralph Symonds of MI5. Wright, Martin and de Mowbray were in their different ways the dominant personalities. Martin, unlike Wright, is a very short man and, at first glance, looks like an insignificant railway booking office clerk. He has a piercing gaze, which those who dislike him tend to call fanatical. De Mowbray is tall, thin, a Wykehamite, the intellectual of the group. Even before encountering Golitsin, de Mowbray was a man of theories. There was said to be some dissent at times in the Committee, although the hard core had striven to give an impression of unanimity. Those on the Committee were essentially analysts, counter-espionage men. De Mowbray, for example, had never run agents. Martin had made his name as an interrogator and Wright, of course, was a technician. They were wedded to the theory that if something went wrong there had to be a logical cause. In the absence of experience in the practical confusion of day to day working with agents, they naturally turned to a conspiracy. Why were the defectors choosing the USA? The answer was that they must be frightened to come to Britain. There were, of course, other reasons, notably money and the good life. Once the Committee was at work it had to find 'penetration' to justify its existence, so its members came to hear very much what they wanted to hear.

It met once a fortnight in conditions of extreme secrecy, after normal working hours. It was answerable to the two heads of Service, White at MI6 and Hollis' former deputy, Martin Furnivall-Jones, who had succeeded to the Director Generalship on Hollis' recommendation. Furnivall-Jones, who had been Director of Security in MI6 had known of the Mitchell Enquiry, an establishment of the Fluency Committee, which he had supported. However when the true believers tried out their Hollis theme, Furnivall-Jones regarded it as wild. Hollis himself, before he left, had come to know what was being said and there was a Peter Wright story that has been regurgitated in various books and articles about this last meeting. One of the later versions is in Chapman Pincher's *Too Secret Too Long*:

'Shortly before he retired he called the committee chairman, Peter Wright, into his office and staggered him by asking, "Tell me, why do you think I am a spy?" Seizing his opportunity, after his initial shock, Wright gave his reasons and added, "Do you dispute these undoubted facts?" Hollis shrugged and responded, "All I can say is I am not a spy." "But is there any evidence to swing the balance your way?" Peter Wright persisted. "No," Hollis replied. "You think you have the manacles on me, don't you?"'

From this Pincher, presumably reflecting his informant, drew the following conclusion:

'If Hollis was a spy, he would have reported his situation to a Soviet controller, who would have sought advice on his behalf from the Moscow Centre. In that event Hollis' initiative with Peter Wright would have been in keeping with the Centre's requirement to discover how much was really known against him in the confident belief that, whatever might be proved, he would never be prosecuted or subjected to public censure.'

It is a matter of words. Wright and the people to whom he has told the story seem to regard the exchange as a confession. On a more rational reading, there is certainly the alternative that a weary Hollis was simply being sarcastic. The status given to the story, almost as 'evidence', is an example of how murky things are in the world of allegations and hints that characterise the Hollis affair, rather than a piece of proof.

Furnivall-Jones' resistance to the Fluency Committee's targeting Hollis did not last, but first the committee members obtained permission to have Mitchell brought back from retirement and interrogated. He was cleared, but to the satisfaction of only some, with dissenters remaining. Mitchell having been put aside, the Committee turned its attention on Hollis. Wright was a busy man: there were the continuing investigations on the Blunt case as well as the Fluency Committee. As well as the wider question of penetration he was to be rewarded for his work in 1969 when his duties were redefined to function as a 'special adviser to the counter-intelligence branches on the techniques of counter-intelligence and the continued investigation of suspected penetration.'

The Fluency Committee brought Golitsin back to England in 1967 and, as Angleton had done in the CIA, they showed him personal files and case files. Golitsin's analysis was, not surprisingly, that the guilty mole was Hollis, who had allegedly only been identified to him under a code name. Golitsin had now much of the first draft of *New Lies For Old* completed and he renewed his old acquaintance with Martin in 1965, while establishing a new relationship with Stephen de Mowbray. The defector also reiterated his theory that Hugh Gaitskell, the former leader of the British Labour Party had been poisoned by the KGB in 1962, a proposition which found ready listeners.

In its first formal report in 1967, the Fluency Committee concluded that MI5 had been penetrated by one or more agents and named Hollis and Mitchell as the leading suspects. They now sought permission to carry out an interrogation of Hollis. The report seems to have been shelved by Furnivall-Jones for two years and in 1969, the year Wright's role had been redefined, the Fluency Committee was replaced by another joint body, code named K7, which was to monitor suspected penetration. K7 recommended calling in Hollis for interrogation and, in 1970, the former Director General, now aged sixty-four, came in for some hours. He did not break down and confess, but predictably those who were against him circulated rumours that his responses to questions had been unsatisfactory. On any reading of Hollis' character, he had probably never been much good at answering questions. In the first half of 1972, K7 submitted its formal report on the Hollis case. There are some differences of opinion over just what it did say. The Hollis-is-guilty team say that the majority upheld their view, others say that it merely rehashed circumstance as evidence and even so its conclusion was not as firm as others claim. Furnivall-Jones decided that the matter was closed and it remained so until he retired in April 1972.

Furnivall-Jones was succeeded by his Deputy, Michael Hanley, who had himself, in the sixties, been temporarily under suspicion,

32

when a defector's lead seemed to match his personal background. Hanley was the bluff Yorkshireman. His hobby was church music and he was proud of being a choir master. He cheerfully admitted his technical ignorance and was fond of saying something like, 'this bloody game used to be about people, now it's all about pieces of equipment'. What mattered about Hanley is that he was a supporter of Wright's. Within a year Wright was to become a special consultant for the Director General and, in 1974, he was to sit alongside Hanley at probably the most important international conference of the Director General's tenure. Wright was able to convince his boss that the Hollis case should be reopened.

As the investigation dragged on, Hollis died in October 1973 of a stroke. His obituary in *The Times* was a sympathetic one written by Sir Dick Goldsmith White, by now a Cabinet-Offices Intelligence Co-ordinator. In 1972, there had been a scare that Blunt, still being regularly visited by Wright, was going to die, but he did not. The threat of his death sparked a reassessment of the material from the Blunt tapes taken by Wright. By then Wright seems to have become increasingly sceptical that Blunt was telling him the truth, although earlier he seems to have convinced himself that there had been a good relationship. On any reading of character, an eight year relationship between a fastidious, homosexual art historian and a deliberate, plodding scientist turned spycatcher, who makes it very clear that he thought heterosexual philandering was bad, let alone homosexual playing around, had to be bizarre.

The angry widow of a few pages ago may well have had a point. Was Blunt being cynical with Wright, merely throwing him stale irrelevant names? Meanwhile, K7 steered towards a second report on Hollis, again the subject of contradictory and confusing leaks. Some claim its case was stronger, others stressed that finally it was all unproven.

Wright, however, was at Hanley's elbow to press his interpretation of the report. He argued vigorously that Hanley had no choice but to inform the other members of the Anglo-Saxon intelligence club of the K7 report. In 1967, at the instigation of Angleton, what amounted to a regular conference of counter-espionage specialists was established, to meet every eighteen months under the code of name of CADZAB.

***As Golitsin told Hollis, one of his colleagues had informed
him of a plot to murder an unnamed western political leader.***

The first was held that year in Australia and it was a measure of
how far it was Angleton's creation that Golitsin was the star
speaker. Sir Charles Spry, Director General of the Australian
Security Intelligence Organisation since 1950, who was the host,
was already an admirer of the defector. In May 1974 another
CADZAB conference was held in London. Spry no longer represented Australia, having retired and been replaced by Peter Barbour.
Hanley, with Wright at his side, reported to the assembled counter-
espionage experts from the United States, Canada, Australia and
New Zealand, and invited them to make damage assessments on the
basis that Hollis had been a Soviet agent.

For Australia and New Zealand it could be said to be serious,
because despite what was said in court in Sydney, their liaison and
interaction with M15 had been particularly close. For Australia the
situation was complicated by Golitsin's insistence that ASIO, also,
had a mole. He had visited Australia on other occasions apart from
1967 and been given access to personal files, so that he could apply
his methodology. Barbour was less of an admirer of Golitsin, but he
had another problem. The participants of a CADZAB conference
regarded them as their own business and not a matter for intefering
politicians. While Angleton could get away with that hidden away in
his bunker in the CIA, it posed a problem for Barbour in his relations
with his Labor government. In March 1973 there had been a
showdown when the Minister in charge of ASIO, the Attorney
General, Senator Murphy, had insisted on entering the offices of
ASIO to inspect files, when he thought he had been misled, a visit
emotionally described by many spooks as 'a raid'. Barbour was also
under attack in his organisation for being soft with the socialists.
Barbour didn't communicate the Hanley statement on Hollis and the
Labor government only learnt about it next year, along with a
version of the Golitsin claims about a mole. Barbour went to a
diplomatic job. The fall-out range of Fluency was considerable.

One of Hollis' offences, in the eyes of Fluency group members,
was that he had been unimpressed with Golitsin and, in particular,
dismissive of a story that the KGB had poisoned Hugh Gaitskell in
1962 to make way for the left-winger Harold Wilson. As Golitsin

34

If the Soviets were prepared to kill to put Harold Wilson in
power, he might be more than just a left-winger. He might
be a Soviet agent.

told Hollis, one of his colleagues had informed him of a plot to murder an unnamed western political leader. Gaitskell, who had died from a sudden illness in December 1962, a year after Golitsin defected, was the one who filled the bill. Golitsin asked if Gaitskell had gone to any Soviet function before the illness. When his question was followed up, it was established that Gaitskell had visited the Soviet consulate a short time before to obtain a visa and had taken coffee and biscuits. It was yet another defector story, but one which wouldn't be forgotten by some MI5 men. If the Soviets were prepared to kill to put Harold Wilson in power, he might be more than just a left-winger. He might be a Soviet agent.

In the world of counter-espionage, hypotheses multiply almost endlessly, and when examined they are usually found to owe their development as much to prejudice as evidence, although prejudice masquerades under the name of analysis. For some on the right wing of politics, Labour has no legitimacy, and no right to govern. So it follows that a Labour government is essentially an aberration, a Trojan horse for something worse. Linked with this is the obsession against trade with the Eastern Bloc, a characteristic of all Western intelligence services since the Bolshevik revolution. Such trade is bad because it allows the enemy to support itself and, even worse, such trade can be used as a cover for espionage. The endless campaign against this trade has included such devices as MI5 in 1924 helping to sabotage a Labour government which had signed a trade treaty, down to the latest hardline US book on the KGB, *The New KGB: Engine of Soviet Power* by two ex-intelligence officers, W. R. Corson and R. T. Cowley. Published in 1986, this details more than fifty pages of what they call 'the commercial stations of the KGB, ie any Soviet trade organisation'.

That there are KGB (and CIA and M16) operatives under commercial cover is not to be denied, the problem is that the compulsive fear that many western counter-intelligence officers have of the effects of East-West trade, leads them to believe, that the advocates of such trade are suspect. A follow-through from this is that visits to Eastern Europe, even though they may have the appearance of being for leisure, are in some way questionable. So when Harold Wilson came back to power in 1974 the mixture was ripe for stirring. Wilson was in favour of East-West trade, he was friendly with businessmen who engaged in such trade and had actually visited Eastern Europe eleven times. Finally, there was Golliwog's (this was the nick-name his British friends gave him) story about the Gaitskell murder. Golitsin's patron, James Jesus Angleton, of the CIA, had even produced some research which indicated that Russian doctors had published investigations into the disease which had killed Gaitskell, such medical research being per se sinister. Rumours about Wilson being a secret communist had been current during his first period of prime ministership. They had, in the way of urban myths, passed into the creed of those who wanted to believe them.

When after his retirement in 1976, Harold Wilson first made claims that MI5 had operated against him, it was treated as an aberration of a mind, perhaps tired by too much partisanship. The allegations were made in the course of interviews with two BBC television journalists, Barrie Penrose and Roger Courtiour. The claims were all mixed up in thoughts about the Jeremy Thorpe affair, then well under way and the role of the South African Secret Police, BOSS, in England. Within a year, however, in July 1977, Chapman Pincher published a curious article in the *Daily Express* to confirm that Harold Wilson had been bugged at Number 10 Downing Street. His article amounted to a justification of what had been done. Indeed it quoted how 'extremely bitter' security chiefs were that Wilson had allowed his suspicion to be used as the basis of a smear against MI5, an argument somewhat akin to a rapist complaining that his victim had scratched him. As it happened, what Wilson did amounted to nothing more than a scratch. There was an investigation and, on 23 August 1977, the then Labour Prime Minister Jim Callaghan made a statement:

'The Prime Minister has conducted detailed enquiries into the recent allegations about the Security Service and is satisfied they do not constitute grounds for lack of confidence in the competence and impartiality of the Security Service or for instituting a special enquiry. In particular the Prime Minister is satisfied that at no time has the Security Service or any other

British intelligence or security agency, either of its own accord or at someone's request, undertaken electronic surveillance in Number 10 Downing Street or in the Prime Minister's room in the House of Commons.'

It will be appreciated that the denial when read was confined to surveillance at Number 10 or at the Commons, and only to electronic surveillance. Next year Pincher justified himself in a book, *The Inside Story*, and gave several hundred words from a reliable intelligence contact who told him just how the bug 'would have been placed' and who certainly seemed to be an expert.

There the matter might have rested. Cynics in different countries like to say there is nothing more ex than an ex-party-leader. The pace of politics moves on. Even Pincher's *Their Trade is Treachery*, published in 1981, had only a passing reference to Wilson's bad relations with MI5, although there were three pages about a businessman friend, engaged in the East-West trade, who had gone bad. When news of Wright's manuscript had filtered around the relatively small publishing world of Australia, compared to the large pools of London and New York, the Wilson revelations tended to feature third in people's minds, after the 'truth at last' on Hollis and the nuts and bolts of a counter espionage officer's life. However in trial hearings in Sydney, the defence solicitor, Malcolm Turnbull, within the limits imposed by not being able to quote directly from the manuscript, has made the Wilson claims very visible. There had been some behind the scenes concessions from the UK government's public relations machine on the allegations. The line now is that there may have been a few mavericks. Indeed, pressed in court in Sydney, the Cabinet Secretary, Sir Robert Armstrong, said something very much like that.

The difficulty is that the figure which appears to be in Wright's book about the number of officers involved is not one, not two, not three but thirty. Now that's a lot to be involved in such an operation. The second difficulty is in Wright's official work history covering the period as presented in the court in Sydney. It reads:

'1973. Took early retirement at his own request. Re-employed as a consultant to the Director General on his former grade. Responsible for technical matters.

1976. Resigned finally shortly before his sixtieth birthday

'Many criticisms can be made of Lord Wilson's stewardship ... the view that he ... was a likely candidate to be a Russian or Communist agent is one that can be entertained only by someone with a mind diseased by partisanship or unhinged by living for too long in an Alice-Through-the-Looking-Glass world

(August) on emigration to Australia.'

A comment from a Tory backbencher MP, Jonathan Aitken, in the House of Commons on 16 and 19 December, 1986, is apposite.

'It is almost inconceivable that any operation of the kind that seemed to have been alleged could have been carried out on a completely unauthorised freelance basis. One only has to think of the mechanics of an operation of that kind. To get into a former Prime Minister's residence without authorisation and set up technical equipment and then take the tapes away and have them read, analysed and stored at headquarters, enters the realms of speculation, fantasy, as does the original allegation. Nevertheless, there is an unanswered question ...'

Chapman Pincher's claim in an interview during the trial is of interest:

'...there was no way – and I think this is a total myth – that any of these people did it without the person above them being aware that they were doing it and then it was up to the person above them to go, if necessary to one above him to see 'Is this all right Joe' ... But this idea that these were a wild bunch who were just doing what the hell they liked, I'm sure is totally unfounded.'

There is fire in the smoke, that much is certain and the issue will not go away in 1987. Those, however many they were, had certainly breached the principle that the Security Service should not engage in party politics. But apart from principle, their judgment was ludicrous, as Roy Jenkins sardonically told the Commons on 4 December:

'Many criticisms can be made of Lord Wilson's stewardship – I have made some in the past and I have no doubt that I may make some more in the future – but the view that he, with his too persistent record of maintaining Britain's imperial commitments across the world, with his over-loyal lieutenancy to

Lyndon Johnson, with his fervent royalism, and with his light ideological luggage, was a likely candidate to be a Russian or Communist agent is one that can be entertained only by someone with a mind diseased by partisanship or unhinged by living for too long in an Alice-Through-the-Looking-Glass world in which falsehood becomes truth, fact becomes fiction and fantasy becomes reality.'

It would be very hard to destroy the buggers' case more effectively. While Wright was doing whatever 'technical matters' meant in the earlier description, he was still very actively concerned with the continuing saga of the Hollis case. The dramatic revelations to the other intelligence agencies at the CADZAB conference might be thought to have been enough. It was near enough to an acceptance, a humiliating acceptance, by the Director General, Sir Michael Hanley, that Hollis had been an agent. The shame had been kept secret from the politicians, but the professionals now knew. While Hanley had given ground, critics were not to be assuaged. So they sent Stephen de Mowbray to do a 'walk in', to borrow a term from the defector world. A few months after the CADZAB conference, de Mowbray confronted the Cabinet Secretary of the time, Sir John Hunt, at Number 10 Downing Street and demanded a meeting with the Prime Minister. De Mowbray didn't get the meeting, but Sir John could recognise trouble and, according to Wilson, recommended an enquiry. Wilson agreed, probably, one might suspect with not unmixed feelings. Lord Trend, Sir John Hunt's predecessor as Cabinet Secretary, was appointed to carry out an enquiry. He took a year, interviewing personally all the malcontents and reviewing the evidence. Lord Trend found, although it was impossible to prove the negative, that Sir Roger Hollis had not been an agent of the Russian intelligence service and that the matter had not been covered up in the internal investigation. De Mowbray, as spokesman of the group was informed orally of the findings towards the end of 1975. The hardcore three, De Mowbray, Martin and Wright, were left bitter and unconvinced, particularly as they had deluded themselves during their interviews that Trend was on their side.

Martin retired, taking a job at the Commons, de Mowbray left, and in 1976 Wright went out carrying the burden of the dislike, even hatred of many of his colleagues in M15 and M16. Hollis was not the last man to use the word Gestapo. One particular feud which raged with intensity was with Anthony Simpkins, Furnivall-Jones' Deputy Director General and the in-house historian of M15. The Fluency Group saw him as the man who had diverted their report. The personal trivia which was deployed in the struggle shows up in repetition of the leakers' story about Hollis' habit of telling dirty yarns. This is peddled as though it proves something sinister about Hollis, rather than how boring were the conventions of grown-up boys' bar talk of that generation. Another story proving the dastardly nature of Hollis was how he bought a large amount of discount scotch from the canteen before he retired.

On the other side, one common description that comes out of the older MI5 and MI6 says, in different words, how Wright seemed to like being hated, as though it proved him right. One can recognise their point. Watching Wright in the witness box, with his fringe of hair, a natural tonsure, it's not difficult to see him in the robes of a Dominican inquisitor, secure against his victims, armoured in infallibility. The old hands of the Fluency Committee had scattered but the man who had given so much or so little, depending on the mood of Peter Wright, Anthony Blunt, was still living in the London flat he had taken after retiring from the Courtauld Institute in 1974. He had earlier finished his term as Surveyor of the Queen's Pictures in 1972, but had been given an honorary appointment as Advisor. In 1976 a journalist, Andrew Boyle, had begun working on a book on the Cambridge spies, and had quickly enough picked up the Blunt story. By 1978 the Labour Government had heard enough about the progress of Boyle's book to know that there was a prospect of disclosure. The book was published in November 1979 and when Blunt's lawyers sought an advance copy, *Private Eye* picked up the story and ran it. *The Climate of Treason*, as the book was called when published, simply identified Blunt under the pseudonym of Maurice. Again, it was *Private Eye* who named him without hesitation. Wright was in Tasmania, but nonetheless it is very clear that Boyle had access to someone, or some persons, in the spook world who knew all about the Blunt interviews with both Martin and Wright, because a close reading of the book shows that the sources are clearly not the small number of politicians in the secret. Blunt's exposure was a great scandal, combining high culture, homosexuality and the royal family. After Margaret Thatcher made a statement, Blunt gave a press conference to a limited group of reporters, which he handled rather badly.

In 1978, when Labour was still in government, a draft statement had been prepared to cope with any public revelations on Blunt. When the Boyle book came out, this statement was worked over by the Cabinet Secretary, Sir Robert Armstrong, and on 15 November, using a Labour backbencher's question as a peg, Mrs Thatcher spoke briefly in the House of Commons, setting out the facts and justifying the 1964 immunity deal. In particular, she referred to the new information received in 1964, without naming Michael Straight, and went on, 'It did not, however, provide the basis upon which charges could be brought.'

In distant Tasmania, where he now lived, it was this sentence which enraged Peter Wright. The earlier feelings of toleration he had towards Blunt, when the man was his source, had evaporated. To him now, it was a tragedy that Blunt had never been charged, and it was dishonest of Mrs Thatcher to say that the evidence wasn't there. He was to say this again and again at the trial in Sydney and in talking to reporters outside. It was all tied in with the Establishment, it was the Establishment's fault that Blunt hadn't been charged.

Wright had kept up correspondence in England with his friends and one of those in whom he confided his opinions was Lord Victor Rothschild , to whom he had been introduced, it happens, by Roger Hollis in 1958. The third Baron Rothschild, Nathaniel Mayer Victor, is something of a Renaissance man. His family name, Rothschild, is, of course, the synonym for great wealth and banking.

From the early nineteenth century, Nathan Mayer Rothschild, the founder of the English dynasty, was the major financial adviser to the British government. The family's wealth and influence grew over the rest of the century, not only in England but also in France. Nathan Mayer's grandson, also Nathan Mayer, was the first Lord Rothschild and lived until 1915, long enough to know Peter Wright's correspondent, the third Lord, as a young boy. The Rothschilds, apart from making money, had maintained a tradition of public service, both to the nation and to their community. The prominence of the family caused prejudice, but the Rothschilds never dissembled their Jewishness. As one recent historian put it: 'Throughout, the Rothschilds maintained their pride and their dignity, and they helped to give their co-religionists faith.' As well as patronage of the arts, there emerged a tradition of scientific interest. Victor's uncle was an eminent zoologist, while his father, even as an amateur, became the world's foremost authority on fleas in his spare time. While the family's banking interests have remained strong in France, this century has seen a decline in their status in the City of London.

Victor did not go into banking. At Cambridge, where he was at Trinity, like Blunt and Burgess, the young heir took a science degree. He played cricket for Nottinghamshire, drove fast cars and, although admitted to the society of the Apostles, liked the company of women. Lord Rothschild is firm that he was never a Marxist, although from this time he called himself a socialist and when he went to the Lords was counted as a Labour peer. As an Apostle, he was inevitably a friend of Burgess and Blunt. After Cambridge, Burgess in particular then continued his friendship not only with Victor but also with his family. One of Burgess' favourite stories in later life was how Victor's mother was so impressed with his political and financial acumen that she made him her investment adviser, although, more realistically, Rothschild's sister, Miriam, thought it a tactful generous gesture on her mother's part to help the brilliant friend who had trouble settling down.

At the outbreak of war, Victor, by now the third Lord, went into MI5. There is some conflict as to who was the actual tenant of Victor Rothschild's flat at 5 Bentinck Street in London, off Oxford Street. Most reports have said that Blunt was the tenant, but more recently Lord Rothschild has said that two women, one of whom was, Theresa (Tessa) Major whom he later married, were the tenants and it was they who let Blunt and Burgess become sub-tenants. The flat, in the centre of wartime London, with Burgess as tenant, inevitably became the focus of a hectic social life. Two visitors, Goronwy Rees and Malcolm Muggeridge, the latter from his mature puritan perspective, have given highly colourful descriptions of the parties and diversions of the flat. Rothschild said that he rarely went there.

For years after Burgess' defection it would seem indeed almost twenty years up until Blunt's exposure counter-espionage officers

It is possible to pick up, in the leaks that have emerged about 5 Bentinck Street from so many people in the security services, a certain prurience on the part of the investigators about those people having such a good time. Wright would have remembered that he was mucking about with magnetic mines, while Burgess and Blunt were picking up rough trade boys and taking them home to a Lord's flat.

tried to find order and chaos in the comings and goings of Bentinck Street. Wright was the last of them, picking over names for clues. The trouble is that anyone experienced in the real world would know that trying to find order and significance in the social pattern of young people's lives at any time, let alone in the disrupting circumstances of war, is a pretty futile exercise. However, it is possible to pick up, in the leaks that have emerged about 5 Bentinck Street from so many people in the security services, a certain prurience on the part of the investigators about those people having such a good time. Wright would have remembered that he was mucking about with magnetic mines, while Burgess and Blunt were picking up rough trade boys and taking them home to a Lord's flat.

Rothschild was to pay for his generosity in letting out the flat and in recent years has tried strenuously to play down any close connection. Throughout the war he had worked in the small anti-sabotage section of MI5. As it happened, the Nazis were too erratically disorganised to mount a serious sabotage campaign in England. Still, Lord Rothschild dealt with one of their few serious attempts, a bomb planted in a case of onions imported from Spain, and for dismantling the fuse of the bomb, Rothschild was awarded the George medal. After the war he returned to science and became a Fellow of the Royal Society. In 1956 he published the definitive text on fertilization. A few years before, he had found the time to compile and publish a catalogue of his own collection of eighteenth-century printed books and manuscripts. He had gone into industry as the head of the oil company Shell's research unit. Peter Wright met him when he was in that job, and characteristically recalls the precise number of laboratories around the world under Rothschild's control – thirty- eight. The Lord had kept up his connections with MI5 after the war which, doubtless, made it easier when he was questioned after Burgess' and Maclean's defection. Suspicion did not seriously attach to him. Dick Goldsmith White thought highly enough of Rothschild to recommend him to Wright, although it was Roger Hollis who effected the introduction.

Wright saw Rothschild often. There was a tone of respect, even awe, in Wright's voice in the Sydney courtroom when he said: 'Victor knew everyone. I met more distinguished people at his house in Cambridge or his flat in London than anywhere else.' With Victor Rothschild, scientist, the boffin could relax and take without affectation the benefits of being with Lord Rothschild. Others enjoyed the Rothschild hospitality and charm, even, one might suspect, generosity.

The Lord was a good committee man for the governments of differing political colours. He was head of the Central Policy Review staff under the Conservative Prime Minister, Ted Heath, an organisation known colloquially as the Think Tank, which was an attempt to find a means of feeding new policy initiatives into government and, especially, the bureaucracy. Although there were high hopes it was not a particular success; bureaucrats don't like such organisations and can nobble them effectively. Roy Jenkins, Home Secretary in the Labour government in 1976, appointed Rothschild chairman of the Royal Commission on Gambling, a fairly heavy job to take on.

Every country, large, small or medium, has a pool of Lord Rothschilds, men or women with a solid record of achievement in academia or commerce, an assured income, a sense of public service and a capacity for being a good committee man. They are the people appointed to the BBC board, or to the Australian Opera, or to sit on a state government's cultural council, or to serve on a zoological garden's trust. Some are useless and pompous, others have intelligence and initiative, but they all suffer one common temptation: a sense of how things can be arranged behind the scenes. They become fixers, in the not unpleasant sense of the word. One problem is that this world becomes as necessary to them as their career twenty years ago may have previously been. Then they come to discover that their appointments really depend on governmental patronage, and that their generation of politicians have moved on. If it is hard enough for politicians to admit they are yesterday's men, it is perhaps even harder for that kind of noblesse oblige committee man to realise that his time has passed.

This is the pattern that emerges from Lord Rothschild's later life and seems to be what landed him in trouble. When *The Times* calls you 'an infernal busybody', as it did Lord Rothschild in December 1986, something has gone badly wrong. If Rothschild, even though having long since retired, was a sort of honorary member of the spooks' club as an old MI5 hand and a friend of Wright's, he can hardly have not picked up some rumours about the Fluency/K7 mole investigation. He certainly knew about Blunt long before the news became public. In an interview, published in *Conspiracy of Silence*, Rothschild said: 'Many people, I suppose, suffer blows which seem devastating, crushing and beyond belief. I have had three such blows, the last only twenty years ago when I was told by the "authorities" that a former close friend of mine had confessed to having been a Soviet agent for many years.' While he was questioned again after the Blunt confession, Rothschild would have been confident he was cleared. After all there was the example of how he had uncovered Philby in 1962.

In 1976, the year Wright retired from MI5, he found himself able to turn to Lord Rothschild for financial help. He was due for a lump sum of 5,000 pounds from the Service on his birthdate in August but, as he wanted to leave for Tasmania early, Rothschild gave him a bridging loan of 5,000 pounds. It was hard to believe that in the discussions about the loan, Wright didn't explain his reasons for leaving MI5, the failure of anyone to expose Hollis and the scandal as he saw it of continuing penetration. The two men corresponded between 1976 and 1978, with Rothschild, the good fixer, trying to organise an increase in Wright's pension, an effort which failed.

Then, in August 1980, 'out of the blue', Wright received a letter from Lord Rothschild, in which, as Wright said in court in Sydney, 'he told me that following Blunt's exposure, people were accusing him of having been another spy, on account of his friendship with Blunt. He asked me to write out a list of his achievements in MI5, which he could publish if necessary .' Wright wrote back agreeing, but said he couldn't afford to come to England to do the job. Rothschild phoned him, directed him to go to Hobart airport to meet a courier, who would take back Rothschild's letter and give Wright a first class return ticket to London. Wright cashed the ticket so that his wife could accompany him for medical reasons and arrived in London in the second half of August.

Over their first meeting in London at Rothschild's flat in St James Square, they reached agreement that Wright would come to Cambridge on the next day; there he would draw up Rothschild's list of achievements. Lord Rothschild has made no comment on Wright's account, but there are questions that arise. Wright was not in MI5 during the war when Rothschild heroically ran his anti-sabotage section. He could only have personal knowledge of what Rothschild had done after 1955. Possibly Shell laboratories had collaborated with MI5, as indeed Marconi had done when Wright was employed there. Rothschild's tip-off on Philby was in 1962 before Wright was in counter-espionage, but possibly Rothschild helped later with character sketches or judgments on the follow-up of clues from Wright's interview with Blunt. None of this couldn't have been written up and posted from Tasmania.

However, when Wright arrived in London he brought with him 10,000 words of a dossier he had started to compile in anger after Thatcher's misleading speech on Blunt to the Commons. It was 'a considered analysis of the problem of Soviet penetration in the past and how the continuing problem could be met in the future.' Wright didn't, at that stage, blame Mrs Thatcher for what she had said; he felt that she had been misled. Wright indeed affirmed that he still saw her as a 'new broom'. He hoped 'somehow' to bring his dossier to the Prime Minister's attention.

All of this he told Victor, who, however, had some more gloomy views. It would be pointless to give it to Mrs Thatcher, she would pass it on to MI5 and they would simply rubbish it.

'He said to me: "You know, she was sitting on that couch only a few days ago. She doesn't understand about intelligence matters." Victor did not elaborate, I knew him well enough to know the significance of what he had said and not to question him about it.'

The good Dr Watson put straight by Holmes. Next day they went to Cambridge and it took Wright a day and a half, he said, to write the list of Rothschild's achievements, and when it was over they added more. Meanwhile Rothschild had read Wright's dossier and thought it 'very good, but it was hopeless putting it through official channels.' The Lord then went on to suggest that the dossier should be published as a book but that Wright would need a ghost writer, and 'asked if I had ever met Chapman Pincher'. Even in such friendships as Victor's and Peter's there are sometimes lacunae. Wright did not tell Rothschild he had met Pincher before. Rothschild anyhow went on to say that such a book would probably prompt a parliamentary enquiry into the intelligence and security services. He then rang Pincher at about 4 o'clock and the author arrived at 6.30 pm. In the spirit of cloak and dagger Wright was introduced to Pincher as 'Phillip' and conversely Pincher gave 'no indication of recognition.'

It must be said that, since this came out in the trial, Pincher has denied that he ever met Wright before that day in Cambridge. It may be that he has forgotten the previous meeting because it seems curious otherwise. Pincher's book *Inside Story* refers to Wright's father, G.M. Wright, the Marconi man, and says that he had done work while at Marconi for MI5, and as well mentions Sir Frederick Brundrett, Wright's patron, some four times and speaks of him as 'my close friend'. There are also other differences between Pincher and Wright about the money discussions on that day. All we have for the relationship with Rothschild over those couple of days is Wright's story; the Lord, on legal advice, has made no statement. There is a ring of plausibility to the broad outline, but the details are often confusing.

The entrance of Chapman, or Harry as he is generally known, Pincher in to any story involving Security and Intelligence Services in Britain is almost inevitable. Pincher, unusually for a Fleet Street journalist in the post-war years, had scientific training. He carved out a niche for himself in science-writing overlapping into defence science, and in more recent years, according to the judgment of some, made himself into an authority on security and intelligence matters. Pincher has written for the *Daily Express* over those years and its loud brand of chauvinism chimes in very much with his gung-ho style. The good of the country is inevitably identified with the source, adapting without a blush Charlie Wilson's 'what's good for General Motors is good for the USA'.

Pincher sometimes likes to see himself as the scourge of the bureaucrats, military and civil, and it is true that, from time to time, he cudgels them with feathers. Pincher as an author is something of a name dropper, a regrettably common journalistic device. Because journalists are cut off from so many of the real stories, the temptation is to be grateful for a bit of recognition. Along with this goes gratitude for the exclusive story. Pincher has always shown a fascination for the security services. In the competitive world of Fleet Street, Pincher is jealous of his rivals there who write on intelligence matters.

A recent arrival on the scene has been Nigel West whose real name is Rupert Allason, son of a Tory MP and a prospective Tory MP himself. West has rapidly produced a series of books on MI6, MI5 (two), Special Branch and GCHQ. He certainly has some very good sources, appearing to have had access to internal official histories written of MI5 and MI6. West represents a supportive view for the Security and Intelligence Services, and is not quite as vehemently partisan as Pincher. For example, on Golitsin, he is cautious compared to Pincher who still calls the Russian probably the most important defector ever. Apart from venturing into his rival's territory, West, in *A Matter of Trust: MI5 1945-72,* rather put the veteran down, in a faintly patronising way, with a story of the divisions in MI5 when years ago Pincher approached the service with an offer to help them by cultivating a Russian diplomat with whom he had some social connection. West said that some favoured using him '. . . the other view was that Pincher had been intrigued by the Security Service and this was an attempt for him to learn something of its methods and personnel . . .' There was some contact with Pincher which ended in 'a gentle brush-off'. Hell hath no fury like an old bull journalist scorned.

Among the most interesting reading to emerge during the trial in Sydney, which certainly produced some absorbing material, was a letter from Pincher to Wright in Tasmania in 1983. The letter was written after the book which Pincher and Wright had collaborated on, *Their Trade is Treachery*, had been published, and it seems that almost two years later Wright was still worried about the legal fallout. West's book referred to in the letter is *A Matter of Trust: MI5*, which was to feature largely in the trial in Sydney. The Martin mentioned is Arthur Martin who was sacked by Hollis and 'Phillip' is the code name for Wright agreed upon at the Cambridge meeting and still being used. The letter reads in part (the emphases are Pincher's own):

'Dear Phillip,

Your letter of 9.1 has just arrived. I can see no reason why we should change our postal arrangements. I am sure that we are in *no danger*.

On New Year's day I was shooting with . . . [someone who] told me about West's book. It is an extraordinary story and I urge you to have nothing to do with West or with anything associated with him.

For reasons I do not understand Martin agreed to see West . . . West then wrote his book and in it . . . quoted Martin by name . . . is so stupid and naive that he then sent Martin a copy of the script for his comments. Martin was terrified and immmediately took the book to the office in an effort to get himself out of the mess. The office . . . then issued an injunction to have the offending parts removed for, had the book been published, the Government would have had no option but to prosecute both Martin and West. West had included several names including yours. He was required to remove them but still kept you in as Peter W. (see enclosed page) . . . He also works with . . . Penrose and Freeman. I am sure he will have told them about you. If they turn up at your house have *nothing whatever* to do with them. . . . [The Government is] still considering whether to prosecute Martin but cannot do that without prosecuting West . . .

I can assure you that there is no intention whatever of taking action against me *which means you too.* I lunched with Dickie Franks recently and he told me that they had my book weeks in advance and came to the conclusion that they would rather I did it than anyone else. They had heard that West, Duncan Campbell Penrose etc were on the trail and preferred my authorship. Further I have been functioning for some months as specialist adviser (paid) to the Parliamentary Defence Committee and have just been appointed chief adviser on an inquiry into positive vetting. I am also elected to an MOD Committee to study censorship problems arising out of the Falklands affair. So I do not think we are unpopular.'

The release of the letter in Sydney indicated how far the rift between the collaborators had gone. In London, Pincher told *The Times* that, although Wright was under the impression that he, Pincher, had destroyed Wright's letters, this was not so. The letters would reveal the true nature of Wright's persistent demands for more money.

However, in Cambridge that evening, under Rothschild's benign chairmanship, all went well. Wright said later the agreement was that he should get half the royalties and that Rothschild should use his Swiss bank to channel those royalties to Tasmania. Wright now affirms that he did not suggest the idea of the book. 'My original intention was simply to bring what I knew in front of the Prime Minister.' Wright, in court, put a long argument that he believed that he was being used as part of a double operation.

'It never occurred to me that Rothschild would lend himself to a scheme of this kind without some degree of official approval. Victor was always very secretive and it was not done to ask him questions. He loved intrigue and conspiracies and was always engaged in secret deals and arrangements, especially with politicians. He loved to exert influence behind the scenes. His wealth and position are so great that I could not believe that he would risk it for such a scheme if it was not at least tacitly approved . . . It struck me as particularly odd that Rothschild should suddenly seek to secure the publication of MI5's secrets about the molehunts, since he had always before counselled caution. Before 1980 he always used to tell me that he felt confident that he would be able to secure something through his political connections.'

It will be clear that in many ways Wright is a naive man, although he has thought himself cunning, as with, say, the interrogations of Blunt. An alternative theory to his in 1980 was that Rothschild's political connections were not as powerful as they might have been. He was after all a man who had once called himself a socialist and who had worked for Ted Heath, not the best of qualifications in the age of Thatcher.

Pincher took the dossier away and then in October flew out to Tasmania for a week to talk to Wright. It is clear from the size of the book when it was published in March, that Pincher had it in the pipeline anyhow, but the Wright material, tying in so well with his framework of belief, and providing useful headlines, was worth a lot to him. Ultimately Wright was to get 30,000 pounds in royalties. For any author or anyone in the publishing business, the round figure is curious; also the amount, given hardback sales, paperback sales, serialisation and American rights, seems too low. Perhaps some of the source of the later bad feeling between Pincher and Wright is a dispute over what that oral agreement might have been in Cambridge. Pincher spoke several times of how the truth about the deal would emerge in the Sydney courtroom, but counsel for the UK government did not oblige, putting only a few questions about the deal, and none of them concerning royalty amounts.

In court in Sydney, however, Wright's announced cause of disappointment with Pincher was that 'the last chapter of the book concluded that there was no need for an enquiry'. So Wright felt badly let down, because the point had been to get an enquiry. But far from convincing Thatcher, the book had provoked her to making what Wright viewed as another misleading statement. Wright and Pincher, bound to each other by the journalist's necessity to keep the source in contact, and Wright's need in exile for continuing attention, kept up their correspondence.

While disillusionment set in long ago with Pincher, Wright shows no signs of similar disenchantment with Lord Rothschild. An observer can get the impression that the acquaintance with Rothschild is one of the things that Wright has valued most in his life. At the beginning of his references to Rothschild in court, the expert on the penetration of the services gave Rothschild and his second wife, Tessa, of the Bentinck Street flat, a ringing endorsement of innocence: 'I am absolutely certain that neither of them at any time spied for Russia.'

Even when he spoke in the witness box of Rothschild's capacities for intrigue, there was no criticism: indeed there was a kind of deference. In conversation with journalists outside the court, Wright regarded the differences with Pincher with a kind of high good humour, some provoking his big grin, but with Rothschild's name he switched to a familiar and respectful tone.

The winter nights are long and cold in southern Tasmania, where the Wrights settled to be near one of their children but also to be rid

The land the Wrights bought was an old apple orchard and they live in a couple of conjoined timber, apple-pickers huts. The money, the locals point out, has all gone into the property

of an England which, for the old boffin, had lost its purpose. They sold up their share in an Arab stud in England and brought out together with their furniture and their books, a grey stallion, Pizzicato, whose death early in the life of the stud caused a financial crisis. They bought land in a valley, a couple kilometres out of the country town of Cygnet, which is about fifty-five kilometres south of Hobart. Named by a French explorer in 1793 the area was mainly used for apple and potato-growing, with timber-felling in the hills until the entry of England into the Common Market, which crippled the local apple industry. The land the Wrights bought was an old apple orchard and they live in a couple of conjoined timber, apple-pickers huts. The money, the locals point out, has all gone into the property, which is well-fenced. Now with less land than in 1976, the twenty-three hectares they hold are valued at about $74,000 for rating purposes. (Their original investment was $11,400.)

It was an odd area for the English spook to end up in. Originally settled by the Irish, it still has a higher Catholic population than anywhere else in the island. With about 800 residents, the town of Cygnet runs to three hotels, three churches and three service stations. Wright used to go into the local Returned Soldiers licensed club in the early years but, because of illness, hasn't been seen recently. The locals all say that since his various sicknesses the work of the stud has fallen almost entirely on his wife, Lois. Wright comes to town in his flat tray Landrover for supplies. If MI5 had tapped the local council's for hire photocopier, which Wright uses, they could have learnt the secrets of the manuscript years ago. The couple keep to themselves, the people who know them speak with real warmth of Lois, 'a real English lady'. Perhaps their only contribution to wider local life has been to display an election poster at their fence for the local Liberal (conservative) member. The property is hilly, running off Slab Road, some bush, cypress pines and willows along the small creek in one corner. The stud's registered name is 'Duloe Arabian'. A service from his black-brown stallion, Indian Treasure, comes for about $800. The stud has a good name among fanciers and breeders, although most of the sales are on the mainland. Arab horses are a distinct luxury for the well-off, so the market fluctuates very much according to economic times, particularly in rural sales — it would not have been so good in recent years. Duloe Arabian runs about twenty Arab mares as well as a changing number in for service and agistment. The Wrights are, like a number of their neighbours, city people who have retired to take up old agricultural land, but most of the retired people don't run anything as serious as a stud.

Wright in exile is a long way from his old friends and family. The latter, of course, means different things to different people. One of the more bizarre anti-Wright stories that surfaced in the English press during the trial was an interview in the *Daily Mail*, who sent their chief reporter out to have a talk to Wright's sister, Elizabeth. Published under the heading 'Wright's Trade in Treachery, by his Sister', the story quoted her as calling her brother unreliable and manipulative, a devious embittered man with a history of embroidering fact with fiction. 'If Peter is not totally discredited by his activities, I shall be very upset . . . I would have thought he was unemployable, he was so unreliable. You could not believe a word he said. He lived in a fantasy world. How he got into MI5 always puzzled me.' After talking about how, if Peter wanted to fix you, he would 'organise a devious plot to undermine you,' the sister played her last card, 'he was always a difficult child, always liked his own way.' Someone had to show Wright the cutting in Sydney, and when one reporter eventually plucked up his courage, Wright read it expressionlessly, handed it back, said, 'Haven't seen her for thirty years,'and walked off.

Slab Road, outside Cygnet, is a long way from family and friends in England. The stud should have been absorbing enough for both of them, but Wright, the old sick man with his heart condition, diabetes and shingles, also had his dossier which grew steadily into a book. There was his correspondence with Pincher, Lord Rothschild and others, who shared his belief and the BBC World Service to bring him the voice of Margaret Thatcher, who had let him down.

In Tasmania, while he worked on his dossier, Wright had only the occasional letter from Pincher. There was some desultory discussion between them on the possibility of collaboration on a book which would deal with penetration on both sides of the Atlantic. Pincher remembers it rather as being more about Anglo-American intelligence relations. The journalist didn't tell Wright that he was working on another book, *Too Secret Too Long*, to be published in 1984. Comparing the two is interesting. Pincher's basic informants in the second book are rather more sophisticated than in the first, and the quality of the argument, while still deeply flawed, has improved.

Meanwhile Wright had been approached by Paul Greengrass, a television producer with Granada TV's 'The World in Action' programme, late in 1982, but he had rejected the proposed interview. Greengrass was persistent and used the case of Michael Bettaney, the MI5 officer who had been charged with attempting to contact the Soviet Union in September 1963, as a fresh argument to persuade Wright of the need to speak out about his knowledge of penetration.

Finally, in December, Wright agreed to do an interview and it was done in Tasmania the next month. However, it was July 1984 before the programme went to air, making Wright the first and so far the only one of the Fluency group rebels to go public. While Wright was pleased with the programme, it finally made him an outcast as far as the security and intelligence services were concerned. He had been reminded in a letter in July 1981 of his duty of confidentiality. When, after the Granada programme, he agreed to his dossier being passed on to a Conservative member of parliament, Alister Kershaw, who on his own initiative handed it over to Margaret Thatcher, he found that Lord Rothschild had been right.

Kershaw sent it back with the news that the Prime Minister had passed on that it was all old hat. Further, Kershaw relayed a warning that he would be prosecuted if he returned to England.

It was a rejection which hurt; when Wright says that in 1980 he still thought of Margaret Thatcher as a new broom, someone he could convince if only he could get through to her, he was speaking the truth. Margaret Thatcher is, after all, closer to the boffin than she is to the Tory grandees. Wright was able at first to convince himself that even if she had misled parliament over Blunt, it was someone else's fault, or the Establishment's fault, but the statement in March 1981 following the publication of *Their Trade is*

Treachery provoked him to anger which showed even in the witness box, four years later. While Wright couldn't admit it, one of the most hurtful things that Thatcher had done was to destroy the delusion that he and others had clung to about Lord Trend's position on Hollis. Even after de Mowbray had been told, the hard core believed the Trend report really upheld them, but that it had been covered up. They convinced others of this too. Jonathan Aitken, the backbench Tory MP in his letter to Thatcher in 1980, warning her about rumours and reports, said:

'• That as a result of great anxieties within the Security Services, and following a later review of the Hollis-Mitchell cases, Lord Hunt, the then Secretary of the Cabinet, in approximately 1975 asked his predecessor Lord Trend to write a report on the penetration of the Security Services. It is alleged that Lord Trend's report concluded that high level Soviet penetration had taken place and that Hollis was probably the Soviet agent responsible.

• That Hollis and Mitchell between them recruited other unidentified Soviet Agents into the Security Services. It follows from this that our Security Services may still be severely penetrated today.'

Pincher, in *Their Trade is Treachery,* had said that 'Trend concluded that there had been a strong prima facie case that MI5 had been deeply penetrated over many years by someone who was not Blunt', and that Trend 'named Hollis as the likeliest suspect'. Mrs Thatcher was cutting in her characteristically jerky prose:

'Lord Trend said neither of these things and nothing resembling them. He reviewed the investigations of the case and found that they had been carried out exhaustively and objectively. He was satisfied that nothing had been covered up. He agreed that none of the relevant leads identified Sir Roger Hollis as an agent for the Russian intelligence service, and that each of them could be explained by reference to Philby or Blunt. Lord Trend did not refer, as the book says he did, to the possibility that Hollis might have recruited unidentified Russian agents into MI5. Again, he said no such thing.'

It was pretty devastating. Mrs Thatcher had made it clear that Lord Trend was unconvinced by all the bulk of circumstantial

But to be rejected by someone he'd had faith in, the new broom, has been bitter. His statement to the court in Sydney had more than four pages on 'the Thatcher statements . . .' half of which were censored. She'd gone over to the Establishment:

evidence such as the microphones which didn't produce any results in the Soviet embassy in either Canberra or Ottawa.

Pincher evaded the criticism of Mrs Thatcher in the second edition of *Their Trade is Treachery*, when he fell back on trying to discredit Trend by referring to Harold Macmillan's clearance of Philby in 1956 as comparable.

Wright's response to the inconvenience of Mrs Thatcher's statements on what Trend's report actually contained is simply to ignore it. To buttress the case that Mrs Thatcher had misled parliament he honed in on one particular word, 'based'. Mrs Thatcher had said that the 'case for investigating Sir Roger Hollis was based on certain leads that suggested, but did not prove, there had been a Russian intelligence service agent at a relatively senior level in the last years of the war.' 'Based' to most readers would mean the foundation and starting point for that period and what came later, but Wright treated the word as if it meant that the only evidence Trend looked at was the world war evidence. His solicitor, Malcolm Turnbull, evidently on his instructions, tried very hard to make something of the word 'based' in the court hearing but, as he struggled manfully, it sounded thinner and thinner as the base, using the word properly, for an indictment of Mrs Thatcher. Wright, in his statement in court, said of the Prime Minister's statement that it is 'simply not correct to say that the extent of the penetration was thoroughly investigated'. What on earth then had the Fluency Committee and K7 been doing all those years? However, reason is irrelevant. Wright is the true believer and, just as Golitsin believes that Dubcek was a disinformation plot, Wright will maintain his belief against anyone else's opinion.

But to be rejected by someone he'd had faith in, the new broom, has been bitter. His statement to the court in Sydney had more than four pages on 'the Thatcher statements in the Commons', more than half of which were censored. She'd gone over to the Establishment:

'Britain's leaders . . . have shut their eyes to the problem of

Soviet penetration ... the British Establishment has never accepted that it was, en masse, penetrated by the Russians. It may be that the Establishment fears the public debate of this problem will cause the people of Britain to have less faith in its leadership than the Establishment would like it to have ... People have mistakenly seen the penetration problem as having been limited to a few colourful, often homosexual, Cambridge intellectuals. It went much farther and deeper than that. It revealed fundamental weaknesses in British society. Understanding the past will enable us to prevent repetition in the future. In my life I have seen so many people in power turning a blind eye to this sort of thing.'

Wright was in the witness box in Sydney to fight the top people who had turned a blind eye. He had written a book which struck at the fundamental weaknesses of British society, created by them. He was prepared to break secrecy, because the leadership had let Britain down. To read his statement through in full is to realise that, in a way, the Russian intelligence service and penetration had become secondary. Wright's struggle was by now against the great and powerful, and by exposing their secrets he would hurt them. MI5 was his life and home for twenty years, the exposure of its members' outrageous plotting against a Prime Minister must wound the organisation grievously. But Peter Wright doesn't care. He is Samson, eyeless in Gaza.

Armstrong disgraced his country, MP says

...or revealed in spy evidence

Ingham news blackout on MI5 secrets case

By Anthony Bevins
Political Editor

THE PRIME Minister's press secretary, Bernard Ingham, yesterday imposed a news black-out on anything to do with the Australian secrets case as an MP accused Mrs Thatcher of using civil servants to betray and attack Sir Michael Havers, the Attorney

only to attack MPs, but also to scatter seeds of division which are growing between the Prime Minister and the Attorney General.

"In a shabby betrayal of a Cabinet colleague, the Prime Minister is inducing civil servants to attack Attorney General."

...said that the House ...the Prime

...decision to launch ...court case.

It has repeatedly been reported in newspapers recently that Sir Michael was responsible for

told the Commons yesterday th ...the trade of a Prime Minister wh ...lacked the courage to admit fa ...ure and cut up her ministerial co league "is one of treachery."

Brian Sedgemore, Labour for Hackney South and Shor ditch, told MPs that Sir Robe Armstrong, Secretary to the Ca net, had given evidence in t Australian court about the We minster lobby briefing system.

He reported that the Head the Home Civil Service had sa that those briefing lobby journ ...ets "seek to influence opini ...accepting responsibil ...in the public ...Gove ...ment there."

□ Chapman Pinch ...Peter Wright, his m ...or his 1981 book sugge ...MI5 boss Sir Roger H

...atcher faces tough week on MI5

MAN PINCHER — THE MAN WHO WAS THERE, TELLS HOW THAT SPY BOOK REALLY CAME TO BE WRITTEN

Mrs Thatcher an...

...secrets stupidity

By Edward Pearce

...H Sir Robert ...strong, that coy prim-...riage among first-division ...servants, held up in ...gga Wagga, subjected to ...interrogations and ...cking doubts of colonial ...rristers, lamentably ...willing to be advised by ...e best wisdom of the Brit-...h Civil Service on the need ...rally 'round young Bingo ...trouble, one

other freedoms. You will find no defence of State convenience, the wisdom of the older and more eminent heads, or any other sort of polite authoritarianism in the pages of Friedrich Von Hayek. Mrs Thatcher's great glory was that she did not belong to the old Establishment, the word-in-your-...ter-not-let-this-

defenc ...ters is ...man tryin ...he can't a

As fo ...they all ...Grandfa ...mark w ...ing to ...States. ...ing to ...only fr ...in the ...w ...guilty ...tion g ...days

Sir Robert's ordeal – the trial in Sydney 2

Malcolm Turnbull and his wife Lucy, the defence team for Peter Wright.
Photo: Colin Townsend

Peter Wright had tried and failed with Chapman Pincher, Granada TV and Sir Alister Kershaw, but boffins don't give up. After the Granada exposure there was, inevitably, interest from publishers and literary agents in the old man in Tasmania. There was something near to a contract from Hamish Hamilton, but nothing came of it and afterwards Wright spoke darkly of MI5 pressure. Then in November Brian Pearlman, managing director of William Heinemann, came to Melbourne on his annual visit but slipped away to Tasmania with the managing director of Heinemann Australia, Nick Hudson. Paul Greengrass came out about the same time to talk with Wright about collaboration. A deal was struck, but to keep away from the Official Secrets Act, Heinemann Australia was to be the publisher. *Spycatcher* became the firm's top secret project, but like many secrets it was impossible to keep for too long, although the firm tried.

Hudson's wife, Sam, typed up Wright's dictated material at home at night. It was then forwarded to an Amsterdam cover address and Greengrass went there to work on the transcript, beyond the power of MI5. Messages to him were in a crude code: 'Rubber Duckie' was Sam's pseudonym, while carrying over from Pincher and Rothschild, Wright was 'Phillip'. Some people at Heinemann Australia began to feel that Hudson was getting too absorbed in the whole

Peter Wright had tried and failed with Chapman Pincher,
Granada TV and Sir Alister Kershaw, but boffins don't give
up. After the Granada exposure there was, inevitably,
interest from publishers and literary agents in the old man in
Tasmania.

project, even though early direct expenses were not great. Wright
has said that he got 18,000 pounds advance, but some of this went
to Greengrass, with more up front for him as a collaborator, but a
declining royalty share later. American interest was canvassed, but
Heinemann didn't want to be tied to a firm contract, although one
company indicated it would be prepared to start talking at $100,000
advance. Hindsight might suggest it would have been better to take
the money and use American publication to drive a breach through
the UK secrecy wall.

It's surprising the secret held so long. But someone in the British
government reads the *Observer* as well as the Melbourne *Age* News
Diary column, even if they take their time brooding over the
contents. On 31 March 1985, there was a brief item in the *Observer*
telling of the publisher Heinemann's plans to publish the memoirs of
ex-MI5 man, Peter Wright, in Australia in order to forestall any
attempts to stop the book. Next month in Melbourne, the News
Diary column worked up the item a bit. Heinemann, it said, had
rented a warehouse in Amsterdam to serve as a distribution centre
for Europe if MI5 tried to impound the book, confusing the
Greengrass cover office. The wheels of Whitehall grind slowly and,
after more time than it took a reasonably fast sailing ship to get to
Australia, the Sydney Establishment law firm, Stephen Jacques
Stone James, wrote letters of ultimatum to Wright in Tasmania and
to the manager of Heinemann in Australia, at two different
addresses. Unless they heard within seven days, the firm's client, the
UK government, would 'consider such action to protect the interests
of the Crown as they may be advised'.

Six days previously in London, John Bailey, the Treasury
Solicitor, had written in similar terms to the managing director of
the home firm, William Heinemann Limited. In Australia, Wright
acknowledged his letter with thanks in a curt 'Its contents have been
noted,' as did the Australian publisher. Brian Pearlman,
Heinemann's managing director in England, wrote indignantly

about being given an ultimatum in August: his legal adviser was on holidays. However Heinemann did meet Bailey early in September and after that meeting the Treasury Solicitor demanded a permanent undertaking that they would not publish Wright in any form, to be given by 17 September. Whatever the deadline in the UK, in Australia the UK government moved more rapidly, gaining temporary injunctions on Wright and Heinemann Australia on 13 September.

The United Kingdom action was to be tried in the Equity Division of the Supreme Court of New South Wales. For a lay person few topics are more eye-glazing than the by-ways of legal history, and it sometimes appears that the legal historians like to keep it that way. In the standard Australian text on Equity, a former judge writes in the Foreword, 'The lawyer dreads the layman's question. What is equity? Well, no crisp answer will satisfy the earnest enquirer.' Quite. For the purposes of this case all that need be said is that the Equity Division of the New South Wales Supreme Court is where a dispute over confidentiality will end up. In say Victoria where the publisher's head office is, or Tasmania where Wright lives, there is no separate Equity Division, but wherever judges are sitting on confidentiality, they will be ruled by the network of precedents and principles that are called Equity Law as distinct from Common Law. The generalisation closest to the truth is that Equity Law fills the gaps, it is an attempt to create judge-made law to cope with certain areas where there are no statutes or Common Law. If that is understood, it can be seen that the right of judges to order discovery of documents to ensure a fair trial, as the judge in this case was to do, is at the very heart of Equity. The notion that the court should be overborne by a mere affidavit from whatever source, senior public servants or otherwise, is repugnant to the proud, if abstruse, principles of Equity, particularly where the flame is kept alive, as it is in New South Wales, by the maintenance of a separate Equity Division. If that were not enough, all the texts agree that the law relating to confidentiality is far from rigid. All this means that the style of an Equity Court hearing is very different from, for example, a criminal trial before a jury where a judge must take extreme care to maintain the forms of impartiality. In an Equity Court there is a continuous dialogue between the judge and counsel. Propositions

63

are produced, queried and debated. Much of the outrage at the active court room role of the presiding judge, Mr Justice Powell, from government sources and their press sympathisers in England was based on a fundamental misunderstanding of the style of an Equity hearing.

The prospect of an appeal from the Equity Division to other forums where, perhaps, more deference might be shown to a Cabinet Secretary's affidavit was much less promising than a legal team in England might have grasped. Mr Justice Powell had to take into account a body of recent case law in Australia which took a distinctly robust, undeferential view of the rights of courts to scrutinise the affairs of organisations like the Australian Security Intelligence Organisation (ASIO) or even the MI6 equivalent, the Australian Secret Intelligence Service.

Perhaps the most important of all the cases was that heard in the High Court in 1980, of the *Commonwealth of Australia v. John Fairfax,* particularly as the presiding judge, Mr Justice Mason, had especially addressed himself to the fundamental principle of Equity in relation to the disclosure of confidential information. The case arose from the serialisation in the *Sydney Morning Herald* and the *Age,* in Melbourne, of extracts from a book *Documents on Australian Defence and Foreign Policy 1968-75,* published simultaneously by Angus and Robertson. The book, as Mr Justice Mason noted in his judgment, 'contained general information taken from official documents relating to intelligence services,' among other topics. The government had mounted its case on two foundations: first, that publication of the documents in full breached copyright and, secondly, that it would be against the public interest because the information was confidential and the recipients were under duty not to disclose it. As it happened, the Australian government won on the copyright question while losing on the public interest point. The book was later published avoiding extensive direct quotation of the documents in line with the copyright point.

Mr Justice Mason in February 1987 took over the position of Chief Justice of Australia in succession to Mr Justice Gibbs. The core of his position came in the following extract:

'The equitable principle has been fashioned to protect the personal, private and proprietary interests of the citizen, not to protect the very different interests of the executive government. It acts, or is supposed to act, not according to structures of private interest, but in the public interest. This is not to say that equity will not protect information in the hands of the government, but it is to say that when equity protects government information it will look at the matter through different spectacles.

'It may be sufficient detriment to the citizen that disclosure of information relating to his affairs will expose his actions to public discussion and criticism. But it can scarcely be a relevant detriment to the government that publication of material concerning its actions will merely expose it to public discussion and criticism. It is unacceptable in our democratic society that there should be a restraint on the publication of information relating to government when the vice of that information is that it enables the public to discuss, review and criticise government action.'

He did provide the rider:

'If, however, it appears that disclosure will be inimical to the public interest because national security, relations with foreign countries or the ordinary business of government will be restrained there will be cases in which the conflicting considerations will be finely balanced, where it is difficult to decide whether the public interest in knowing and expressing its opinion outweighs the need to protect confidentiality.'

But even after the rider it was a very tough-minded view laying down that claims of public interest had to be tested and questioned more closely. In effect, it was not just enough for a public servant, of whatever level, to affirm public interest in relation to national security in an affidavit. The court would have to consider the argument. The case was to be cited continually throughout the hearing in Sydney.

Justice Mason himself had referred among other cases to the matter of *Sankey v. Whitlam* which had reached the High Court in 1978 and had resulted in a very clear statement that protection of Crown privilege was not absolute or permanent. Sankey, a private individual, had brought a prosecution alleging breaches of the Crimes Act by the former Prime Minister, Gough Whitlam and other ex-ministers of the Crown. The claims arose from the government's approval in 1975 of a large overseas loan. The then Chief Justice, Mr Justice Gibbs, in his judgment said then:

'It is in all cases the duty of the court and not the privilege of the executive government to decide whether documents will be produced or withheld . . . If a strong case has been made out for the production of the documents, and the court concludes that their disclosure would not really be detrimental to the public interest, an order for production will be made.'

An early benchmark defining the attitude of the High Court to the security organisation, ASIO, came in 1982 in a case where the Church of Scientology sued the Director General of ASIO, Mr Justice Woodward. Like most matters involving the Church of Scientology it was all very complicated, but what matters is that the majority of the court ruled that the question of whether intelligence was relevant to security and whether a document was relevant to the purposes of security could be determined by a court. Mr Justice Mason was one of the majority and said that while 'no one could doubt that the revelation of security intelligence in legal procedure would be detrimental to national security,' it did not follow that ASIO's activities should be completely free from legal review.

Again, in 1984, the High Court addressed itself to the question of the power to direct ASIO to produce material. The case *Alister and Anor v. The Queen* came as an appeal by members of a religious sect, the Ananda Marga, from a number of charges including attempted murder. They had sought, at their trial in the New South Wales Supreme Court, the production of ASIO material relating to an informant, Richard Seary, who was the main Crown witness. The trial judge had refused. The High Court divided three-two in favour of the production of any documents 'that enable the court to discover whether any such documents existed and then to inspect them for the purposes of determining whether they should be disclosed to the accused.' The Federal Attorney-General had objected on the grounds of national security. Chief Justice Gibbs, with the majority, rejected the Attorney's claim, saying 'I am not at all convinced that the public interest requires that ASIO should be able in all cases to refuse to disclose whether any document exists, and to refuse to produce it if it does exist.'

Not only had the internal security organisation, ASIO, come under scrutiny, but the overseas organisation, the Australian Secret Intelligence Service (ASIS), had been the subject of action and discussion in the High Court.

Not only had the internal security organisation, ASIO, come under scrutiny, but the overseas organisation, the Australian Secret Intelligence Service (ASIS), had been the subject of action and discussion in the High Court. But apart from that, in Australia, the existence of the equivalent of MI6, that organisation that Sir Robert Armstrong could not acknowledge, the Australian Secret Intelligence Service had been officially acknowledged in the Report of the Royal Commission on Security and Intelligence by Mr Justice Hope in 1977; since then it has even been in the Budget, albeit with a rather deceptive one line entry.

On 30 November 1983, a number of ASIS officers carried out a realistic hostage-rescue exercise in the Sheraton Hotel in Melbourne, an exercise that got out of control. A hotel door was broken down with a sledgehammer and the masked members of the party ran through the ground-floor foyer brandishing two machine-guns and a pistol; all without any warning to the hotel or its clients. The Victorian police, who also knew nothing of the exercise, chased and arrested four of the men. The police demanded their names and those of all those involved. The participants themselves sought an injunction to restrain the Commonwealth government from giving their names to the State police on the grounds of confidentiality in their contract. The majority of the High Court threw out the application. The participants had sought to invoke national security but that was rejected. One judge, Mr Justice Brennan, invoked the principle 'if an act is unlawful – forbidden by law – the person who does it can claim no protection by saying that he acted under the authority of the Crown' and went on:

'The principle is fundamental to our law though it seems sometimes to be forgotten when executive governments or their agencies are fettered or frustrated by laws which affect the fulfilment of their policies. Then it seems desirable to the courts that sometimes people 'are reminded of this and the fate of James II ...'

Much of the criticism, whipped up in England, of the presiding

67

judge seemed to treat him as some kind of bizarre eccentric, but there was, in fact, in Australia a very solid basis for the discovery of documents even if they came from or were related to security organisations. Underpinning this was a firm legal doctrine that no institution was above the scrutiny of the courts and that national security as an argument had to be justified.

In Melbourne in the months preceding the injunction, the Wright project had become even more important for Nick Hudson of Heinemann. His job was in danger, for a complex of internal company reorganisation reasons, even though he had worked for Heinemann for twenty-six years. In October, at the Frankfurt Book Fair, the international market place for the sale of translation rights, Hudson, himself a German speaker, took up his place by his company's stand wearing a badge, which said, in German 'Forbidden to talk about the spy book'. At home, the legal bills were ticking up, and the advice was very pessimistic and very expensive. Hudson had been referred to the text-book authority on equity, R.P. Meagher, QC, who held out no hope. Indeed lawyers to whom Hudson spoke seemed not to understand the public interest and freedom of speech issues he was trying to canvass. There is a story current among the publisher's staff about some lawyers in the corridor, after a meeting with Hudson, laughing about how he didn't understand the hopelessness of his case. Costs were mounting, later an estimate of six figures was current in the company. Then in November Hudson and the firm parted company. While Heinemann was sorting out its internal affairs, the major players in the court case were lining up.

The trial was to be heard by Phillip Ernest Powell, or Perc, as he is known to his older friends, who has been a Justice of the Supreme Court of New South Wales since 1977. Powell was aged fifty-six during the hearing, almost fourteen years from the statutory senility of the judges' retirement age, as he liked to remind the court during more complex arguments. The allocation of cases in his division is worked out at a judges' meeting and those who know say it is fairly informal. If Powell had put up a bid for a case, the attitude would be if he wants it, he can have it.

Powell's reasons for interest are easy enough to discern. As a citizen soldier, or territorial in English terms, in the fifties, he had been a captain in the Royal Australian Intelligence Corps and he was a voracious reader of history, as well as spy thrillers. During the trial he was able cheerfully to upstage counsel, in particular, Theo Simos, QC, for the UK government, by his range of reading. His sense of irony and self-deprecation did not always translate well into headlines: an early reference to a 'Lowly Colonial Judge' was to be interpreted as a chip on the shoulder. The *Daily Express* and *Sun* found his court to be a forum for Pom-bashing, which was seen as the source of all Sir Robert Armstrong's problems.

Powell's colleagues at the bar in Sydney were amused and then baffled when told he was supposed to be an Anglophobe. Could this be the man who kept the range of Twining's teas in his chambers, recalled with gusto his appearances before the Privy Council, admiring Lord Scarman above all, and finally, as he was to show in the court, took pleasure in identifying the judges of England, their promotions and books. Those who know Powell talk about him as an old-fashioned Tory, apolitical and certainly no Labor lawyer. He won the Equity Prize in his final year, while taking first-class honours. Apart from his practice, Powell has been an adviser to the Australian parliament's Senate Standing Committee on Regulations and Ordinances and the editor of *Mercantile Law*.

He was educated at Sydney High School, an elite government school of the city, during the war years. Powell managed to be a champion hurdler and later captain of the New South Wales athletics team. The ultimate handyman, Powell designed his own home. His great love in poetry is the Australian vernacular verse writer, C.J. Dennis, who wrote about the street larrikins of Melbourne, from whom he can recite huge slabs. (It was a measure of control that the Judge only referred to C.J. Dennis once during the case, and also a measure of their different styles that Malcolm Turnbull, for the defence, appreciated the reference, and Theo Simos, for the government, did not.) Powell's practice was mainly commercial, but he did some work for one of the bigger unions, the mainly pastoral Australian Workers Union, as well as for the State of New South Wales in the national wage case. Everything about Powell marks him as a traditional lawyer of his generation, except perhaps the fact that, in private, his language could be more colourful. For his generation, the peak of their professional careers were appearances in London before the Privy Council, before this

Indeed, it was the Privy Council which in 1980 was to give Mr Justice Powell one of his most notable victories.

option was abolished.

Indeed, it was the Privy Council which in 1980 was to give Mr Justice Powell one of his most notable victories. Cadbury Schweppes Pty Ltd, the maker in Australia of a drink called 'Solo' sued a smaller firm called Pub Squash Company Pty Ltd, claiming their rival had stolen the advertising campaign and deceived the market. It was a substantial case: twenty-six days and sixty-four witnesses. Mr Justice Powell dismissed the claim and Cadbury Schweppes went to the Privy Council, which unanimously upheld the colonial judge. The judgment of the Council was delivered by Lord Scarman, whom Powell, as a counsel, had so much admired. It was shot through with compliments: 'Their lordships would not seek to better the trial Judge's description . . . a quite remarkable passage . . . entitled to the greatest respect . . . did not allow the structure of his judgment to mislead him . . . analysis . . . cannot in their lordships' view be challenged.' Finally, 'the Judge had not only to conduct an elaborate and detailed analysis of the evidence, which he certainly did, but to bear in mind the necessity of the balance.'

None of the Judge's career can be said to add up to the curious picture presented of Mr Justice Powell as some kind of coarse, hick-lawyer-Anglophobe, out of an early Ronald Reagan movie. The Judge was harsh with the UK government because its tactics, particularly during the preliminary hearings, angered him as a judge. Those who sit in the equity jurisdiction deal very largely with the debris of commerce and, in that world, time is money; a delay gives a desperate defendant time to juggle his funds, or makes it not worth the plaintiff's while to continue, and vice versa. Equity judges become used but not reconciled, to a great variety of tricks and when Mr Justice Powell saw the government of the United Kingdom doing the same he saw red. As far as judicial interventions during the hearings went, Mr Justice Powell had learnt about those early in his career. When still practising, he used to tell his juniors, 'Let the Judge go on talking, never interrupt him.'

'The long term in office of the Liberals has resulted in their becoming part of the establishment, and this has attracted to their ranks men adverse to change of any sort . . . No matter

70

how great a conservative one is, one would have to admit that times change and it is thus logical to say that policies must also change lest they become outmoded' – *The Sydneian* 1970.

The political thoughts of Malcolm Turnbull, in his mid-teens in the school magazine, do not exactly indicate a red-ragger, although he was to be described as a maverick again and again during the trial. Sydney Grammar School has not been a nursery for rebels, but rather a training ground for good solid professional men. Malcolm Turnbull, even at school, sharply divided people – into those who liked him and those who disliked him. Those who liked him admired his brilliance, his achievements. Those who disliked him are often imprecise, but seem to be trying to say that he is a little too ambitious. In his final year at school he took the English prize and the oratory prize, as well as being a senior prefect. Turnbull's background was conventional enough, coming from the reasonably well-off Australian upper middle class; his father Bruce was a hotel broker and later investor. However, his mother and father separated when he was nine and she, Coral Lansbury, went to live in the United States. Turnbull has never made any secret of this fact but, like other children of split marriages, he found the break shattering. Those who know him talk of the effect showing in an edginess and abrasiveness that conceals an insecurity.

Coral Lansbury was unusual for her generation in being a woman in her own right. She wrote radio and television plays for both the ABC and the BBC. She was a cousin of Angela Lansbury, the actress, and a niece of George Lansbury, the British Labour leader in the 1930s. She took a PhD and, when she left to go to the United States, built a new career as an academic. She is now a professor of English at Rutgers University, in New York state. For good measure, she has published books on Trollope and Elizabeth Gaskell; her two most recent publications are *The Old Brown Dog: Women Workers and Vivisection* and *Sweet Alice.* The latter is described as a rich mixture of biting satire, knockabout farce and uproarious comedy by a female Tom Sharpe. Coral Lansbury is a formidable lady and established a firm presence in the court gallery, impossible to ignore, stylishly dressed and certainly no blue stocking. In Australia for a holiday, she took some audible pleasure in her son's achievements in cross-examination.

By contrast the father was a quiet, even shy man. People speak of him as a typical Australian. He died in a commuter plane crash in the early seventies, leaving his son a substantial amount of money as well as a country property at Aberdeen, a rich rural area by Australian standards. At the University of Sydney, Turnbull seemed more destined for journalism than the law, working for the *Bulletin*. When he got the Rhodes Scholarship for his year, he went to Brasenose still undecided on his career, and while in England worked on the *Sunday Times*. Turnbull doesn't talk much about Oxford; people get the impression that he didn't much like the place. On return Turnbull went to the Bar, but then gave that up to become a solicitor, so that he could be an in- house lawyer for Kerry Packer. Packer's empire was at a peak when he joined, embracing magazines, television stations and a host of other companies from ski resorts through the World Series Cricket to salt mines. Turnbull established a good reputation as being a no holds barred defender of press freedom. He got good money for it. The strength of Turnbull is that when he takes something on it becomes absorbing, even a crusade. It may have been Packer, media magnate, paying the money, but for Turnbull each case involving freedom of speech was a personal struggle.

However, working for Kerry Packer brings handicaps as well as benefits. The intense competition and enmity in media rivals that of Fleet Street in the thirties. Just as Lord Beaverbrook was a demon figure to many, so, in his time, has Kerry Packer been a man people like to hate. This is helped by the fact that Packer is a massive punter, unabashedly prepared to bet millions of dollars. It was the association with Packer that probably cost Malcolm Turnbull Liberal Party selection for the blue-ribbon Federal House of Representatives seat of Wentworth. Nevertheless, he gave it a very close run.

During the Wright case it was possible to find a feeling in some media people that it was all a Turnbull affair. Given that Packer was the enemy, this feeling was a kind of justification for being indifferent to the possibility of giving publicity to his man Turnbull. Visiting English journalists were surprised that the Australian coverage of the Wright case was not as extensive as they thought it would be. Certainly, the Australian press are not as keen on spy sto-

Certainly, the Australian press are not as keen on spy stories as their English counterparts, but it was true that some of the press coolness at the executive level had its sources in some of that feeling about Packer and Turnbull.

ries as their English counterparts, but it was true that some of the press coolness at the executive level had its sources in some of that feeling about Packer and Turnbull.

For all that he worked for one of the big men, there is still a streak of the outsider in Turnbull. A sub-editor on the *Guardian*, putting a head on a diary item about Turnbull, called him 'a razor-edged loner', taking his cue rather intelligently from the copy. Sitting l5,000 miles away, he still got it right; it was close to the essential Malcolm Turnbull.

Turnbull married Lucy, the daughter of Thomas Eyre Forrest Hughes, QC, the most expensive silk in Australia today, and this is sometimes taken as a reading of his desire to get into the Establishment. However, in terms of Sydney and the wider politics, the interesting thing is that Hughes, like his son-in-law, is a bit of an outsider. At school he was the English-Catholic-family boy among the Irish Australians at the Jesuits' St Ignatius College. Later on in politics, he was a Catholic in the Liberal Party, which had almost no Catholics at all. Hughes eventually went out of politics when the Liberal Party overthrew John Gorton as Prime Minister. To him, Gorton had been a political leader to whom he had held a personal sense of loyalty which he couldn't transfer. Hughes hasn't actively sought the bench although it is probably true he could have had a position in any jurisdiction quite easily. While he was once seen as a stitched-up conservative, he is now more relaxed, prepared to surprise people by taking a brief for Mr Justice Lionel Murphy, the High Court judge and former politicial rival who was threatened with deposition by parliament.

Lucy, Turnbull's wife, a recently qualified lawyer, assisted him in the Wright case. It was a cut-price affair. Wright didn't have much money, and the publishers, by the time they turned to Turnbull, were on the edge of giving up. Legal opinions obtained had been deeply pessimistic until Turnbull came along. Geoffrey Robertson, the Australian-born hard-case lawyer in London, had told William Heinemann that Turnbull was probably their last chance, he was a fighter and so Turnbull was hired. Once Turnbull was on the case, there was no question of losing; he had identified with Wright and the justice of his cause. And it was possible to see how Wright sometimes his support needed almost desperately.

Turnbull's position as a solicitor, standing up in court and conducting the case, was acceptable under Australian practice. But if he were a barrister he would not have been able to act outside the case as a solicitor could, and indeed should, to wheel-and-deal and protect and advance his client's interests. A solicitor's objectives, if he is fulfilling his obligations to his client, should be to reach a settlement which can avoid the expense of litigation. Turnbull was, to use a London example, trying to be a Lord Goodman, the famous solicitor-fixer, and he strove to get the UK government to back off from its injunction or at least to offer to edit the book.

Theo Simos, QC, was a rational choice for the plaintiff given that the UK government hoped to fight the case on the grounds of confidentiality. Simos was acknowledged as one of the small group of top equity lawyers in Sydney, and had lectured on the subject at the Law School. He had a Bachelor of Arts and a Law degree from Sydney University, as well as postgraduate degrees from Oxford and Harvard. A studied and courteous man, he was popular in the profession having been both secretary and treasurer of the Bar Association. Like Turnbull, he was educated at Sydney Grammar, but twenty years earlier. Simos is a second-generation Australian Greek. The family came from the desperately-poor Aegean island of Kythera, in its time renowned for the sponge fisheries, a very dangerous occupation. They established themselves in the mountains town of Katoomba outside Sydney, and in 1916 opened the Paragon Cafe, now described as part of the National Estate, with a classical art deco interior as well as handmade chocolates which are famous throughout Australia. The family are now well-off enough to own a house in Sydney's comfortably stylish Centennial Park, next door to the Nobel Prize author, Patrick White.

Against Turnbull, the hare, Simos appeared to be as a tortoise. His policy was consistent, sticking to confidentiality as the main core of his case. Simos, like most equity lawyers, is prepared to negotiate, but he was hampered by the need to refer everything back to London. Several times in the case it was the evident that the back

74

If MI5 had their liaison officer in court, he was under deep cover, never speaking to the rest of the English team. There was one mysterious man in yellow string trousers, Indian jacket, shoes, no socks, clutching a book called Zen Flesh, Zen Bones, who was perhaps the modern spook in disguise.

seat drivers in London not only did not understand the Judge, but also did not understand how the law of Australia had evolved. Simos had been briefed by Stephen Jacques Stone James, the solicitors who had sent the original ultimatum letters to Wright and the publishers in 1986. Richard Feetham, one of the partners of the firm, a South African expatriate who had been a lower court judge in that country, had the passage of the case. Stephen Jacques (pronounced Jakes) is one of the half dozen or so top commercial firms in Sydney and one of the top twenty in the country. Partners don't come cheap. The rate for someone like Feetham is something like $200 for an hour (divided into six-minute units) and that's without the backup charges for other staff. Simos would have been on about $2000 per day. William Calwell, who had done some of the preliminaries, was the junior, although he took silk during the case. The rest of the UK team came from England. John Bailey, the Treasury solicitor, the public servant in charge of the government's litigation, was there almost to the end of the trial. One of the assistant Treasury solicitors, David Hogg, was also flown out. Bailey looked like anyone on the London underground, but Hogg was a little more Oxbridge. Sue Marsh, a senior principal from the Attorney-General's office, looked like an extra at an Iris Murdoch party and showed considerable capacity to vary the sober colours women lawyers must wear in court. Sitting in the gallery was the deputy head of the news department of the Foreign Office, Ivor Roberts, who had spent two years in Canberra and was married to an Australian. His job was to handle the English press, which he did very smoothly, never wilting under the pressure of the more undisciplined liberal wing of the press.

If MI5 had their liaison officer in court, he was under deep cover, never speaking to the rest of the English team. There was one mysterious man in yellow string trousers, Indian jacket, shoes, no socks, clutching a book called *Zen Flesh, Zen Bones*, who was perhaps the modern spook in disguise. Otherwise, it was hard to see what reason he had for being so interested in the case.

But for all the lawyers, the most important member of the defence team was Robert Temple Armstrong, GCB, KCB, CB, CVO, Secretary of the Cabinet of the United Kingdom government since 1977, and head of the Home Civil Service since 1983.

The politicians for whom Armstrong has worked personally are a roll-call of the last fifty years: Reginald Maudling and, Rab Butler, two Tory might-have-been Prime Ministers; Roy Jenkins, Edward Heath, Harold Wilson, James Callaghan, and Margaret Thatcher. Armstrong was actually private secretary to Harold Wilson at the time of the alleged buggings in 1974. Sir Robert had come to Australia by virtue of his office, which made him the government's principal adviser on security and intelligence matters. It is the practice in English government to have a strong section of the Cabinet Office concerned with overseeing the security and intelligence services.

Over the years since his appointment, and again during the trial, Sir Robert has been the subject of a number of newspaper profiles, but the writers have found him an elusive man to pin down. It was easy to pick up the obvious: son of Sir Thomas Armstrong, the organist at Christ Church, his Oxford college, time for the boy at Eton and then the classics at Oxford, entry into the Civil Service in the Treasury in 1950. From then onwards it was an escalator ride up all the way. The profiles tell of his work on the Covent Garden Opera House board and his passion for Wagner, a taste which doesn't equip you for the witness box. There was only one surprise, the break up of his marriage in 1985 and remarriage to a woman who did the catering at Downing Street. By general consensus his greatest achievement is the Anglo-Irish Agreement. One gets the impression he is very much the mandarin's mandarin. Although the press profiles found nice things to say, the press don't much like him and he doesn't much like them. One profile during the trial had it that 'he is not a believer in secrecy for its own sake'. If that were the case his dissimulation over the days in the dock would have led to plaudits from Machiavelli. The projection is wrong. Sir Robert very clearly thinks secrecy, not only confidentiality, is a very good thing, indeed the very basis of good government. On his return from Sydney, typically enough, one of his first acts was to tell the

Birmingham City Library that they could not publish the diaries of Neville Chamberlain, the Prime Minister at the time of Munich, which they hold.

Malcolm Turnbull was before the court early in February for a brief hearing. At another hearing late in March, Mr Justice Powell showed, for the first time, some signs of impatience to get the matter under way. Calwell, for the UK government, asked for more time to prepare their case. Mr Justice Powell, commenting it is 'time to get the matter into the marketplace', gave them three weeks. Turnbull foreshadowed one of his main lines of defence when he maintained that much of the material in the manuscript was already in the public domain and there was nothing in it that could assist a hostile power.

Much of the legal manoeuvrings over the next six months dealt with two pieces of housekeeping that had to be cleared up before the trial. Each side was entitled to submit interrogatories, that is, questions on points of fact, approved by the Judge, to make for a fair hearing and to cut down trial time. Interwoven with these questions was the discovery of documents, to be disclosed by the Judge's order from each side to the other. In the more commonplace cases in equity, such as commercial disputes, the sorts of documents produced would typically be company accounts, such disclosure being generally acceptable. When national security was alleged to be involved, however, it had become a more complicated issue, as indicated in the Australian High Court judgment cited earler. The UK government was to fight tenaciously against disclosure, carrying its case against Powell to the Appeals Court twice.

In early June at one hearing, counsel for the UK government, Calwell, made it clear that it would resist any compromise on the book. He stated that three of the chapters in the 100,000 word manuscript were permissible but, as for the rest, only the odd sentence was unobjectionable. At a later hearing that month, when he complained about the singular lassitude on the part of the plaintiff, Mr Justice Powell opened up on a theme which was to exasperate him throughout the rest of the preliminary hearings. In July, foreshadowing further delay, Calwell, still appearing for the UK government, told the court that he had to go to London that month to confer and that there was still no final indication from the United Kingdom government on the number of witnesses. Mr

Justice Powell said that he wanted the trial on as quickly as possible because of the age of the defendant, a point he referred to on a number of occasions. On the same day the High Court in London imposed on the *Observer* and the *Guardian* a ban on reporting or publishing any material obtained from Peter Wright, including allegations that the Service had committed unlawful and criminal acts. However the court did not maintain a previous injunction against reporting the open court proceedings in Australia. The judgment relied heavily on an affidavit supplied by the Cabinet Secretary, Sir Robert Armstrong. Mr Justice Millet said: 'I have no doubt that the effective functioning of any security service force requires its affairs to be kept secret.' The position the Australian High Court had adopted in recent years on the balance of the disclosure clearly had no influence. An appeal by the two newspapers against the terms of the injunction later that month failed.

Back in Sydney, on 12 August, the UK government had an ominous foretaste of the robust scepticism of the presiding judge. Looking at the assertion that the publication of the book, dealing in part with relations with other agencies, would help hostile foreign agencies, Mr Justice Powell said that he felt the distinction was sometimes 'utterly unreal, for example, to say that knowledge that MI5 had had trouble with Edgar Hoover of the FBI, could hardly be said to help Moscow Centre.' On the same day, Malcolm Turnbull signalled one of his planks when he said that the manuscript of Wright's book contained information on twenty-three criminal conspiracies and twelve instances of treason by members of the British Security Service. He was foreshadowing the 'unclean hands' argument which is said to justify a breach of confidentiality to enable the disclosure of a crime.

Two days later, the UK government tried to head off open debate on these charges by conceding 'for the purposes of these proceedings and not otherwise' the truth of the undisclosed allegations made by Peter Wright in his book and on Granada Television, and those television revelations made by ex-MI5 employee Cathy Massitter. (She resigned in 1985 and went public, particularly on taping of trade unionists and civil libertarians.) It was a not uncommon device in Equity courts, a way of clearing the ground, but naturally enough the concession led to headlines in England,

and the confusion still lingers. Turnbull called it a cynical exercise of manipulation. In Whitehall, the briefers were quick to explain to journalists the concessions were only a legal technicality.

At the end of August, Mr Justice Powell delivered a judgment on the disputes between the parties over the interrogatory questions and outlined the points at issue. The defence was claiming that the information in the manuscript was in the public domain and no longer confidential, that it was already known to the Soviet Union, or in any case it was so out of date that it wouldn't hurt the United Kingdom government. In addition, in the public interest, details of crimes and breaches of government directives should not be suppressed. The plaintiffs stood on their confidentiality argument, irrespective of whether the matter in Wright's book was true or false, had been previously published or would cause harm. It was an attempt to narrow the whole topic of the hearing which proved to be unsuccessful.

September and October saw a flurry of exchanges of legal documents, though the UK government sought to resist the discovery of documents. However, the real action in that period was taking place on the telephone. Malcolm Turnbull, solicitor, was trying in a number of different ways, to bring pressure to bear on the UK government to back down or at least agree to a censorship of the manuscript. Turnbull was a personal friend of Jonathan Aitken, MP, the man with an interest in spook matters who had written to Margaret Thatcher in 1980 on the allegations and rumours about Hollis et al. Turnbull contacted Aitken with a compromise proposal and Aitken passed it on by letter to the Attorney General, Sir Michael Havers. After what Aitken took as initial warmth in response, the answer came back as a 'flat no'. Turnbull was also helpful to journalists as, of course, were the Whitehall briefers. He warned that a toughly fought case would mean political trouble for the United Kingdom government, the Labour opposition was certain to take the case up. One of the journalists, Chapman Pincher, put a twist on that later to make Turnbull sound like a Labour operative, but Turnbull, whose political record has already been noted, was simply playing the tough lawyer. Indeed it had become clear that, as with all his cases the young solicitor had come to identify with the old man, even to be protective of him, and the best service he could do was to find a way out to avoid an expensive legal case. But Turnbull failed. Indeed Turnbull's taking phone calls and making his own was picked up by some people around government in Whitehall and stored away for future use.

On 4 November, the Judge gave the defence about half of what they'd wanted in disclosure of documents. In effect, the material on government reactions to certain books published by Chapman Pincher and Nigel West, on the Wright/Granada TV programme, and the Cathy Massitter programme, as well as papers relating to Margaret Thatcher's statements on Blunt and Hollis would have to be delivered up. The United Kingdom was to produce them by the 12th, only five days before the opening of the trial. Predictably they did not and on Friday 14th tried to reopen the case again with the Judge, bringing a harsh rebuke for 'serpentine weaving'. Simos and the Judge clashed over a period on the breadth of 'public interest'. In the course of these discussions on what the public should be entitled to know, the Judge tossed down as a hypothetical case the question of whether or not the public should know if Roger Hollis was the model for Bill Haydon. Simos, confused by the similarity between the Le Carre character's name and that of the Australian Foreign Minister, Bill Hayden, looked blank and finally, picking up the reference, had to confess that he hadn't read Le Carre. At the end of the day, Simos announced an appeal, which it seemed might threaten to delay the whole case when it opened the next week.

Offstage in Canberra that week, a curious little sideshow was being played out. Margaret Thatcher had made a late personal appeal to the Prime Minister, Bob Hawke, for Australian intervention in the case in support of the UK government, intervention meaning Australian representation by counsel and arguments in favour of the continued suppression of the book. The Hawke Labor government had had their fingers rather badly burned earlier on in a muddled affair involving David Combe, a lobbyist who had been a former ALP official, and his social relations with a KGB man. There was a Royal Commission into the affair and in the course of it one senior cabinet minister was rapped for letting out something trivial from the Cabinet Security and Intelligence Sub-Committee, so discussion on the Thatcher request had been tightly held. The Sub-Committee met on the Monday of that week and did not reach a deci-

There is a commercial television advertisement in Australia for a non-alcoholic drink served in bars called Claytons, which is tagged 'the drink you have when you're not having a drink'. So the Australian government's very half-hearted move was tagged around Canberra as 'the Claytons intervention.'

sion, although someone, presumably with a vested interest in trying to stampede people into intervention, leaked to the press that there had been a decision. There was a brief discussion about the question in Cabinet the next day, and the Committee met again on Friday. The line being run around parliament house on intervention was that the barriers had to be maintained because otherwise every ASIO man would be writing his memoirs. There was some caution, however, in the government and the Director General of ASIO, Alan Wrigley, was not himself over the top in his support. It was the Canberra bureaucrats who were more keen. The government decided against briefing counsel to intervene on the floor of the court and as a compromise let Michael Codd, the Permanent Head of the Prime Minister's Department and Chairman of the Permanent Heads' Committee on Security and Intelligence, present an affidavit in support. Given the response Codd was to provoke from the Judge, in the long run the UK government might have wished that he hadn't been allowed to come forward. The Australian Solicitor General, Dr Griffith, sat in the court with a watching brief the public-interest-immunity questions of principle, which always worry a government, but as no significant issue arose, he didn't address at all. There is a commercial television advertisement in Australia for a non-alcoholic drink served in bars called Claytons, which is tagged 'the drink you have when you're not having a drink'. So the Australian government's very half-hearted move was tagged around Canberra as 'the Claytons intervention.'

The trial was to be held in Court 8D in the bunker-like Commonwealth-State court building on Queens Square in Sydney's central business district. Like most court rooms in the building, it has no windows and the dreariest possible utilitarian furniture. The capacity for the press and the spectators was less than adequate: ten seats in the press gallery, eight in the jury area (which were taken over by an unwritten acceptance by the core of the English press), twenty-eight seats in the public gallery, usually half taken by the press overflow. The seats were almost always full and the tolerant Judge allowed up to a dozen or so to crowd standing near the door. On peak days, some press, having missed out, sat on the floor to take their notes. The public gallery had its usual run of court building regulars, pensioners, both aged and invalid who find their theatre in the courts and tend to whisper loudly when bored. Barristers and solicitors from other cases, settled or adjourned, tended to drop in to see the star case of the moment.

While the hearing was getting under way in Australia, in question time in the House of Commons, Roy Jenkins spoke of the 'increasing ludicrousness of the government's posture before the Australian courts,' and went on to ask the Prime Minister to recover her 'sense of proportion on this issue'. As well, Jenkins said 'as the Home Secretary who saw the Trend report,' he wanted to affirm that he believed in the strong probability of Sir Roger's innocence. Mrs Thatcher invoked sub judice to repel Mr Jenkins' question, and others. However a little later the Speaker, Bernard Wetherill, ruled that actions taking place in an Australian court were not sub judice. Neil Kinnock went for the attack to ask the Prime Minister to concede that as the matter was no longer sub judice she would have to answer. In a dust-up, the Tory Conservative Leader of the House, Mr John Bitten, intervened to question the Speaker's ruling and got a flea in his ear, with 'I prepare myself very carefully for question time every day and for any eventuality and I took this matter into account today.' Confronted with this uncompromising approach from the Speaker, Mrs Thatcher retreated by saying it would be 'unwise' and 'rash' to comment on a court case and invoked national security. The Commons descended into a wrangling confusion on points of order and the government lost the headline battle in the papers next day, with the emphasis being given to the Speaker's ruling.

In Sydney, on the first day (18 November), it was a crowded Court 8D, with an overflow prepared to queue outside for hours in the hope of getting a seat.

Sir Robert did not have a long walk to the witness box: there were only a few steps from his chair at the rear of the plaintiff's team. He settled himself and thanked the Judge for the offer of a break if he felt fatigued, an offer he never took up. Turnbull was on the other side of the court in a sober, well-cut double-breasted suit, blue tie, but with one of his collar-tips sticking up; he is one of those who never quite look dapper no matter how expensive the suit. Sir Robert had his Christ Church tie, dark suit, soft collar blue shirt – 'Jermyn Street', according to one knowledgeable journalist, although he couldn't quite explain why.

Simos established who Sir Robert was, and that he had sworn the affidavits presented to the court, then it was the turn of the defence. The first question set up the crucial issue, the credibility of Sir Robert Temple Armstrong. Turnbull: 'Sir Robert, is everything in these affidavits true?' The answer was a brisk 'yes'. The same clipped response came when Turnbull sought to probe the UK government's consistency or otherwise on the publication of disclosures about the Security Service. Sir Robert was adamant; the government view was consistent, because that was what he had said in one of his affidavits. Pressed as to whether that was his sincere belief, the Cabinet Secretary felt confident enough to venture beyond the one word answer with the statement: 'It is my belief. If I have a belief it is a sincere belief.'

Turnbull's cross-examination style was circuitous, deliberately. He got to many issues the long way round but with most he got there eventually. It was not your cabinet briefing session with a minister, usually polite, asking the mostly obvious questions and the deferential lesser public servants in the background. The apparent disorder would offend Sir Robert's sense of form as much as the recurring barbed questions. However Turnbull's techniques did work; on a number of occasions coming back to a topic he teased the witness into modifications, almost amounting to contradictions.

Sir Robert looked puzzled when the first case Turnbull chose was Cathy Massitter an ex-MI5 employee who in 1985 went public and accused the Security Service of extensive illegal telephone tapping. Sir Robert found it easy initially to brush Miss Massitter aside. Her allegations had been the subject of an investigation by Lord Bridge, who had reported to the Prime Minister that no telephone interceptions had been conducted otherwise than in accordance with the properly laid down rules and procedures. The Judge showed off his knowledge of English legal personalities with 'I assume that is

Lord Bridge of Harwich', which was readily confirmed by Sir Robert. Turnbull showed rather less regard for Lord Bridge. As he pointed out in one question, Lord Bridge's internal investigation took four days when his enquiry had to cover some 6,129 warrants issued over fifteen years. In reply Sir Robert merely said he understood that it had been a full investigation.

Then Turnbull set out to enmesh Sir Robert in the implications of the August admission that, for the purposes of the case, the allegations of Wright and Miss Massitter were true. Why then wasn't the Home Office investigating Miss Massitter's allegations? 'I don't know, because it isn't,' said Sir Robert. A little later the witness disclosed the thinking behind the UK government's August concession: 'My understanding was that we were not concerned in these proceedings with the truth or otherwise of the allegations as a result of the admission we made.' What he and others in the plaintiff's team had thought was that they were off the hook. Now Sir Robert was in the box and had realised that he was being cross-examined anyhow on the claims. The device had misfired. Pressed further on Lord Bridge and his investigation, Sir Robert Armstrong agreed that it could only be a matter of trust when he came to give his findings from the unpublished evidence. That was all of Miss Massitter for the present, although she would return. 'Matter of trust' provided the cue for Turnbull to turn the cross-examination to Nigel West, a pseudonym of Rupert Allason and his book *A Matter of Trust: MI5 1945-72*, which had been published in 1982. To the first question on the book, Sir Robert admitted that the government had a copy of the original manuscript even before the book was published. Simos was quick to object to any questioning on the book pending the hearing the next day of the appeal on discovery of documents on internal UK decision making, including its reaction to West's book. Mr Justice Powell allowed the cross-examination pending the outcome of the appeal and neatly summed up the issues of such cross-examination. Would it provide evidence of (implicit) authorisation and would the allowing of the publication of certain material be an admission that such publication was not to the detriment of the government?

Without difficulty Turnbull drew from Sir Robert Armstrong the agreement that legal action had been commenced to restrain publication of West's book and further that after discussion and agreed deletions there had been a consent order to clear the way for publication of *A Matter of Trust*. Had all the material obtained by West in breach of confidentiality from his admitted former-MI5 sources been removed? Sir Robert had affirmed as much in his answers to those interrogatories made before the hearing, however sensing the danger, he fell back on saying that to the best of his knowledge the answer was true based on what the Attorney-General, Sir Michael Havers, believed at the time. His caution was to be justified as Turnbull moved in.

The defence solicitor read out an extract from the UK government's affidavit when they sought an injunction against West. In particular the government complained that the manuscript contained names of former MI5 officers and also organisational charts of the Security Service. Yes, Sir Robert agreed, the government claim had contained such a statement. Turnbull pounced. He opened a copy of *A Matter of Trust* and pointed out when published it did contain the names of ex-officers and furthermore, organisational charts up to 1965. For the defence it was a breakthrough on the claim of inconsistency, the first of a number and served to strengthen the authorisation argument.

That done, Turnbull went on a fishing expedition on West's sources. Sir Robert agreed that it was known that Arthur Martin had supplied information to West and it was also believed there were some other ex-MI5 officers. So, Turnbull asked, had all the information supplied by Martin in breach of confidentiality been removed? Sir Robert Armstrong, now more cautious, shifted his ground saying that those responsible for the agreement allowing publication believed it 'would be removed'.

Turnbull filed the topic away, although he would return to it, and moved on to nag at the notion put forward by the government that ex-MI5 officers had an 'absolute' duty of confidentiality. Weren't there breaches of the absolute duty of confidentiality which, because of the content of the information, might not be detrimental to the national security? Sir Robert played back: 'the information may not; the source from which it came may be'. It was a wedge and Turnbull took the tactical opportunity to make the offer on Wright's behalf that his book should be handed over for vetting. Sir Robert didn't

Mr Justice Powell asked Sir Robert: 'Let's assume that in his book Mr Wright says that the standard small arms weapon issued to MI5 agents is a Walther PPX, or even one of them borrowed from Mr Ian Fleming, a Beretta, how could that conceivably affect the national security of the United Kingdom?'

take up the offer and brushed aside the question of scale of detriment with, 'Our argument is the breach of the duty of confidentiality'. Although Turnbull returned to the possibility of the vetting of the book at intervals throughout the trial and the Judge himself made a number of comments indicating that he might be prepared to do a 'blue pencil' job, the UK government never wavered. The final reasoning for this adamant line is hidden in the minds of a few people: Margaret Thatcher; Sir Robert Armstrong himself; the head of MI5, Sir Anthony Duff; the MI5 legal adviser, and possibly, but not certainly, the Attorney-General, Sir Michael Havers. All that an outsider can say is that Sir Robert's distinctions in his answers as to why no compromise with Wright was possible simply don't stand up. There was a deal possible with West over material he had obtained in breach of confidentiality, why none with Wright? As time went on the plaintiff refined an argument to meet the case: the insider/outsider distinction.

However on this day a harried Sir Robert fell back on the claim that the publication by Wright even of some information that was already in the public domain could cause detriment to the national security. 'All of it?' asked Turnbull. 'All of it could,' came the official answer.

This brought an intervention from Mr Justice Powell, demonstrating his knowledge of, among other things, James Bond novels. The Judge commented that he found himself 'straining a little' to follow the distinction and asked Sir Robert: 'Let's assume that in his book Mr Wright says that the standard small arms weapon issued to MI5 agents is a Walther PPX, or even one of them borrowed from Mr Ian Fleming, a Beretta, how could that conceivably affect the national security of the United Kingdom?' Sir Robert said that information coming from an insider could be helpful to a hostile intelligence service or a terrorist group.

Turnbull then zig-zagged back to the West manuscript, a topic

Sir Robert was probably happy to have left behind — he was going to have to become accustomed to this defence tactic. If there had been a breach of confidentiality even after the agreement with West, Sir Robert said that it would not have been a matter for him but rather for the Attorney-General, that is, Sir Michael Havers, to launch any proceedings. For the first, but not the last time, Sir Robert was to seek to shift ultimate responsibility to the Attorney-General. This was to prove an error, a very considerable error.

As the going got rougher that morning, Sir Robert started to show a faint stutter, when Turnbull pressed him. At one stage the defence solicitor described Sir Robert's answer as 'almost weasel words'. Simos objected, 'I don't know what "weasel words" means,' which gave Turnbull his cue: 'It has been judicially defined as meaning words which are devoid of content, just like an egg which has been sucked out by a weasel.'

At the beginning Sir Robert had leant forward slightly in his chair, the picture of a thoughtful man, ready to help. Now under pressure he pushed himself back in the chair. His anger showed in a frown (he had the eyebrows for a good one) and the upward tilt of the jaw. It was then that one realised whom he had reminded one of all along: he might have been a brother of Alistair Sim, that old-style British actor who could bring a certain authority even to being headmaster of St Trinian's. The tension flared into the first really personal exchange.

Turnbull: 'What are you saying?'

Sir Robert: 'I am saying what I have said in my answers, Mr Turnbull.'

Turnbull: 'I am sorry there is a big barrier between you and I in terms of the English language. I recognise that we have a local dialect.'

Sir Robert: 'That is not troubling me, actually.'

Turnbull: 'That is good.'

Sir Robert: 'Mine may be troubling you, but that is another matter.'

Turnbull: 'No, it is fairly clear. We watch a lot of television.'

Mr Justice Powell cut in with a quip to settle them down, telling Turnbull: 'That's your free ad for the day.' Turnbull and Sir Robert cooled down and a few minutes later were able to share a joke about their common lack of mathematical ability. Turnbull said that he had had to go to the law for that reason and Sir Robert responded, 'I had to become a civil servant.'

Even so Turnbull turned the exchange around with a capping comment: 'You could have joined the Secret Service and you would never come to court.' A light exchange, and only a brief interlude in a relentless cross-examination on the process by which agreement had been reached to allow publication of the West book. Finally, just before the morning tea break, Turnbull got the concession he wanted: Sir Robert agreed that he could no longer contend that there was no breach of confidentiality in the West book as published. It was a useful score for the defence; if authorisation for those breaches of confidentiality was given to West, why not to Wright?

After the break, as Turnbull nagged on at the West book details, Simos struck back by objecting that the West book was simply not relevant. Mr Justice Powell overruled him and in doing so commented: 'It is relevant for the defence to establish if it is a fact that much or perhaps even only some part of this material (in Wright's book) is already in the public domain; allowed or authorised to be published by the plaintiff, in which event the defendants could say that the allegation made against them is unfounded.' This first indication of judicial thinking can have done nothing to cheer the plaintiff.

Pushed on the answer that he'd given an oath in the interrogatory documents before the hearing which had suggested that all objectionable matters had been removed from the West book, Sir Robert fell back to, 'If it has misled, I regret that.' This drew a harsh response from Turnbull: 'Sir Robert, your whole life has been involved in writing submissions, writing documents, expressing yourself fully and clearly, has it not . . . yet you are confronted with an answer which a court has ordered you to answer on oath and you answer it inadequately.' Sir Robert's faint stutter came back as he denied that his answer was inadequate expressing his regret if it had been 'interpreted that way'. The cross-examination arising from the West book ended with a discussion on truth.

Turnbull: 'Sir Robert, how high on your scale of values is telling the truth?'

Sir Robert: 'It reckons very high.'

Turnbull: 'Is it the highest?'

Sir Robert: 'There are a number of things I wouldn't wish to grade in order of priority.'

Turnbull: 'Would you tell an untruth to protect what you perceived as national security?'

Sir Robert: 'I would not wish to do so.'

Turnbull: 'You may not wish to do so, but can you tell us whether you would under no circumstances tell an untruth to protect national security?'

Sir Robert: 'I don't think I can answer a question like that, I have not been faced with such a situation . . .'

Turnbull: 'You have never been put into a position where you have had to tell an untruth in order to protect sources or operations of MI5?'

Sir Robert: 'I cannot recall being in such a situation.'

Turnbull: 'A little while ago you said you had not been. Now you are saying you can't remember.'

Sir Robert: 'I do not distinguish between those.'

Sir Robert might have expected more questions on the West agreement, but Turnbull switched abruptly to Chapman Pincher's book *Their Trade is Treachery.* His cross-examination style only appeared abrupt; in fact he had borrowed from journalism and literature. At the end of a chapter in cross-examination, Turnbull liked to have a hook to the next section, and his little passage on truth was really only a curtain-raiser to the Pincher book cross-examination. Sir Robert must have been glad to say goodbye to West, but he would find Chapman Pincher's book more dangerous.

Turnbull handed the Cabinet Secretary a letter from himself to Mr William Armstrong, the chairman of Sidgwick and Jackson, the publishers of *Their Trade is Treachery.* The letter dated 23 March 1981 was one of the documents successfully sought by the defence. Turnbull read an extensive extract from the letter:

'I have seen the extracts in the *Daily Mail* today from Mr Chapman Pincher's forthcoming book *Their Trade is Treachery.* The Prime Minister is in my judgment likely to come under pressure to make some statement on the matters with which Mr Pincher is dealing.

I believe you will agree with me that, if she is to make a statement, it is in the public interest that she should be in a position to do so with the least possible delay. Clearly she cannot do so until she has seen not just the extracts published in the Daily Mail but the book itself. I should like to be able to put her in a position where she could make a statement this Thursday (26th March), if she should wish to do so.

I should therefore be very grateful if you would be willing to make one or (preferably) two copies of the book available to me as soon as possible today or tomorrow.

I can understand your need and wish to protect the confidentiality of the book until publication date, which is (I understand) 26th March. I can assure you that, if you are able to comply with my request, that confidentiality will be strictly observed, that the copies will not go outside this office and the Prime Minister's office, and that until the book has been published there will be no disclosure to the Press or the broadcasting authorities of the contents of the book.

I can also assure you that the only purpose of this request is to equip the Prime Minister to make a statement, if she should need or be minded to do so, with the least possible delay. The request is not made with a view to seeking to prevent or delay publication, and I can assure you that we shall not do so'.

That done, Turnbull put it to Sir Robert that the letter conveyed the impression that the government did not have a copy of Pincher's book. (In interrogatories, Sir Robert had stated that the government did procure a copy in February.) Sir Robert's response was that the letter did not say the government hadn't a copy, but had been worded in such a way because he wished to protect the source from which the advance copy had been obtained by not disclosing that the government did have the copy.

Turnbull had Sir Robert cornered. 'You misled Mr William Armstrong, did you not?'
Sir Robert: 'If you put that interpretation on it. I was bound to do so. I wished to protect the source.' Hammered in a stream of questions on whether the letter misrepresented the facts, Sir Robert's last answer was 'If it did so, if you say it did, if you say that is what the letter was doing, very well.'

The Judge intervened to try and take the heat off Sir Robert and

Turnbull: *'What's a misleading impression, a kind of bent untruth?'*
Sir Robert: *'As one person said, it is perhaps being economical with the truth.'*

direct the issue back to national security, but the witness didn't pick up the out, and indeed denied that the form of the letter was more to protect national security than to protect the confidentiality of the source. Turnbull didn't let up:

Turnbull: 'So it contains a lie?'

Sir Robert: 'It is a misleading impression, it doesn't contain a lie, I don't think.'

Turnbull: 'What is the difference between a misleading impression and a lie?'

Sir Robert: 'You are as good at English as I am.'

Turnbull: 'I am just trying to understand.'

Sir Robert: 'A lie is a straight untruth.'

Turnbull: 'What's a misleading impression, a kind of bent untruth?'

Sir Robert: 'As one person said, it is perhaps being economical with the truth.'

A ripple of laughter pricked the tension in the court room and the Judge again moved to ease things by saying that he must pass that saying on to one of his brother judges to which Sir Robert responded, 'It's not very original, I'm afraid.' But the laughter gave little respite. Turnbull wanted to know what assurance there was that the witness wasn't being economical with the truth to the court and was told, 'I am under oath in this court.' The follow-up was obvious:

Turnbull: 'You don't convey misleading impressions under oath but you do so when you are not under oath?'

Sir Robert: 'I don't wish to do so at all, under any circumstances. There are occasions when, as there was an occasion here, when it seemed necessary to do so. I regret that, but it seemed necessary.

Turnbull: 'Necessity is your guide, is it?'

Sir Robert: 'It sometimes has to be.'it is,

Sir Robert's next task was to handle the role of his Prime Minister, Mrs Thatcher. Before she had made her subsequent statement on 26 March on the Pincher book, denying the Hollis claim, she had not read the lot of the book, just the 'immediately relevant bit' and a summary of its contents as well as a damage assessment, which had said the publication would raise doubts in the minds of friendly services about the reliability of British security. Turnbull's next question was sharp and to the point: 'Why didn't you stop the book?' Sir Robert had placed the blame for the decision to let publication go ahead on the broad shoulders of the Attorney-General, Sir Michael Havers: ' ... the Attorney-General in his discretion did not seek an injunction. What his reasons were for that, I'm afraid I can't speculate, as he does not give reasons.' As he got back into his stride the Cabinet Secretary gave a constitutional lesson to the court: ' ... the Attorney-General, acting as a law officer, is not subject to consultation, he is acting on his own and not as a pursuit of collective responsibility.' It was a no nonsense answer which served to close off the topic, for the moment.

But Turnbull went back to the interrogatories sworn by the witness in the security of Whitehall weeks ago, when things seemed simpler. One of them said that the government had been advised there was no basis for legal restraint on the Pincher book. So there were reasons, advice from whom, asked Turnbull. Sir Robert dug in. It was all the Attorney-General and he couldn't answer for the Attorney-General, and he could add nothing more because he knew nothing about law. At this stage the court rose for lunch and Sir Robert could have felt a little easier. The blame, if blame it was, for not proceeding against the Pincher book, was laid at the Attorney-General's door and the Attorney-General was a long way away from any Australian court. But solving short term problems in Court 8D could quickly create problems elsewhere and it did. After lunch proceedings were varied by a gallant try by Ken Horler, QC, on behalf of the New South Wales Council for Civil Liberties to seek leave to appear. Horler said he was present because the Commonwealth of Australia had failed to intervene on the public interest issue to protect freedom to publish. Simos objected, Turnbull left it to the Judge, who briskly refused, telling Horler he had no legal power to allow his association to intervene.

The Cabinet Secretary back from the break was confident, more like the Sir Robert of the early part of the evidence. Turnbull took him back to the Attorney-General's decision with a complicated question. There were, he suggested, three sorts of considerations in looking at a book like Pincher's: law officers had to have a reasonable case on confidentiality or the Official Secrets Act; the Security Service had to decide that it would be damaged by publication; finally there were the practical politics of whether it was worthwhile. Sir Robert agreed to the propositions and Turnbull then asked did the Attorney-General make all three decisions? Yes, according to Sir Robert, 'but they are not three separate decisions, it sounds a bit theological, but one decision.' There was a nice bit of oneupmanship to make a play on trinitarian theology but Turnbull was equal to the challenge:

Turnbull: 'Are you a heretic or not, having said that?'
Sir Robert: 'I probably am.'
Turnbull: 'Well, it was Arius who lost his . . .'
Sir Robert: 'I'll stick to Athanasius.'

The theologians invoked by the two men fitted each of their characters neatly. Arius, Turnbull's authority, was the heretic Bishop of Alexandria who cast doubt on the divinity of Christ. Athanasius, the theologian favoured by Sir Robert was a pillar of orthodoxy, who triumphed over Arius and who gave definitive expression to trinitarian theology in the Athanasian Creed. If Sir Robert had time to think he might have recalled that Athanasius had gone into exile on six occasions.

But he didn't have time to think. Pressed again why the Attorney-General didn't seek an injunction against Pincher, Sir Robert answered that there was 'insufficient material on which to obtain an injunction'. This led him on to difficult ground in trying to explain the differences between Nigel West's and Chapman Pincher's books, given that each of them contained material allegedly obtained from ex-MI5 men. Sir Robert offered the fact that it was known that Arthur Martin supplied material to West, but the names of the Pincher sources were not known at that stage. It was not particularly convincing and became less so as Turnbull nagged at the point for another quarter of an hour. Under pressure Sir Robert conceded that *Their Trade is Treachery* was a 'bombshell' when it came out and 'few things, if any' could be more damaging to a security service than the allegation that its Director General had been a Russian agent.

As the argument ground on, the Judge, while ruling on an

Turnbull: 'Now I put it to you, Sir Robert, that you and the Prime Minister and the Security Service agreed to let Pincher write this book about Hollis so that the affair could come into the open through the pen of a safely conservative writer rather than some ugly journalist on the left.'
Sir Robert: 'It is a very ingenious conspiracy theory, and it is quite untrue. Totally untrue.'

objection, made a comment which showed him to be singularly unimpressed by the distinctions Sir Robert was striving to make. 'I must say, for what it's worth, without knowing what was given to the Attorney-General, I find it difficult to distinguish the Pincher book from the West book, and to understand why action was taken in relation only to the former.' The Judge recalled how in the General Motors-Holden case, a case about alleged confidential information, he as the Judge had been prepared to grant an injunction against publication, even if the source of the controversial document was not known.

Hidden away in the haggling was a passage subsequently to prove most embarrassing to Sir Robert and by extension to his government. Turnbull asked the witness when he first became aware Pincher was writing a book about the Hollis investigations. The Cabinet Secretary answered that while he couldn't remember, it must have been about February 1981, a few days in advance of the page proofs becoming available to the government, but said his memory was hazy. With hindsight it can be deduced that Turnbull had something up his sleeve but on the day he simply moved back to the Attorney-General and his responsibilities. After a little while the defence shifted to the character and reputation of Chapman Pincher. Sir Robert agreed that he was known as conservative in his political views but saved the Conservative Party embarrassment by explaining that he thought Pincher was a conservative 'with a small c'. Turnbull got Sir Robert to agree that the Hollis allegations were being talked about before Pincher's book came out, and then snapped out a question which articulated one of the crucial planks of the defence case.

Turnbull: 'Now I put it to you, Sir Robert, that you and the Prime Minister and the Security Service agreed to let Pincher write this book about Hollis so that the affair could come into the open through the pen of a safely conservative writer rather than some ugly journalist on the left.'

Sir Robert: 'It is a very ingenious conspiracy theory, and it is quite untrue. Totally untrue.'

Having raised that banner, Turnbull went back to consistency. If Arthur Martin had supplied material to West, why hadn't he been prosecuted under the Official Secrets Act? Well, that was a matter for the Attorney-General. Why was Sarah Tisdall prosecuted under the Official Secrets Act in 1984 for leaking to the *Guardian* some documents concerning the Defence Minister's parliamentary tactics: 'I can't tell,' said Sir Robert, 'why the Attorney-General had exercised his discretion differently on the two cases.'

Turnbull revived the West book and the decision not to prosecute, bringing something of a tinge of exasperation from Sir Robert, who said that he had answered the question that morning. 'I wasn't satisfied with your answers,' said Turnbull. Sir Robert's faint stutter returned and he again fell back on the Attorney-General. In one legal skirmish, Mr Justice Powell commented, 'One of the problems that does worry me is that it appears there are matters on which Sir Robert, who is the primary witness for the Crown, is quite incapable.' About ten minutes later, as Turnbull pressed Sir Robert on his written answers to the interrogatories, the Judge put a rather worldly view:

'I have come to expect over the years that the person who has to put his oath to a piece of paper says to those advising him "I didn't quite say it that way" and the solicitor says either "Shut up you fool" or "It reads better that way" and I do have the feeling here that Sir Robert had questioned the matter with those in the Treasury Solicitor's Office and been told "That's it, you sign it".'

It was pure Perc Powell. While some in the court looked closely at the Treasury Solicitor, John Bailey, contemplating his telling Sir Robert 'Shut up you fool', Mr Simos was quick to his feet to say 'With respect there is no basis for that view.' The Judge responded '. . . there are clearly things of which Sir Robert has no personal knowledge, yet he has been put up to answer interrogatories.' It was the Judge who intervened a little later with some questions to Sir Robert on the interrogatories which allowed him to state his belief that they were all correct and sufficient. Still it was clear that Turnbull had notched up some more points.

In the last quarter of an hour Turnbull squeezed Sir Robert again on the question of why no action had been taken against the reputed informants of Pincher. Sir Robert said that a list of suspects had been narrowed down to three, after publication. What steps then had been taken to interview them? None. Pressed, Sir Robert was prepared to say, 'I wish it had been done'. Defending the time it took to get to the short list of three, the Cabinet Secretary said it was 'a very long book with a great deal of detail in it.' By now Sir Robert was tired and for the first time, sounded on the edge of open anger; his stutter had gone.

Turnbull at the end turned to the 'Westminster Lobby System', the practice of politicians and senior civil servants of giving out information to the media on an unattributable basis. Sir Robert agreed that such a system existed as a means of briefing and proffered the view that something like it existed in most free countries. So Turnbull delivered his last punch for the day:

Turnbull: 'I put it to you that the publication of this book was analagous with the great Whitehall tradition of the Lobby System. You wanted the information to get into the public domain but you didn't want it to be seen as coming from the government so you let Pincher have access to it and publish it.'

Sir Robert: 'That is quite untrue.'

It had been Turnbull's day. He had shaken the credibility of the principal Crown witness, not once, not twice but on at least half a dozen points. In particular the claim of consistency in the UK government's treatment of the publication of material obtained through breach of confidentiality was in shreds. Turnbull had the pleasure of hearing the Judge comment unfavourably on the plaintiff's attempts to draw distinctions between *A Matter of Trust* and *Their Trade is Treachery*. To have undermined consistency opened the way for him to press the arguments of public domain and authorisation. However, his sweetest victory for the day, sweet for any cross-examining counsel, was to have drawn Sir Robert into the damaging 'economical with the truth'.

For Sir Robert, the most powerful civil servant in the United Kingdom, the Prime Minister's confidante and a man known not to suffer fools or failure gladly, the day must have been one of the worst in his life. His training had not prepared him for the gladiatorial world of adversary cross-examination. Nor, it seemed, had his advisers prepared him either. Now he was on his own, because as long as he was in the box he could not discuss the case with his advisers. A vital element in his defence against Turnbull had been what might be called the 'Attorney-General did it, guv' ploy. Indeed Sir Robert clutched at the Attorney-General with all the vigour with which a child grips a security blanket. However, as any child could have told Sir Robert, security blankets can be unceremoniously yanked away. Perhaps, just perhaps, at the end of the day, Sir Robert might have thought that despite the unpleasantness he had at least held the fort and would be given credit for that by his peers. However, when he scrutinised the transmitted facsimiles of the London press the next morning, such hopes would be crushed. It was the matter of those four words 'economical with the truth'.

It sounded good at the time, witty, a thrust back at Turnbull in court room joust. The provenance was respectable, Edmund Burke, but it looked terrible in a headline. History is unkind; men and women are likely to be remembered for their one-liners.

It took more than a week for *The Times* to deliver the authoritative verdict on the origin of the phrase in its leader. The writer started somewhat tartly by correcting the belief grown up that Sir Robert was the author of the phrase. 'Some have suggested that he will be remembered in years to come as the author of this immortal phrase, if for nothing else. His authorship has been generally accepted and perhaps he has been too preoccupied to disclaim it.' The last is a little unfair, Sir Robert having admitted immediately in the court that it was not original.

There had been a rival claim on behalf of C. P. Scott, but the leader writer had no doubt. In a letter to a fellow-MP published with others in 1796-1797 under the titles of *Letters on a Regicide Peace* Edmund Burke had written:

'Falsehood and illusion are allowed in no case whatever but as in the exercise of all virtues, there is an economy of truth. It is a sort of temperance by which a man speaks truth with measure, that he may speak it the longer.'

There was another candidate put forward in the letters columns of

Mr Justice Kirby raised the point that some insiders would be of such a low level as to be insignificant. What about the contents of the Whitehall cookbook? If published would that be a breach of confidentiality? 'Yes,' said Simos.

The Times later, Samuel Pepys, but it was not as convincing as the Burke attribution. The leader writer managed to find another Burke extract in support of the principle that reasons of state did not in any circumstances permit disclosure of certain matters, which pleased him as an argument, it would seem, against Peter Wright. What the leader omitted to do was to establish how economy of truth, as envisaged by Edmund Burke, would apply to Sir Robert's letter to Sidgwick and Jackson.

The morning of the 19th saw the case transferred to the Appeals Court, presided over by the Chief Justice of New South Wales, Mr Justice Street, sitting with the President of the Appeals Court, Mr Justice Kirby and Mr Justice McHugh. The judges sat in the Banco Court, the grandest court in the building with accommodation for about ten times the number of spectators that could cram into Court 8D. Appeals courts are very much a lawyer's pleasure. For the layman the action is often rather esoteric. Anyone who felt Mr Justice Powell intervened too much in his court would have been even more disconcerted by the style of the three judges this morning. In the tradition of Appeals Court judges they interjected often and with deflating precision, against both Simos and Turnbull. Simos, arguing against the Judge's order for the discovery of documents, had a difficult time with his insider-outsider argument. Mr Justice McHugh asked, 'Surely it could be open to the trial Judge to form the view that publication by an outsider caused more detriment.' Simos stoutly answered, 'No.' Mr Justice Kirby raised the point that some insiders would be of such a low level as to be insignificant. What about the contents of the Whitehall cookbook? If published would that be a breach of confidentiality? 'Yes,' said Simos. Mr Justice Kirby with studied politeness said, 'That seems a rather extreme proposition.' But if Simos had his interventions, so too did Turnbull, who was more tentative, even almost nervous. It was dull complex stuff, difficult to report. By lunch their honours had made up their minds: leave to appeal refused. Discovery of documents was still very much on, but the UK government still had a few more devices left.

Mr Justice Powell was rather chirpy when the court resumed in the afternoon: the Appeals Court had vindicated him. After a few quips from His Honour, Sir Robert was back in the box, working his way through a thicket of distinctions between insiders and outsiders. Sir Robert clung to the belief that it was a question of black and white, one was either an insider or an outsider, but Turnbull didn't have much difficulty in demonstrating various shades of grey. There was no let-up in the afternoon in the nuances of antagonism between the two. When Turnbull asked whether Sir Robert himself was an insider or an outsider, Sir Robert smiled: 'It is a nice question. It is depending where you are looking at it from.' Turnbull snapped back 'What about a nice answer?' and got 'I am clearly not part of the intelligence or Security Service. I clearly have some knowledge of these matters.'

Then it was on to Chapman Pincher. Sir Robert agreed that Pincher had good sources. Pressed as to why nothing had been done to silence him, Sir Robert said: 'Making the Security Service leak-proof is not a matter of suppressing Chapman Pincher is it?' but did admit 'One would like to discourage his sources, certainly.' Pressed again on why nothing had been done about *Their Trade is Treachery* Sir Robert once again brandished the Attorney-General as the decision-maker.

Next Turnbull proceeded to deal with the ex-MI5 and MI6 sources in *Conspiracy of Silence*, just published in London. What had been done about Arthur Martin? He had been reminded that his case was under consideration. What about Sir Dick Goldsmith White, had he been reminded? What about the twenty-four other ex-MI5 and ex-MI6 officers quoted in the book? They were all being reminded. The gallery laughed. It was actually the second laugh they got out of that slab of cross-examination. When Sir Dick Goldsmith White's name was invoked Turnbull commented that as well as being the head of MI5 he was also head of MI6. Sir Robert chastely answered, 'He had other jobs.' Turnbull, amused, repeated the question. Sir Robert side-stepped it with 'He was also head of that other organisation.' Sir Robert would not let the word 'MI6' cross his lips, lest official confirmation should at last be provided that its thousands of employees actually existed.

It was the turn of insider-outsider dichotomy again. Turnbull set out to suggest that, say in the case of a war, some history by outsiders, that is historians, could be more authoritative than that by an insider, say a general. Trapped by his own position, Sir Robert was adamant: ' . . . a personal memoir of one man, if he is what we call an insider, would carry greater authority because he is an insider.' No, he would not accept the proposition that some outsiders could ever have more authority on the intelligence services than an insider. Turnbull put up the example of a low-grade clerk insider who was not in a position to write about anything much authoritatively and got a mandarin response: 'I don't believe the outside world would necessarily take as sophisticated a view as you and I.' And amplified the point, [We are] talking about a relatively unsophisticated public.'

Turnbull was delighted and coaxed Sir Robert with 'We are both Oxford men,' before he struck with the proposition that Sir Robert appeared to believe that the majority of the people he served were unsophisticated. Sir Robert saw this headline coming and tried to back off, the stutter returned. After a series of exchanges, Turnbull trapped him into giving an answer that probably more than half of the population of Great Britain were unsophisticated, although he then tried to qualify, 'in matters of this kind'. Turnbull, in full flight, sought Sir Robert's opinion on Australians, but the now wary witness backed off saying that he didn't know whether there were any unsophisticated Australians. The Judge broke it up with the comment 'Fifteen all, Mr Turnbull.' To which Simos, loyally doing his job for the plaintiff, interjected 'Forty love'.

The solicitor and the witness plodded through more questions on the insider-outsider and history. Would the memoirs of a cabinet minister have more authority than an historian's work? There was no doubt in Sir Robert's mind, they would. At that stage, the Judge intervened more seriously. He had read years ago an account of the Nuremberg trial, written by Lord Kilmuir, one of the prosecutors, and then a more recent book by an historian with far more detail and better research, and perhaps for that reason more authoritative than that of the participant. Sir Robert didn't budge, 'Lord Kilmuir must surely carry greater weight.' The Judge raised his eyebrows in the direction of his wig.

Turnbull took Sir Robert off on another historical tack, the rigid British rule against the release of any intelligence records however old. It was true that the witness had recently reaffirmed that policy in the case of the records of the Secret Service Committee of the UK government in 1919-21 which had been sought by researchers. Looking for other examples Turnbull wanted to know if the ban could go back to the Agadir crisis of 1911 (involving German interests in Morocco). Sir Robert agreed that 'if there are any such papers,' a qualification arousing the spectre of a forerunner of the shredder, 'nevertheless they should not be made available.' The question of how current operations of the Security Service could be affected by the release of pre-World War Two material, brought the objection from Simos that Sir Robert's answer would be obviously confidential. Turnbull then tried the example of any Security Service activities among Russian emigres in London in the 1920s. Sir Robert, conceding that it was a long time ago, said that he couldn't say that it wouldn't be of interest (presumably to hostile agencies) to have that information.

A key plank of the plaintiff's case in Sir Robert's affidavits and in the supporting affidavits from Michael Codd, the Secretary of the Australian Prime Minister's Department, was the damage that might be done to relations with other security and intelligence services if Wright's book were published. Sir Robert's first affidavit set it out:

'(a) the intelligence and security services of friendly foreign countries with which the British Security Service is in liaison would be likely to lose confidence in its ability to protect classified information.

(b) the British Security Service depends upon the confidence and co-operation of other organisations and persons. That confidence would suffer serious damage should the Second Defendant [Wright] reveal information of the nature described above.'

Over the next hour or so Turnbull probed this point. Sir Robert's responses seemed so odd as to be almost perverse, until right towards the end, a couple of frank answers revealed what he was thinking and, indeed, provided the significant part of the explanation of why the UK government had mounted the whole extensive exercise against an old man in Tasmania.

Sir Robert: 'I can't answer a question about the CIA, I'm afraid.'
Turnbull: 'Why not?'
Sir Robert: '. . . Because I have nothing to do with them.'

Turnbull put it to Sir Robert:

Turnbull: '. . . It is the practice of the CIA to permit former employees of the Agency to publish works about their life in the Agency so long as that information is in the public domain or regarded as being of historical interest only. Isn't that true?

Sir Robert: 'I don't know.'

Turnbull: 'Sir Robert, really.'

Sir Robert: 'I can't answer a question about the CIA, I'm afraid.'

Turnbull: 'Why not?'

Sir Robert: '. . . Because I have nothing to do with them.'

Turnbull then put it to him that the Wright book would have been cleared under the CIA standards and indeed if written by a CIA man would have been cleared years ago, so why should the Americans think the less of MI5 if the book was published? Sir Robert said that he thought it was 'quite possible' that they would. Pressed on why the Americans would apply different standards, Sir Robert said 'they might,' though he didn't know why, 'they might easily do so.'

When the Judge intervened to seek clarification, Sir Robert revived the argument that it was all about confidentiality. 'The CIA might still feel that we have not taken sufficient steps to preserve the duty of confidentiality.' The Judge expressed himself 'rather puzzled' and produced from his own reading the example of *The Secret War,* by R.V. Jones, a scientific intelligence expert in World War Two. Jones had been at the heart of scientific innovation during the war. Why hadn't his book been banned?

Turnbull then put figures on the clearances by the CIA Manuscripts Review Board which, since 1978, had reviewed some 400 manuscripts by 200 authors, of whom only four had not been employed by the agency, and all had been cleared in whole or in part. Sir Robert said he would accept these figures as an assumption. After a few more minutes Turnbull asked:

Turnbull: 'Don't you think that before you come to this court to give us your opinion on what you think other intelligence agencies, including the Americans, think, you should find out what their policies are?

Sir Robert: '. . . I didn't know I was going to be asked about the policies of the CIA.'

To an observer it was puzzling. How could Sir Robert have seriously thought that he wouldn't be asked about CIA manuscript policy? Surely at the planning meetings in London he or someone must have raised the question of the publication of so many books in America. Had John Bailey, the Treasury Solicitor said 'Shut up you fool' and told the Secretary not to find out anything about CIA policy so that he could truthfully say he knew nothing about it? Or was it simply oversight: sloppy preparation which hadn't provided for every contingency. How could it be that no one in the Cabinet Office, Home Office, MI5, or MI6 had thought 'This could be an issue in Sydney and we'd better do a couple of pages and get it into the briefing papers?'

It was only in the closing few minutes of cross-examination on this point that it all became blindingly clear: Turnbull was going at Sir Robert on whether it would be 'logical' for the CIA to have thought the worse of MI5 because of the publication of Wright's book. The cross-examination had somewhat bogged down. Indeed the Judge intervened at one stage to remind Turnbull of the late J.W. Smyth's classic principle on cross-examination: 'If you don't strike oil within ten minutes, stop boring, and if you do, get the hell out of there.' (J.W. Smyth, QC, a legendary Sydney figure, was a really savage and brutal cross-examiner who would have done much more terrible things to Sir Robert than Malcolm Turnbull had done.)

Turning it around, Turnbull asked 'Does MI5 think the less of the CIA because of its manuscript clearance policy?' There was a flicker of a superior smile from the witness as he answered:

Sir Robert: 'I think it would be thought that the CIA is actually more leaky than some other security and intelligence agencies and that this policy would be part of it.'

Turnbull: 'People [that gave us] Philby, Burgess, Bettaney, and Maclean say that the CIA is apt to be more leaky?'

Sir Robert: 'I think you could match that list of spies in America very easily.'

Turnbull: 'You say it is leakier?'

Sir Robert: 'I said that it is more disposed. More disposed to leak. I think more information comes out of the CIA than out of the Security Service without authority.'

So there it was. Sir Robert didn't 'care' about the CIA policy, he didn't need to know details about their manuscript review policy, because even the fact that they had one was a symptom of leakiness, decadence, if you like. Britain, by sticking to absolute confidentiality from former spooks would show them. The question about the British spies from Turnbull was quickly met, *tu quoque,* they had spies too. So we saw now at least part of the reason for the mounting of the elaborate, expensive and tottering legal case: it would show the Americans that the British were better than them at keeping secrets (give or take a few spies). Certainly there was an element of vengeance against the inconvenient Peter Wright, the need to frighten off other would-be authors, but underlying it all was the need to show the Americans. It was, in the old fashioned sense of the word, straight-out chauvinism.

If Sir Robert was pleased with his exposition, he had little time before being dragged back to the question of consistency. Turnbull moved on to Peter Wright's appearance in July 1984 on a Granada TV programme 'The Spy That Never Was'. Sir Robert was a bit vague about when the government had heard of the programme, although he firmly rejected Turnbull's suggestion that it might have been weeks, rather than days, before. Nothing had been done to stop the programme because it wasn't known that it was likely to be damaging. Turnbull pulled that apart: what did they think Wright would be talking about if it wasn't Sir Roger Hollis? According to Sir Robert, it was only on the morning of the programme when *The Times* carried a more detailed reference, that it was realised what Wright would say. So why, the defence asked, didn't they get an injunction in the eleven and a half hours left before the programme went to air? Sir Robert was again vague, shifting the problem off towards his familiar scapegoat, the Attorney-General. The exchange gave Turnbull a few bricks for his inconsistency argument, but it was also another hidden time bomb which he was to explode later.

At the close of the second day Sir Robert looked more sure of himself. While to the outsider his cavalier attitude towards whatever CIA practice on manuscripts was seemed to have damaged if not crippled the argument about friendly liaison services, Sir Robert, from the way he answered wouldn't have perceived it that way at all. The verbal evasion over MI6 again might strike outsiders as bizarre, but Sir Robert was doing his job. He had, once again, invoked the Attorney-General as the ultimate decision-maker on *Their Trade is Treachery,* firmly and without equivocation. On this and a couple of other points it might now be seen with hindsight that he was being neatly positioned once again by Turnbull.

In London that day, Dale Campbell-Savours, a Labour back-bencher who had become the House specialist on the Wright case, in a Commons question had named eighteen former MI5 and MI6 officers for discussing aspects of their work with the authors of *Conspiracy of Silence.* Sir Michael Havers played a straight bat and answered that no proceedings were contemplated against the officers. On the next day, Kinnock tried to raise a question on why Pincher's book had not been prosecuted. The Prime Minister merely restated that there would be no answer while the case in Sydney continued. On the same day, Campbell-Savours named another five former officers, this time for passing information on to Nigel West.

Sir Robert Armstrong's third day in the box might have been expected to settle down to the more mundane aspects, after the highlights of the first few days. But it did not. There was the curious affair of Chapman Pincher and the Attorney-General, Sir Michael Havers, having a little chat on the moors of Yorkshire on New Year's Day 1983, then the introduction of Lord Victor Rothschild's name. Although the court went into closed session on Lord Rothschild, before it did so, Sir Robert's answers on Lord Victor were so chill, even frigid, as to indicate that whatever his past connection, the powers that were were seeking to distance themselves from the Baron. Arthur Martin came under the spotlight again, and the afternoon bogged down in arid semantic quibbling on whether or not Margaret Thatcher had misinformed parliament with the Hollis statement in 1981.

On Sir Michael Havers, Turnbull's opening was blunt. Wasn't he one of Pincher's 'better contacts' in the government? Sir Robert had 'no knowledge of that'. The defence put up, as one of Pincher's better and frequent contacts, the name of Sir Arthur Franks, who was described as head of MI6 from 1976 to 1982. Turnbull's question touched off ten minutes of haggling that Sir Robert and Simos twisted and turned to ensure that 'MI6' did not cross Sir Robert's lips. The Judge pointed out that a significant number of books had referred to what he called 'the other side of the penny'. Turnbull complained that things were being reduced to the level of farce, but Sir Robert stolidly held out.

Questioned on Chapman Pincher, Sir Robert said that he had only met the journalist socially at evening functions and never discussed government business with him. Turnbull then suddenly closed his trap on Sir Michael:

Turnbull: 'On New Year's Day 1983 Sir Michael Havers was out shooting with Chapman Pincher, was he not?'

Sir Robert: 'I do not have the faintest idea.'

Turnbull: 'New Year's Day 1983, you would agree, was only about six weeks after the injunction was lifted on West's book, was it not?'

Sir Robert: 'It was about that.'

Turnbull: 'It would be about six weeks. I put it to you that Sir Michael Havers at a shooting party on New Year's Day disclosed confidential details about the West case to Chapman Pincher.'

Sir Robert: 'I have no knowledge of that.'

Turnbull: 'I further put it to you that in conversation Michael Havers told Chapman Pincher that Arthur Martin had provided secret information, secret documents, concerning various enquiries into Soviet penetration in MI5, to Nigel West.'

Simos objected. Mr Justice Powell, like anyone else in the court room, could see that Turnbull had in his hand what appeared to be a copy of a letter. The Judge told the defence that the letter, while not a formal exhibit, could be put in the hands of Sir Robert, and he could check and he could be asked whether he had any knowledge of the matters in it. Turnbull said he would take away the letter, edit it. The Judge worried out loud that there might be a problem of distorted reporting if the letter were produced, however there was quite enough material for fairly spectacular reporting from the early question. Having been earlier identified as the man who had made all the final decisions not to prosecute Chapman Pincher, or to compromise with Nigel West, Sir Michael now had some rather serious claims made against him in cross-examination.

It was back to Arthur Martin, but not without a skirmish about where Martin went when he left MI5. The whole world knew it was

Has Lord Victor Rothschild been a trusted confidante of the Conservative government both now and in years past on intelligence matters? Sir Robert replied 'I think that would be an overstatement.'

MI6, but Sir Robert still wasn't giving that away. To defuse things, the Judge ironically suggested that Martin had probably met up with Graham Greene. Turnbull's objective in this cross-examination was that if Martin were able to give documents and material to West thirteen years after leaving MI6, then he'd got them from someone that had been in the Service. If this was true, it could bolster Turnbull's case, as the West book had then been de facto authorised. Sir Robert had some difficulty. If he admitted that it was possible for Martin to get documents out when he was still in the Service, then he reflected on MI5 and MI6. So the Cabinet Secretary had to say that it was improbable that he could have, but then this could open the way for saying that he had got them from someone still in the Service and that was improbable, so in the end Sir Robert blandly answered that there were two improbabilities.

The defence then cornered Sir Robert on the logic of why West himself had not been prosecuted under the Official Secrets Act for receiving the material from Martin. Sir Robert again threw the ball back to the Attorney General; it had been his responsibility.

Cross-examination then dragged through what Sir Arthur Franks, head of MI6, or head of the 'other organisation', said to Chapman Pincher at lunch one day. It was interesting only in so far as it established Pincher's acceptance at the high levels of the security and intelligence community.

Then, about midday, the by now sleepy English press, kept awake most of the night by their late London deadlines, were aroused by the introduction of a new name, Lord Victor Rothschild. Was he a friend of Sir Robert's? 'I know him . . . he has been a colleague of mine.' Were they particularly close? 'No.' Has he been a trusted confidante of the Conservative government both now and in years past on intelligence matters? Sir Robert replied 'I think that would be an overstatement.' Does he have considerable contact and access? Again Sir Robert effectively put down his lordship: 'He is getting on in years and has not been very well and is rather more remote from these things.' Then came the crunch question:

Turnbull: 'Have you received any report from the Security Service concerning Victor Rothschild's role in the publication of *Their Trade is Treachery?*'

Sir Robert: 'I would not wish to answer these questions in open court since in England the information I have on these matters is confidential.'

After a series of objections from Mr Simos the court went into closed session over the protest of Turnbull who argued that any information about the book *Their Trade is Treachery* was in the public domain.

Before the closing of the court however, there was another skirmish, this time over Paul Greengrass, the Granada TV producer of the 1984 Peter Wright show, who had been co-opted as an adviser on spook literature for the defence team. Simos objected to anyone other than legal advisers staying in court. Mr Justice Powell allowed Greengrass to stay but warned him that he would be in contempt of court if he disclosed anything to anyone outside.

While the UK government were pleased to have achieved the closed court, the last comments of the Judge reminded them that they were not in a climate where they could keep whatever might be said secret forever. Mr Justice Powell told those about to leave: 'I wish to make it abundantly clear to those that are here that our purpose in doing so [closing the court] is not to hide information which may be ultimately found to be in the public interest to reveal.' The court was closed for about an hour.

Back in open court after lunch, Turnbull turned to Mrs Margaret Thatcher's statement in March 1981 to the House of Commons dealing with Sir Roger Hollis. It was a passionately held belief of Peter Wright that Mrs Thatcher had misled the House of Commons in the speech. Sometimes he had made the distinction between Mrs Thatcher and her advisers, more lately he had not. He had articulated the accusation openly in the Granada TV programme in 1984. It was not a position calculated to endear him to Mrs Thatcher, as it sounded dangerously like calling her a liar. How the argument was crucial to Wright's critique of the British Establishment and also what it says about his own thought processes has been looked at earlier. This afternoon Turnbull followed his instructions and tried to pin down Sir Robert to an admission that the statement was deliberately incomplete. Late in the afternoon Mr Justice Powell commented: 'We are really, I think, with great respect, debating matters of language, expression, style.' When Turnbull resisted the proposition the Judge came back, 'I can see the point you are making. I just do not think you are getting anywhere.' That day, when looked at closely, is a useful antidote to the impression so vigorously peddled in London that the Judge favoured Turnbull. On at least ten occasions during the early cross-examination Mr Justice Powell intervened in his cross- examination or upheld objections.

For the last few minutes of the day, Sir Robert was switched back to the question of illegal acts by the Security Service and he took a high tone: 'It has no immunity from those laws. It is subject to the same laws of the land as everyone else.' A noble sentiment given that, for the purposes of the case, the truth of allegations by Wright and Massitter of illegal actions had been conceded. Still Sir Robert under cross-examination felt that if there were any breaches they should 'in the first instance' be drawn to the attention of the Home Secretary and the Prime Minister.

Wasn't there a national interest in the public being aware so that such criminal conduct could be rooted out? asked Turnbull. Sir Robert fielded that one quite easily. Yes, there was a public interest, but 'also a great public interest in not damaging the effectiveness of the Service more than is necessary.' So the witness ended his third day looking more cheerful. Though if Sir Robert looked a little more relaxed, three people in England were likely to be distinctly disconcerted by the events of the day.

What had looked like a quiet day for the English press had been turned into a very busy one. The Attorney-General of the United Kingdom had been flushed out shooting pheasants with a man whom only a little while before he'd decided not to prosecute and allegedly talking about the rival journalist's legal problems. Sir Michael had to be very displeased, not the least with Chapman Pincher, who had been indiscreet enough to put something in a letter about their talk (it wasn't difficult for anyone in the court room with a minimum of common sense to work out that the letter Turnbull had in his hand was from Pincher to Wright). Finally, Lord Victor Rothschild could hardly be happy that his name had come into the case. If the verbal devices used by Sir Robert in answering questions reflected Whitehall, and they certainly did, Lord Victor might have suspected some people would not be answering his phone calls in future.

Friday, his fourth day in the box, saw no slackening of pressure on Sir Robert. Early on he was boxed in again on the question of inconsistency on the government's part. They had not acted in 1985 to stop Cathy Massitter's TV allegations, which after all dealt with a much more recent period than Wright's disclosures. Later in the day, Turnbull returned to the Massitter allegations, which had been admitted as true for the purposes of proceedings, and took Sir Robert through his justifications for the phone taps of trade unionists, communists and civil libertarians. It was certainly the first time that any member of the British security establishment had given in public quite such an extended and unabashed vindication of phone tapping.

There was still more on the Attorney General's decision on *Their Trade is Treachery*. As Turnbull ground away with the quotations the possibility occurred to observers that he was setting up Sir Robert for an ambush. It was becoming clear that Turnbull was getting instructions from his client about recent government decision-making processes that inexorably suggested that there had to be a pro-Wright mole somewhere in Whitehall.

As if that wasn't enough variety for a day in court, the allegation that some people in MI5 had spied against Harold Wilson came into the open and provoked a very conscious attempt by Sir Robert to stretch the 1952 Maxwell Fyfe guidelines, under which MI5 is supposed to operate.

The day opened with the foreshadowed attempt of the UK government to refine the true constructions of the 'definitions' of the Judge's order for discovery. In laymen's language, the UK government was trying to limit the judgment. Turnbull was angry with the 'new British' definitions of the documents in the Judge's order for discovery: it was an attempt to reinterpret the order. He spoke of the 'intolerable burden placed on the defendant by the twists and turns of the plaintiff.' It would all be clarified on Monday, the Judge indicated. Before getting to Massitter, Turnbull produced another insider case, that of a former MI5 transcription secretary

Miranda Ingram, who in 1984 published an article on her experiences. Why had she not been proceeded against like Wright? Sir Robert put it back on the Attorney General again. Then, to the Massitter TV programme and Sir Robert came up with an explanation for the absence of action: 'I can distinguish between an account of a full lifetime in service and the kind of material that was in Massitter's programme.'

Turnbull resisted vehemently the proposition that *Spycatcher* was a full account because he said that Wright had deliberately left out a great deal of more recent material. Sir Robert fell back to saying that some of Wright's material would be damaging and he was not prepared to say which material, 'certainly not in open court and I doubt even in camera.'

In the afternoon Turnbull returned to Miss Massitter to probe again the question of just who decided not to proceed against her. It was, of course, the Attorney General. Sir Robert, however, made a slip when he suggested that one reason why no action was taken against Massitter had been that MI5 would have been damaged because certain internal procedures would have been revealed in open court if she had been charged. Turnbull could hardly believe his good fortune. He spent ten minutes battering home the point that there were many precedents for the court being closed for all or part of such hearings, as in Ponting, Prime and Bettaney. Later questions on the Massitter television claims on phone tapping of communists, trade unions, and civil libertarians brought out some interesting notions of subversion and the elastic limits of the state's power to phone tap. There was the case of Syd Harraway, a union shop steward at Ford during a particular dispute. Sir Robert responded: 'Who was a communist, that is, I think admitted . . . I assume that for the purposes of this discussion that it is admitted. It [tapping] might be designed in such a situation to discover what effect the activities or views or opinions or pressures of the Communist Party were having on the conduct of negotiations.' Later on Sir Robert affirmed his particular view of the function of the Security Service: 'I regard it as within the business of MI5 to seek to discover the extent of subversive influence so the possibility of the use of industrial means to undermine parliamentary democracy . . .' Though confusedly put, it was an almost limitless charter

When Turnbull asked him whether Harman and Hewitt were communists, Sir Robert replied 'I do not know,' it would seem prudently protecting himself against the possibility that they were undercover members.

to tap any trade unionist in any dispute.

Sir Robert was then pressed on the Massitter allegations that not only communists had been tapped but also two officers of the National Council of Civil Liberties, Harriette Harman and Patricia Hewitt. Turnbull reminded Sir Robert that the UK government had admitted 'for the purposes of these proceedings' that they had been tapped. On a number of other admissions Sir Robert, when questioned about them, managed to show disdain: he had a way of emphasising 'for the purposes of these proceedings' to indicate that it was a mere tactical device and everyone knew it. There was no such sense of qualification when it came to these two women.

Turnbull: '... the Director General must have assumed that Harriette Harman, now a Labour MP, and Patricia Hewitt, an assistant to Neil Kinnock, were subversives.'

Sir Robert: 'He must have had reason to believe they were having subversive connections or something.'

Turnbull: 'You must live in terror of the next Labour government when it is led by a man on whose right hand sits a subversive.'

Sir Robert: 'I do not think that I live in terror of a future Labour government.'

When Turnbull asked him whether Harman and Hewitt were communists, Sir Robert replied 'I do not know,' it would seem prudently protecting himself against the possibility that they were undercover members. Sir Robert wasn't showing the faintest stutter during the exchange. He was brisk and aggressive and, perhaps wisely, Simos objected and the matter died out, with the Judge commenting that it was not clear whether it was two-one or one-all.

The absent Sir Michael Havers was back on stage on Friday. It was the decision over *Their Trade is Treachery* again. Before the contestants got down to that topic, there was a bit of sparring about the relationship between the Director General of MI5 and Sir Robert. Asked whether there had been a discussion about the damage caused by Pincher's book, Sir Robert replied: 'I think you have altogether too formal a view of the way that relationships occur in these matters.' Then it came, somewhat belatedly on the fourth day, the first 'Yes Prime Minister' reference, up to then all parties having shown admirable restraint. Turnbull asked, 'Sir Humphrey and Mr Bernard? An accurate portrayal?' Sir Robert gave a wince and a fleeting smile: 'I wondered when it might come to that.'

While the witness had been frisky in pursuing the civil libertarians, he looked rather dubious during the renewed cross-examination on the decision of the Attorney-General. The thought must have occurred to him, as it had to a number of other observers in the court room, that either Turnbull had something up his sleeve on the circumstances surrounding the decision of February 1981, or he was wasting an awful lot of time for no good reason. But Sir Robert had committed himself beyond retreat to the picture of the Cabinet Secretary as the mere receptacle of the Attorney-General's decision. Pushed into a corner again today, Sir Robert fell back on 'the Attorney took the decision,' or 'I accepted the Attorney's judgment,' or 'I accepted the Attorney-General's advice. He is a lawyer and I am not,' or finally, 'the Attorney has to take his decisions on his own factors. It is not for me to query or challenge.' On the Pincher book, Sir Robert took a battering on his claim that the decision not to prosecute had been influenced by the need to protect the source who gave MI5 the page proofs. Turnbull pointed out that so many people usually had access to page proofs that it was 'utter humbug' to suggest the source could have been in danger.

Margaret Thatcher came casually into the cross-examination. Turnbull wanted to know if the Attorney General would have discussed his reasons with the Prime Minster. 'Not to my knowledge,' said the Cabinet Secretary and principal official adviser on security and intelligence matters. Curiously, Turnbull moved on without questioning this view of an easy-going Downing Street. As the probing of bureaucratic relations went on, the Judge cut in to confess his puzzlement at the Attorney General's decision not to try and block the book. Mr Justice Powell elaborated: ' . . . A moment, as I understand the law, the advice tendered to the Attorney was unsound. I cannot understand why with six weeks' notice somebody did not hot-foot it up to the Strand and get an ex parte injunction and an "Anton Piller" order [so named from a case involving a ship and involving the seizure of all documents] and at the moment I do not see how they could have failed.'

With a tinge of polite desperation, Simos pleaded, 'Your Honour would not form any view in the course of hearing a case. I know Your Honour would keep an open mind throughout the hearing until the evidence is in and the addresses have been made.' Which brought a characteristic Powell response: ' . . . You have been in my court often enough to know that I have a habit, whether it is an unfortunate one or not – when I am troubled about something, when I am puzzled about something, I tell those involved so that they have an adequate opportunity of removing any error or misconception.' With that the court rose for lunch.

After the break, Turnbull sought disclosure of the informant source of the Pincher page proofs. He handed a name on a piece of paper to Sir Robert and suggested the name was the source, which Sir Robert denied. Next Turnbull said he wanted the name to help support his submission that 'the evidence Sir Robert has given concerning the Attorney-General's advice is palpably false, [because if true] it would mean that Sir Michael Havers was surrounded by legal incompetents which I am sure is not the case.' Still seeking the source Turnbull, if not showing his hand, at least dropped a hint. He told the court that he had 'very precise instructions on who was the source.' Now, to any listener, that had logically to mean that Wright had information directly or indirectly about a key element of the government's discussions on Pincher's book in February and March 1981. It was again an indication that Wright had a mole in the government ranks at that time, possibly even later. If that were the case it would explain the precision of some of Turnbull's requests for discovery. They were not just a fishing expedition, something was known to be there.

As a curtain raiser to the Wilson allegations, Turnbull gave Sir Robert a run-through of the claims made in *House of Commons* by Dale Campbell-Savours that Wright's book had included a reference to an MI6 plot to kill Nasser in 1956. Sir Robert stressed the conditional 'if' when discussing the allegation but then said, even allowing for age, he would still be against any publication. Still in the area, Sir Robert almost failed and admitted the existence of MI6. Asked by Turnbull if he thought it was possible that MI6 would assassinate a foreign leader, Sir Robert said that he thought it was unlikely and after a pause, in the nick of time, added, 'If there was such an organisation.'

On the Wilson plot allegations, Sir Robert was curt and dismissive. He admitted that he knew Campbell-Savours had said something about a plot against Wilson but he didn't know exactly what the MP had said. Turnbull asked him whether the role of MI5 was to defend the government of the day from subversion, but Sir Robert chose to reply that it was rather to defend parliamentary democracy, a shift with quite interesting implications. However, later, Sir Robert addressed the possibility that some officers of the Security Service had been plotting against the goverment. If action should be taken in such a case, then it would be against the public interest to do it in public or 'to use sunlight as a medicine', as Turnbull suggested. Embedded in his answer was an interesting qualification: 'The hypothesis I think was that there were a few officers, ... nothing was said about the whole Service or in fact a substantial part of it . . . ' This was a trifle disingenuous on Sir Robert's part. Although even Turnbull couldn't bring the precise numbers forward (the Judge was shortly to warn him against coming too close to the contents of the book), one didn't have to live in London or to have read the manuscript to know that the figure mentioned by Wright was thirty, which was not a few and indeed could even be said to be a substantial number. Turnbull produced the *Pencourt File*, the first book to deal with the Wilson allegations, quoting the former Prime Minister himself, and sought a comment from Sir Robert. 'There were some extraordinary allegations.' Turnbull was quick to detect a note of distaste in the way Sir Robert drawled 'extraordinary,' and he followed it up with: 'What you are saying is that he, Wilson, was unfit to continue by that stage?' Sir Robert responded flatly, 'There were some extraordinary allegations made.' Turnbull tried to goad, 'Maybe he was Prime Minister of a very extraordinary country?' Mr Justice Powell tried cricket to soothe the contestants with a reference to England's recent form: 'Having won the Test. That makes it extraordinary.' Once the concession that truth for the purposes of the hearing had been made by the UK government in August, it was clear that the full details of the Wilson allegations would not be aired in court. In fact, Turnbull had probably overridden the boundaries in getting in as much as he did. If the truth or otherwise of the bizarre affair of the Wilson plot were to be established anywhere, it wasn't to be in the Equity Division of the Supreme Court of New South Wales.

At close on Friday, Sir Robert was looking more relaxed. It was almost as though the opportunity to put down the Misses Hewitt and Harman, as well as Harold Wilson, had cheered him up. As well, and importantly, it was clear that not too much about the Wilson affair was going to get out.

However, reading the facsimiles sent from London, the weekend press would have certainly revived his gloom. The Sunday papers were disaster areas. The *Sunday Times* main feature illustrated by a rather smug-looking photograph of Sir Robert, was headed 'Fiasco Down Under – The Unmaking of Sir Robert'. He had suffered 'indignity upon indignity at the hands of the defence and the Judge ... forced into a string of embarrassing headline admissions, making the man who is called Britain's most powerful civil servant appear ill at ease, ineffectual and ill-informed.' Hidden away in the middle of the article was an interesting piece of government log-rolling, which must have given Sir Michael Havers food for thought.

'Last week, thinly disguised "government sources" indicated that Havers was most to blame for the debacle in Sydney. He had, it had been whispered, given poor advice to the Prime Minister.'

The *Sunday Telegraph* opened its news story with 'For Sir Robert Armstrong, head of the Civil Service, it has been a miserable week – and there is more to come.' Both newspapers broke, for the first time, the story of Turnbull's use of Jonathan Aitken, MP, as a channel for his rejected proposals to Sir Michael Havers, that a deal was made on cuts in the book.

However by Monday the government's tactics to fight back were sweeping into the Fleet Street papers. The *Daily Express* and the *Independent* were able to agree that Sir Michael was a likely scapegoat, although the *Express* thought Sir Robert would be a scapegoat too and spread the suffering a little wider with the headline 'More Misery For Security Chiefs in Court Ordeal'. An *Express* columnist thought the whole thing was about 'Pom baiting', and that Sir Robert was the kind of Pom that Australians love to torment.

The counter-attack on Neil Kinnock for his impertinence in

raising the question in the Commons was well underway. The *Sun* editorialised on Wright and stated that, 'In this country, such an act of betrayal would have sent him to prison. Instead he shelters behind the laws of Australia . . . just what is brother Kinnock's purpose in sniping and snooping?' The *Daily Mail* also weighed into the attack on 'little Kinnochio'. It was a preemptive strike before the inevitable Commons row later in the week. *Today* dusted off four cases left over from Wright's old list of unconvicted spies, although it did not name them. The *Daily Mirror* went one better with a list of twelve undetected traitors. There were passing references, as there had been in the previous week to how Maggie Thatcher was firm against anyone getting money for secrets.

But the rest of Fleet Street that morning was scooped by *The Times* Whitehall correspondent, Michael Evans, who provided a front page story which was headed 'Wright Was Paid for Revealing MI5 Secrets'. The lead paragraph spoke of an 'extraordinary secret deal' under which Wright got royalties from a share of the sales income from *Their Trade is Treachery*. The story then went on to make the point which the government would have been glad to see in print:

'Until now, it was believed that Mr Wright's sole motive for helping Mr Pincher write his book *Their Trade is Treachery* in late 1980 was that of a crusader exposing alleged traitors inside MI5 in an attempt to clean up British intelligence.

However he had another motive which was money. Under a secret agreement with Mr Pincher, fifty per cent of the royalties from the book was to be paid to a front company of 'consultants'. There was only one consultant, and that was Mr Wright.'

The revelation that Mr Wright was paid 'thousands of pounds' for collaborating with Mr Pincher on his book which was filled with classified information could help the government's case in Sydney. It could do absolutely nothing to help the government's case as it had been presented up till now in Sydney, but it could, and it clearly was, designed to help the government regain the initiative in London. Certainly it was in the government's interests to have *The Times* story published in the hope that the issue would be turned into a greedy-old-man-in-search-of-money story.

Wright had to respond to *The Times* royalty-sharing story and he duly did, at a press conference called at Malcolm Turnbull's office a couple of blocks away from the court room after Tuesday's hearing. The press waited around for about three-quarters of an hour while the statement was prepared. When it came, it outlined what was to be one of Wright's main themes, that is, that he thought Lord Rothschild had approval from someone high up. For an old man his voice was vigorous and he only faltered a couple of times in reading a statement of just over two pages:

'As you will no doubt be aware I have been preparing for my appearance in court next week, and in particular preparing a full disclosure of the circumstances of the publication of *Their Trade is Treachery*. However the government this weekend has selectively leaked parts of my evidence to the Whitehall correspondent of *The Times* in an effort to discredit me in advance. Accordingly I have no choice but to make a public statement which will of necessity contain information which will be part of my own testimony.'

He then told his story of the Rothschild letter, the trip to London and on to Cambridge and the summoning of Pincher, concluding with:

'I had the distinct impression this meeting had been prearranged.

I was terrified of getting into trouble. Lord Rothschild assured me that it was going to be all right. He told me that he would arrange through Swiss banking facilities and pay me half of the royalties of the book. He knew I was in financial difficulty and I was grateful for this assistance. Mr Pincher has told *The Times* that he was not involved in these payments. I can and will prove that he was.

I knew Lord Rothschild to be an intimate confidante of successive heads of British intelligence establishments. I could not conceive of him embarking on such a project without knowing that it had the sanction, albeit unofficial, of the Authorities. I sensed I was being drawn into an authorised, deniable operation to enable the Hollis affair and other MI5 scandals to be placed in the public domain as the result of an apparently inspired leak. All that I knew about Lord Rothschild and the ease with which *Their Trade is Treachery* was published, leads me to the inescapable conclusion that the powers that be approved of the book.'

Next day, in an editorial, *The Times* offered a few tart comments. It summed up on the Rothschild-Wright-Pincher triangle, 'the episode remains curious. Lord Rothschild surely has the responsibility to give his own version when the case is concluded in Sydney.' The general editorial tone and the description of the "noble lord" as an "incurable busybody", faithfully reflected the coolness towards Rothschild shown by the voice of the Establishment, Sir Robert, in the witness box in Sydney. A week later *The Times* put a spin on it with the opinion that the disclosure of the money deal was 'more unfavourable to the government's case than Wright's,' because the status of Lord Rothschild had aroused suspicions of some government involvement in the deal. However *The Times* then went on to argue that 'doubt had been cast upon the purity of his [Wright's] motives and by extension upon the justice of his case.'

On the fifth day Sir Robert was reminded of the only occasion previously where he had found himself under cross-examination, at a House of Commons Select Committee on the Westland affair. The Committee had been set up to look into a dispute within the government and the bureaucracy over whether an American takeover of Britain's last helicopter company, Westland, should be allowed to succeed. The internal struggles had been bitter and had culminated in the resignation of the Defence Secretary, Michael Heseltine, who had opposed the takeover. Sir Robert had given evidence twice before the Committee. A journalist who had attended both the Committee and the Sydney court found the differences substantial: at the House of Commons, Sir Robert had been treated almost with deference. The only unfavourable comment made on evidence he had given (about the motivation for leaks by bureaucrats in favour of the takeover) was when the Committee said, 'We do not doubt that Sir Robert accurately reported what he was told in his enquiry, but we do hope his credulity was as sorely taxed as ours.' What Turnbull achieved in his cross-examination of the affair was to get into the record just how widespread authorised leaking was in Whitehall.

Then he turned to Pincher's earlier book *Inside Story*, published

***Turnbull: 'Sir Robert, last week I asked you a great many
questions about the Attorney-General and the Pincher book.
Have you or any of those advising you sought any
clarification about the reasoning behind the decision not to
seek an injunction?'***
Sir Robert: 'I have nothing more to say on that.'

in 1978. Turnbull took Sir Robert back to 1956 when, according to
Pincher, he had willingly written two stories planted on him by MI5.
There was an occasion later when a Russian diplomat took Pincher
to lunch at a Greek restaurant. After lunch, Pincher approached MI5
offering information which they were grateful to receive. Turnbull
said that the book proved that Pincher had been used in the past by
MI5 as an agent or conduit to get information out into the public
domain. As his cross-examination ran on, Mr Justice Powell
intervened, showing a certain boredom. 'I will not be disposed to let
this run on merely because Mr Chapman Pincher, who may or may
not be a man with a gift for fantasy, wrote some things in a book.' A
little later, the Judge added that the difficulty was 'whether we are
going to be overloaded with material which is at best on the
periphery'. After morning tea, the cross-examination was inter-
rupted when Simos handed up his latest list of the documents under
discovery. For the first time he raised, on the UK government's
behalf, a public interest immunity claim. Turnbull, predictably,
complained that this was the latest disruptive tactic. It was agreed to
hold the argument over until the next morning. It was clear to the
observers that the British were laying the ground for another bid in
the Appeals Court.

Turnbull returned to the task of reinforcing his case of inconsistency on the part of the UK government because of the different
ways in which it had treated Pincher and Wright. Sir Robert had to
admit that the government had taken no steps to block the second
edition of *Their Trade is Treachery* or Pincher's follow-up book
called *Too Secret, Too Long*, even though Sir Arthur Franks of MI6
had warned that the second book was coming. Sir Robert made
heavy weather of justifying the government's inaction. Then
Turnbull darted in with another Attorney-General question.

Turnbull: 'Sir Robert, last week I asked you a great many questions
about the Attorney-General and the Pincher book. Have you or any

of those advising you sought any clarification about the reasoning behind the decision not to seek an injunction?'

Sir Robert: 'I have nothing more to say on that.'

Without any build up Turnbull turned suddenly to the disclosures in *The Times* of Wright's royalty deal. Asked when he first heard that Wright was getting money for his contribution to *Their Trade is Treachery*, Sir Robert said unequivocally that he had never heard of the deal. Asked why Number 10 (ie Downing Street) was briefing to that effect today, the Cabinet Secretary said that he did not know they were doing so. Moving on, Sir Robert agreed that now he knew Wright had visited the UK in 1980. Turnbull brought Lord Rothschild back into play. He asked whether, shortly before Wright had arrived in England in 1980, Lord Rothschild had discussed intelligence matters with Mrs Thatcher in his London flat. Sir Robert said he had no knowledge of such a meeting.

A little later, Turnbull switched for the first time to Sir Anthony Blunt, obviously on instructions from Peter Wright. Once again, as with the Hollis statement, Turnbull's line of questioning reflected Wright's passionately held belief that Mrs Thatcher had misled the House of Commons when she made her speech in 1979 on Blunt, as she did later on Hollis. Turnbull put it that when the PM had said there was no evidence which could be used as a basis of prosecuting Blunt, her statement was simply not true. Sir Robert was brisk: 'I do not accept that.' Turnbull then suggested that the evidence of Michael Straight, the American dilettante Cambridge graduate, whose late confession had led directly to Blunt, could have been used. Sir Robert backed off a little, his recollection on Straight was not absolute. Turnbull also suggested that Mrs Thatcher was wrong when she said that Blunt had collaborated fully, again obviously reflecting Wright's anti-Blunt feelings.

Sir Robert then passed an hour or so of grindingly detailed cross-examination directed to the question of which methods and techniques could be written about. He fell into one trap on the SATYR microphone, a Soviet eavesdropping device from the fifties, when he said that it would be objectionable if there were details about it in Wright's book. Turnbull pointed out with glee that it was in Wright's book and in the only three chapters that the UK government had not objected to.

Sir Robert however recovered, to make a joke later, in the middle of the discussion about a touchy topic with Britain, George Blake and the Berlin tunnel. Asking about Blake, Turnbull said that he was a real insider, 'as far as the tunnel was concerned.' Sir Robert topped it with, 'I guess that's as near as you get to the real mole.' Cheered up, Sir Robert put the Americans in their place again when Turnbull revived CIA manuscript review policy. He observed, 'I think that there are probably fewer disclosures under our system than under theirs.' Turnbull had some hard words about Sir Michael Havers' overnight announcement that there would be a police inquiry into the circumstances of *A Matter of Trust*, calling it hypocritical and window-dressing.

In the closing minutes of the day, Turnbull tried to get, as an exhibit, the letter Jonathan Aitken, MP, had written in 1980 to Mrs Thatcher on the Hollis affair. Simos objected and the question was shelved until the next day.

The fifth day had probably been Sir Robert's best so far. Apart from the slip over the microphone, the Cabinet Secretary had held the line well. There was the Attorney-General question, but that might be thought by now to be just a Malcolm Turnbull ritual.

On the sixth day, Sir Robert might have felt, to borrow a metaphor from the leaky Americans, he was on the home run. He looked more relaxed, even when the Judge, over Simos' objections, allowed the admission of Aitken's letter. Sir Robert agreed that Mrs Thatcher had taken the Aitken letter seriously. While being cold to Lord Rothschild, Sir Robert gave Mr Aitken something of an endorsement when he said, 'I don't think anyone could call Mr Aitken a backwoodsman'. However he was only prepared to say that Aitken had 'some intelligence' experience.

That polite exchange on the status of the Conservative back-bencher over, Turnbull returned to the Westminster briefing system. Sir Robert agreed to the proposition from Turnbull that 'there are at least two time-honoured methods in Whitehall of getting information into the public domain. One is the official statement and the other is the unofficial inspired disclosure.' He denied, however, that there had ever been any consideration of putting anything out about the Hollis question in any way as a response to Aitken's letter. When Turnbull tried to draw Sir Robert into admissions on government reactions to Aitken, Mr Justice Powell came down heavily against the defence on the grounds of relevance. Turnbull succeeded in making the point that the two collaborators, Pincher and Wright, parted company on whether, in 1981, there was a present problem of Russian penetration. Pincher thought there wasn't; Wright thought there was. Turnbull made Pincher's adherence to the squeaky clean service 'the reason why [his book] was not impeded on its passage to the bookstands'.

Still on books and authorship, Turnbull took Sir Robert to *Conspiracy of Silence* and Philip Knightley's *The Second Oldest Profession*. Sir Robert agreed that the drift of both books was critical, indeed almost 'savagely in some respects' of Wright. But criticism or lack of respect for Wright didn't matter at all in looking at those books: it came back to the fact that they had not been published with the special authority of the insider. Turnbull then put Sir Robert under questioning on the case of Geoffrey Prime, the man from GCHQ, the British code and cipher centre, who had spied for the Russians for seven years. Turnbull put it to Sir Robert that what Prime did was vastly more damaging to American-British intelligence relations than anything that might flow from Wright's book. Sir Robert dipped into sexual folklore to answer Turnbull: 'It is the argument that it is all right if it is a little one,' as coming near to articulating what shone through the government's case, that confidentiality, like chastity, admitted of no degree.

Turnbull, still exploring the implications for Anglo-American relations of the Wright manuscript, asked what if his client's doubts about continuing Russian penetration were well-founded? 'As you know I do not believe it to be well-founded,' came the answer. Turnbull then tried to work the government's confession, in August that year, of the truth of the allegations in Wright's manuscript, back on Sir Robert who had a formula to cope: 'I think we admitted the facts but not the conclusions.' The Judge commented wearily that it was another 'semantic exercise'. Turnbull switched to another tack, putting as a hypothesis that if MI5 was still penetrated by the Russians, wouldn't it be a good idea to have a public debate and an enquiry? 'No,' said Sir Robert, 'public debate might enable the penetration to conceal itself.'

Turnbull, baffled on that line, set out to get in as exhibits a wide

Asked if the writer Duncan Campbell belonged to the Conservative Party, Sir Robert commented, in steely tones: 'Shall I say I would be surprised.'

range of publications that had contained confidential material and had not been the subject of any legal action. His first was the autobiography of Sir Percy Sillitoe, the outsider policeman put in by Attlee to run MI5 and whose *Cloak Without Dagger* was published in 1955. Next came a series of articles by Duncan Campbell in the *New Statesman* in 1979 dealing with phone tapping and electronic spying. Sir Robert didn't like Campbell, who had a 'mixed reputation' for accuracy. Asked if the writer belonged to the Conservative Party, Sir Robert commented, in steely tones: 'Shall I say I would be surprised.' Then there were three other cases: the BBC 'Panorama' programme with another former MI5 man, Tony Motion; a Granada TV screening of interviews with GCHQ former employee Jock Kane; and articles by Nick Davis in the *Guardian* in 1984 on the internal workings of MI5. Sir Robert had to admit that no action had been taken in any of those cases.

Turnbull introduced a fresh book *The Ties That Bind* co-authored by Des Ball, an Australian National University academic, and Jeffrey T. Richelson, another academic at the American University, Washington. The book had been published in Australia in 1985 by the English-owned publisher George Allen & Unwin. Sir Robert didn't know the book. Turnbull was able to point out that it contained organisational charts of MI5 and MI6 along with the names of all the directors general since their foundation. It also contained similar information for Australia, the USA, Canada and New Zealand, as well as the names and sites of a large number of the SIGINT code-breaking listening posts throughout the world. Given that Sir Robert was sincere in not knowing the book, it was for the observer another spectacular example of how poorly he had been briefed. The book had more extensive details than any other book published in the western world on how the Anglo-Saxon intelligence club worked and it contained material which certainly in the past would have been the subject of D notices in the United Kingdom. Asked about a book by a Cambridge historian, Dr Christopher Andrew, who had expressed critical views of secrecy as applied to the security and intelligence services, the Cabinet Secretary dismissively said that Dr Andrew was not the only person who had expressed views of that kind. Turnbull then tendered two other Nigel West books: *MI6, British Secret Intelligence Service Operation 1909-45* and *MI5, British Security Service Operation 1909-45* but didn't particularly press Sir Robert on them. The defence also got in, as an exhibit, a letter to Wright in 1976 from Sir Michael Hanley, his former boss at MI5, evoking the weary comment from the Judge 'For whatever it is worth.'

After that, Turnbull loaded in Kim Philby's book *My Silent War;* an article by an ex-MI6 man Robert Cecil on the Cambridge Comintern; as well as a book, partially ghosted by Peter Wright, titled *Handbook for Spies*, written by Alexander Foot, a Russian agent in Switzerland during the war. Then remembering the Judge's invocation of *The Secret War* by R. V. Jones, the definitive work on scientific intelligence during World War Two, Turnbull put in a copy. Finally, there was *The Doublecross System*, by J. J. Masterman, which revealed how the British had successfully turned around the Nazi spies sent into the UK during the last war. Sir Robert had to admit both the last two were insiders and no action had been taken against them. That was the end of the books as far as Sir Robert went and, although Turnbull was to put forward more later, the bulk had come during the Cabinet Secretary's testimony. At the end of the trial, the number of books entered as exhibits related to espionage reached twenty-six.

Moving toward the close of this stage of evidence, Sir Robert gave a few more glimpses into Whitehall complacency about the way things were in the secret world. After Aitken's letter, some consideration had been given to its suggestion of a major enquiry, like the Hope Royal Commission in Australia, but it wasn't given 'major consideration'. On whether or not, since the Thatcher government had come into power, there had been any consideration given to any change in policy on disclosures of security and intelligence matters, the answer was simple, 'No'. It appeared things were always for the best in the best of all possible worlds, to adopt Pangloss. A few more questions and Sir Robert was quit for the moment of open court.

Wednesday 26 November saw the court enmeshed in legal arguments over public interest immunity, the latest legal device trundled forward by the UK government to block the disclosure of the documents as ordered by Mr Justice Powell. Some of the time was taken up by an address by the Commonwealth counsel assisting the Solicitor General, Mr Richardson, on public interest immunity principles, which was so Delphic as to draw the comment from Turnbull that the Commonwealth was 'sort of against us'. Simos mounted his public interest immunity in the face of a very cool attitude on the part of the Judge. Certainly Simos' instructions were haughty. His first plank was that the Judge should uphold public interest immunity without even reading the documents, although counsel said that if the Judge wanted the documents they would, of course, be given to him. If the Judge were to decide, however, that the documents should go to the defence, the UK government would 'test Your Honour's decision', that is, appeal.

Turnbull said that he didn't want to run through all the documents proposed and put forward as a 'sensible approach' that he and Simos should sit down and look at the documents and agree on some compromise resolution, but got no response. However, Turnbull still wanted the list of documents to be discussed, if they were to be discussed, in open court. (Even so, the references to identification by letters and numbers left listeners unenlightened for most of the time.) In the course of the preliminary exchanges before the formal addresses, Turnbull, for the first time, referred to document B1 relating to *Their Trade is Treachery*, a document about which everyone was to hear a great deal before the proceedings were over. In another comment, the Judge, referring to the documents, said that he wouldn't want to look at 'operational material', an important qualification that was to be ignored by the media manipulators in London over the next week. A little later Mr Justice Powell outlined some of his thoughts on public interest immunity:

'The other thing which is a question of very considerable public importance, I think, is quite frankly the role of courts in a democratic society. I do not say this offensively to Mr Mallaby (the UK civil servant who swore the affidavit in support of public interest immunity) or Sir Robert or the Prime Minister or anyone else. I find it difficult to understand why if a court says, in order to do justice between these parties I require documents to be produced subject to

***In other words what has a disclosure of documents to an
Australian court under proper conditions got to do with
American-British intelligence relations?***

some exceptions, if need be, subject to some limitations, if need be, I
require inspection to be permitted and then to be made available for
use by the other side, how can people say the system [MI5] is not
leak-proof?'

In other words what has a disclosure of documents to an
Australian court under proper conditions got to do with American-
British intelligence relations?

At one stage in his argument, Simos called Turnbull's search for
the documents nothing more than a fishing expedition and 'mere
speculation'. It was brave whistling in the wind from the plaintiff
given that, as even the most cryptic details of the list of documents
were revealed, it became clear, because actual dates were cited, that
Turnbull knew very much what he was after. The Judge allowed
himself some comments on the consistency of the UK government's
policy towards non-publication which showed that he was certainly
listening to Turnbull's argument about *Their Trade is Treachery*
and *A Matter of Trust*.

If that is the stated policy and the government, without valid
reason, chooses itself to permit breaches, then it casts more than a
shadow of doubt over a lot of evidence and certainly casts a shadow
of doubt over the validity of the policy.

At the close of the day, Turnbull still had not begun his formal
reply on the public interest immunity issue.

Next morning, Simos opened the proceedings with a change in
policy which was another demonstration of how far the backseat
drivers in London were prepared to over-ride his judgment. The day
before Simos had said that if the Judge wanted to read the
documents the plaintiff would not appeal at that stage, but would
appeal if they were to go to the defence. Now Simos indicated his clients would reserve the right to appeal at the first stage. The Judge
was clearly angry: 'I am quite unable to predict from one day to the
next what is the attitude of the plaintiff in this case . . . [and] if it is to
be a continuing pattern the defendants are placed in an intolerable
situation.'

Turnbull spent his first hour or so on questions of law before get-

127

ting back to his point that the UK government had knowingly acquiesced in the production of *Their Trade is Treachery*, that it was an inspired leak. Turning to the document B1 Turnbull drew the Judge's attention to the date, which he said showed the document, still undescribed, was created within weeks of Pincher's returning from seeing Wright in Tasmania in late 1980 and at least two months *before* Sir Robert had said the government knew about the book. The organisation which had sent the letter was that which Sir Robert had had trouble in identifying, which meant that anyone in the courtroom could deduce it was MI6, the Secret Intelligence Service. Turnbull described it, summing up, as 'the whale in the bay'.

On that basis, the UK government had very good reason to fight to the end for an appeal to stop the disclosure of documents. If what Turnbull was indicating emerged to be true, the credibility of Sir Robert and his civil service colleagues would be gravely damaged.

As Turnbull went through the other documents he was seeking, again cryptically and without detail, it was clear that he was claiming other whales in the bay and, again, the sources in Whitehall of those giving him his instructions were good. It was a rich listening diet for Peter Wright, who for the first time that morning slipped into court and was smiling his big wolfish smile as Turnbull put up his points on the documents. The old man should have been sparing some grateful thoughts for his remaining friends somewhere in those London offices.

Exercising his right of reply, Simos tried to get the whale, B1, out to sea and out of sight by telling the Judge that it was not relevant and, in any case, only speculation on Turnbull's part. Mr Justice Powell was unimpressed. Simos came back by saying that evidence from the document might not be of substantial assistance to the defence case. The Judge thought otherwise and told him: 'If I may be forgiven the illustration there would be another nail in the coffin . . . ' Simos ground back that another nail might not be sufficient reason having regard to the countervailing national security interest. That could be weighed, said the Judge, but as for relevance 'if it is the nail that locks the coffin shut, why isn't it . . .' The court rose just before lunch and the Judge promised judgment on public interest and immunity at 2 p.m.

'I should wish to say that I am afraid I did mislead the court in that matter and in that matter only . . . I now understand that it was not referred to the Attorney.'

Not surprisingly, the Judge came down against Simos and the UK government. In the judgment he leant heavily on that case that had come before the Australian High Court, involving the Ananda Marga and the Australian Security Intelligence Organisation, where the right of a judge to look at intelligence documents had been affirmed. The court had said there could be no blanket public interest immunity; examination depended on the circumstances of a particular case. Mr Justice Powell's position was strengthened by the fact that the majority judgment had been written by the current Chief Justice of Australia, Mr Justice Gibbs. What his decision meant was that the UK government would have to hand over the documents for his scrutiny unless they wanted to go back to the Appeals Court.

Sir Robert's in camera evidence was longer than a day: he was in the box for part of Tuesday afternoon, most of Thursday afternoon and all day Friday. One hour in that closed session on Friday must have rivalled his first day of evidence which had been such a long, drawn-out ordeal ending in damaging London headlines. Sir Robert, his counsel Simos, and the Judge agreed with Turnbull that the questions over those sixty minutes or so would have to be made public. This meant even worse headlines than the week before.

Turnbull in open court had nagged Sir Robert again and again on the decision not to proceed against Chapman Pincher. On that Friday when the defence raised the Attorney General question again and then asked, 'do you have any reason to revise that answer now?' Sir Robert said:

'I should wish to say that I am afraid I did mislead the court in that matter and in that matter only . . . the conclusion that there was no basis for restraint was a view reached by legal advisers after consultation among all the legal advisers concerned and it was a unanimous view. I was aware of the view that was reached. I am afraid I assumed from what I was told that it had been referred to the Attorney personally. I now understand that it was not referred to the Attorney.'

It was a retreat on the scale of that from Stalingrad to Berlin.

Sweet as it was for Turnbull, 'a concession of enormous gravity ...', he must have regretted that it was not in open court, but the quick agreement to the release of the transcript solved that. The logical step now was to find out who made the decision. Although Sir Michael Havers was no longer involved it was going to prove difficult to pin down the others.

Sir Robert said: 'I have been informed that it was a decision taken by the legal advisers concerned. I have not yet found out who they all were. I am afraid there are no papers regarding that decision and I am afraid that it may be impossible to find out who were the people concerned, but that is what I have been informed.'

Sir Robert faced more pointed questions from Turnbull who honed in on the reason for the change.

Turnbull: 'Sir Robert, I want to put it to you that the only reason you have made this concession is because Sir Michael Havers has made it very plain in London that he had no part in the decision not to restrain . . . that is so, isn't it?'

Sir Robert: 'Sir Michael Havers was unhappy with the answers which I gave and having made enquiries, I was intending to find an opportunity of putting the record straight in this matter and your question has given me this opportunity.'

On a couple more occasions in the next five minutes, Sir Robert repeated that he was sorry he had misled the court but he remained unable to help on just who it was that made the decision. No, he couldn't remember who it was that transmitted the decision to him, even. Further questioned, he couldn't recall just how the Prime Minister herself was informed of the decision. However, he did shed some light on the process by which he had changed his mind about Havers. It was only on the phone that morning that he had learnt the Attorney-General was not personally responsible. It had been a call from a colleague at the Cabinet Office that had enlightened him.

Turnbull tried the Prime Minister tack again and was given some rather shaky answers:

Turnbull: 'I put it to you that the final decision not to do anything about *Their Trade is Treachery* was taken by you and the Prime Minister, not the Attorney General. You said that was absolutely untrue. Now who was the final decision taken by?'

Sir Robert: 'Well, I have to say that I think it was the final, I don't think it was taken as a decision in that way. The conclusion emerged from the discussion of business that there was no basis for restraint. That was accepted. I accepted myself and didn't take steps to contest it.'

Sir Robert's answer, was showing visible signs of strain, in syntax at least. In another answer, he apologised again: 'I have tried to tell the truth throughout, Mr Turnbull. In saying that I was misled in this case, that I misled myself . . . but I was wrong.' That night, Turnbull's office helpfully gave out copies of the released transcript, ensuring coverage from Fleet Street next morning of the humbling of the most powerful civil servant in England. While it had been Sir Robert who had voluntarily proffered his confession that he had been wrong on the Attorney-General, it was still very clear, especially with hindsight, that Turnbull knew Sir Robert was wrong all along.

In London, the Kinnock diversion, over a phone conversation he had with Turnbull, the stoked-up sensation of the week, was overwhelmed by Sir Robert's backdown in Sydney. The sober and conservative *Daily Telegraph*, on the Saturday morning, led with: 'Ministers and Officials Out of Step; Disarray in MI5 Affair: Havers Denies Spy Claims'. Alongside was the report ' "I Misled the Court," Armstrong admits.' The lead paragraph of the news story was blunt: 'Mrs Thatcher's government was closer to disarray last night than at any time since the Westland affair as increasing strains over the Australian spy case came to light.' The *Telegraph* and the rest of the papers agreed that Sir Michael had confronted his Prime Minister on Thursday night. The *Daily Express* headline 'Havers Anger'. The *Daily Mirror* had 'Law Chief's Ultimatum to Thatcher'. Havers' only public comment was to the *Daily Mail* where he said that it had been the worst week in his life. The heat was back on the Thatcher government and on the Prime Minister personally.

Next day, the *Mail on Sunday* ran in its first edition the name of Bernard X, the MI5 in-house lawyer, who was said to have recommended against action on *Their Trade is Treachery*. While the government may have been slow to move on various books, it moved quite rapidly that Saturday night and issued a D notice banning publication of Bernard's name and the *Mail* dropped it from its second edition. On Monday the *Independent* was profiling

131

Havers as 'the Tory lawyer who defies his Prime Minister'. The Conservative Press were still concentrating on beating Kinnock down. The *Financial Times* partially summed up prospects with 'Thatcher Faces A Tough Week on MI5' and spoke of the inevitable pressure of political embarrassment. The *Daily Mirror* proffered the view that Sir Robert had made 'a proper berk of himself in the witness box' and tagged him 'a buffoon'.

As if Friday had not been enough, Sir Robert had to go back into the witness box in open court on Monday and, predictably, Turnbull took the opportunity to look again, at the Attorney-General question, this time in pursuit of the identity of the advisers. Sir Robert was more confident now that he had appeared in Friday's transcript. He was brisk in repeating his apology, both to the court and to Turnbull, for being wrong in what he'd said. Indeed later, after another apology, Turnbull reached the stage of snapping back, 'Please stop apologising.'

In the hunt for the responsible legal advisers, Turnbull asked whether one lawyer who had advised against it was the MI5 in-house legal adviser (whose theatrical name is under a D notice, i.e. still banned, in the United Kingdom). Sir Robert said that he had been one of those involved in the decision. Asked again about just how Margaret Thatcher was informed, the Cabinet Secretary gave an interesting portrait of decision-making at Number 10 Downing Street.

Turnbull asked directly whether it was Sir Robert who had informed Mrs Thatcher. The answer came:

'It could have been. It could have been in a meeting where it was just said in passing, by anybody, "there is no possibility of proceeding by way of restraint, so we have to think about a statement". I don't know how it was done. It could have been done at one of my regular weekly meetings with the Prime Minister. I am afraid I simply don't remember. I think it would have been possible even at that stage for somebody to say "Why don't we look at that again?" but they didn't. It was accepted, as I say, as a general view, as part of the landscape as it were.'

Taking Sir Robert through his earlier statements on the Attorney General, Turnbull reminded him that the first had been on the second day of the trial, so he asked the question which had occurred to a number of people: why had it taken so long for the correction? Why had it come on last Friday, ten days after his first statement? Sir Robert said that he had received the phone call correcting him early that morning. Asked again why it had taken so long, Sir Robert blandly answered that he didn't know how much prominence the earlier statement had been given in the London papers. Turnbull switched back to the circumstances of the publication of *Their Trade is Treachery*, going into such detail as to draw the weary comment from the Judge in the closing minutes of the day: 'We are straying a little.' However it can now be seen that his questions were directed to setting up another ambush. At the end of the day, Turnbull promised that there were only a few matters left.

On Tuesday, after the Judge had delivered his latest decision on the public interest immunity and documents issue, against the UK government, and after a brief adjournment to allow the parties to digest it, Sir Robert came back into the box for the last time. Turnbull, for the last few minutes was polite, almost conversational, compared with the relentless pressure and sharpness apparent in the earlier cross-examinations. He was being reasonable, sweetly reasonable, floating the possibility of an agreement on a blue pencil job on the manuscript to allow publication. There was still perhaps a possibility and, if the UK government said no, well that helped to show them as stubborn and unreasonable. Sir Robert said 'no'. Would he perhaps take the Judge to particular passages? asked Turnbull. 'There would be a great many examples, one would gather, so I would stand on the general case,' said the Cabinet Secretary. The Judge, thinking out loud, wondered whether his experience thirty years ago (a reference to his service in Australian Military Intelligence) would allow him to undertake a blue pencilling exercise. The drift of the Judge's comment, more explicit than his previous broad hint, seemed to indicate that he would consider it if asked. Sir Robert and Simos sat mute.

One minor point from Turnbull about named ex-MI5 officers in the manuscript and Sir Robert was out for the last time. But he couldn't be sure of that because there was still a question of whether or not he would have to return to be cross-examined on the documents, that is, if the defence ever got their hands on them. It

The* Daily Telegraph *leader writer said, 'The Cabinet Secretary now resembles a bull so extensively adorned with banderillas that even the most sadistic spectator yearns to see him decently dispatched.'

seemed it would depend on the Court of Appeal.

In Fleet Street that week, Sir Robert's humiliation was quickly overwhelmed by the continued furore over Neil Kinnock and a dramatic, if not melodramatic, initiative from Lord Rothschild. However, before then, the *Daily Telegraph* in an editorial on Tuesday, did make a parting comment on Sir Robert which, coming from a conservative newspaper, must have made Sir Robert think that with friends like this, who needs enemies? The conservative leader writer said, 'The Cabinet Secretary now resembles a bull so extensively adorned with banderillas that even the most sadistic spectator yearns to see him decently dispatched.'

Lord Rothschild evidently hoped for more sympathy from the *Daily Telegraph,* because on Thursday he chose it as the forum for a heartfelt plea for the final clearance of his name of the claims that he had once been a Soviet agent.

'Lord Rothschild CBE, GM, ScD, FRS

December 3, 1986

Dear Editor and Readers

Since at least 1980 up to the present time there have been innuendoes in the press to the effect that I am 'the 5th man', in other words a Soviet agent.

The Director General of MI5 should state publicly that it has unequivocal, repeat unequivocal, evidence that I am not, and never have been a Soviet agent. If the 'regulations' prevent him from making such a statement which, in the present climate I doubt, let him do so through his legal adviser or through any other recognizably [sic] authoritative source.

I am constrained by the Official Secrets Act, but I write this letter lest it be thought that silence would be an indication of anything other than complete innocence.

I shall not make any other public statement to the Press until further notice.

Yours truly

Rothschild'

The *Telegraph* leader writer, much more kind than to Sir Robert, said that the letter, rather touchingly addressed 'Dear Editor and Readers' is 'a cri de coeur [which] could end [Rothschild's] trial by rumour, gossip and innuendo'. Cri de coeur the letter may well have been, but it was also a damn good diversion from the question of just what Rothschild's relations with Wright and Pincher had really been. On this question, the newspapers carried reports that, on the advice of lawyers, Lord Rothschild was not saying anything about his relationship with Wright. It was curious advice as certainly sub judice would not apply in England to a case in an Australian court; indeed, the facts of the hearing had been extensively canvassed, as distinct from simply reported, for weeks in almost every paper in London.

Lord Rothschild certainly proved to have friends. Roy Hattersley, the deputy leader of the Labour opposition, was to be only one of those drawn into advocating a clearance statement. Margaret Thatcher's slowness to give the clearance provoked the headline in the *Daily Telegraph*, 'Anger by MPs on Rothschild: Stonewalling by Thatcher Over Fifth Man Plea'. In the body of the story the political correspondent wrote, 'her stonewalling over the reputation of such a distinguished public figure surprised and angered MPs.' The Baron's letter had spoken of the Director General of MI5 being in possession of unequivocal evidence that Rothschild had not been a Soviet agent. Nigel West in a radio interview the next morning explained just what the unequivocal evidence was, and it proved to be fairly old hat. In 1962 when Lord Rothschild was in Israel he was told by a woman (Flora Solomon) who had known Philby when he was a young man, that he, Philby, had personally confessed to her he was working for the Comintern. On returning to England, Rothschild passed this on to MI5, who at last had the information needed to have Philby confronted. This wasn't much good as 'unequivocal evidence'. As Philip Knightley, an author on the spy world who, unlike many of his colleagues brings a certain scepticism to assertions, pointed out next day that it was common espionage practice for one spy to give up another. So, in the wilderness of mirrors nothing could be said to be unequivocal.

On Friday Margaret Thatcher issued a three paragraph statement from Number 10 Downing Street.

I am advised that we have no evidence that he was ever a Soviet agent.'

'I have now considered more fully Lord Rothschild's letter in the *Daily Telegraph* yesterday in which he referred to innuendoes that he had been a Soviet agent.

I consider it important to maintain the practice of successive governments of not commenting on security matters. But I am willing to make an exception on the matter raised in Lord Rothschild's letter.

I am advised that we have no evidence that he was ever a Soviet agent.'

That the exception was made was a tribute to Lord Rothschild's reputation, but the chill note of the last sentence echoed Sir Robert's tone in the court room in Australia. Next day, pressed in an interview on the topic the Prime Minister said, 'That is a clearance. Leave it at that.'

The week did provide some light relief, with the revelation that the Prime Minister's parliamentary private secretary, Michael Alison, didn't much like Sir Robert Armstrong. At a constituency dinner the previous weekend in Yorkshire, Mr Alison had unburdened himself of a few after-dinner bon mots, not noticing that one of the local Social Democrats was in the audience and was later only too happy to relay them to the press. The MP referred to Sir Robert as a 'Wally among the wallabys', thus, no doubt, getting his own back for the occasions at Number 10 when the Cabinet Secretary had, as befits a very senior public servant, perhaps not taken much notice of an importunate back bencher. Mr Alison had gone a bit further adding, 'We don't know whether to laugh or cry about it all. We don't know whether this is Gilbert and Sullivan or the Two Ronnies. At any rate it's good for a laugh.' Predictably, of course, the MP denied that he had intended to reflect upon Sir Robert in any way.

There was a side-show at an even more distant venue than London that week (day). The High Court in Dublin rejected a British attempt to ban *One Girl's War* by Joan Miller, who had been an assistant to Maxwell Knight, the M15 man who ran agents in the Communist Party of Great Britain in the 1930s and 1940s. Miss Justice Carroll, ominously for the UK government, cited the Australian High Court, *Commonwealth v. Fairfax,* to support her rejection. The publisher

Next day, pressed in an interview on the topic the Prime Minister said, 'That is a clearance. Leave it at that.'

said he would be delighted to produce Wright's book in Eire.

Meanwhile, back in Sydney on Tuesday, the UK government's other witness, Michael Codd, Secretary of the Department of the Prime Minister and Cabinet, appeared to be cross-examined on his affidavit. Codd, in the witness box, was not your smooth, controlled Sir Robert Armstrong. He personified the word 'bristling'. To confirm that he had read the manuscript of Wright's book, Turnbull asked him whether it was right to say that his objection was based not on its contents but on the fact that it was written by a former officer of MI5. 'No. You are not right,' said Codd, and went on to explain that it was the fact that it was a comprehensive account of Wright's experiences and the operations and techniques of MI5.

Codd's aggressive responses implied a contest between Turnbull and himself. Such an approach gives the impression that a witness is trying to take over the court. Judges, any judges, do not like this. The court is for them to control, not witnesses nor for that matter barristers. Codd's style laid him open to correction and, when he fell into errors and misjudgments, a provoked Mr Justice Powell applied the rod with vigour.

Turnbull pointed out that two books had been published relatively recently in Australia by former intelligence officers: *Sub Rosa* by R.H. Mathams, a former Joint Intelligence Organisation scientific intelligence expert and *The Truth Will Out* by Michael Thwaites, who had been one of the Petrovs' handlers. Codd said they were not regarded as breaching national security, which allowed Turnbull to lead the witness into agreeing that regard had to be given to contents, but then, like Sir Robert, he refused to be drawn on specifics about Wright's manuscript. The witness and the defence went through the same skirmish over whether or not Wright had disclosed all his experience. At one stage, Codd refused to answer whether the manuscript referred to computer retrieval practices. However, when Turnbull insisted he should write an answer down on a piece of paper to be handed to the Judge, he did so.

Like Sir Robert, Mr Codd was proudly 'unfamiliar' with the CIA manuscript review policy; indeed, he wasn't aware that it existed and had existed for eight years. Closer to home, he had no idea whether or not Harvey Barnett, the former Director General of ASIO at the time of the Ivanov-Combe affair, was writing his memoirs. After a few more minutes, Turnbull, with a straight face, turned to the Report of Mr Justice Hope and contrived in his opening questions to sound faintly sarcastic about the Hope Royal Commission. The proper departmental secretary vigorously took the side of the Royal Commission, stressing how there had been a bi-partisan response to the Hope reports. Then Turnbull briskly closed the trap: 'Why have you set out to mislead the court?' He then proceeded to disclose himself as an admirer, even a disciple of Mr Justice Hope. What Codd had done in his affidavit was to quote Paragraphs 449 and 450 of the report on the utility of liaison with other services. However, as Turnbull pointed out, a cut off had eliminated paragraphs 451 and 452 which laid down strenuous qualifications on relationships with so-called friendly services. Hope said that liaison should not 'assist any service which does not sufficiently respect civil rights and freedom'. As Turnbull pointed out, the absence of such respect for civil rights and freedom had been admitted about MI5 in August. Codd said he'd seen reports about it in newspapers but didn't consider it important.

Mr Justice Powell, wearing his frown, intervened. Wasn't Codd aware that the material conceded revealed instances of illegalities and improprieties by MI5 officers? Codd said that he wasn't aware that they'd been accepted as fact. Now that he was, said the Judge, did he see the relevance of Mr Justice Hope's comments? The Judge continued to look displeased and, a few minutes later, impartially slapped down Turnbull when he pushed his luck to the limit on another question. When Turnbull pressed the witness as to whether the Australian people would have a right to know about abuses by the security agencies, Codd fell back on the unauthorised disclosure of investigations and operations jargon. The Judge asked sharply: '. . . [if] we did liaise with the security services of Chile and only half the stories of security services in Chile were true, surely to heaven you would not suggest that the Australian government would wish to prevent the Australian people being told the activities that are alleged against the Chilean security system . . .?' Codd spoke of needing to look carefully at the Hope report. 'I appreciate that,' said

Mr Justice Powell, 'but who is to be the judge, you or the Australian people ... I gather you would say you and your professional colleagues.' Codd then spoke of the need to strike a balance between what should be made available 'for public consumption' (a revealing use of language) and the protection of the security service.

The exchange between the Australian public servant and the Australian judge concisely summed up the whole case in a way better than all the counsels' addresses. On one side, the right of the public to know, and on the other, a view of the public as consumers to be given what people thought was good for them. Mr Justice Powell again looked less than pleased and when Turnbull, realising that he had done well, tried on an ironical reference to 'Saint Robert Hope', he got a put down: 'I think that is enough, Mr Turnbull.' For a while afterwards, Codd was cautious. Turnbull led him through other sections of the Hope Report on compliance with international conventions and with statute law in Australia. Having taken him so far, Turnbull then asked a hypothetical question which had the English journalists leaning forward on their seats.

Turnbull: '. . . I stress for the benefit of my friends in the press that this is entirely hypothetical. Let us assume that thirty officers of ASIO were conspiring to overthrow the government of the day, Mr Hawke's government. Let us assume that the plot came to your notice. Would you consider it appropriate for a plot of that kind to be dealt with by a formal public investigation?'

Simos objected and Turnbull, after some toing and froing withdrew, but the hypothetical question was left hanging in the air. It was, to adapt a phrase people had become used to, 'hypothetical for the purposes of the proceedings', but it did fit in with what had been said in other places, that is, that the number within MI5 involved in the Wilson fiasco was larger than just a few. This, of course, was in conflict with the impression Sir Robert had striven to give during his cross-examination.

Turnbull led Codd through some teasing questions on whether he was for or against assassination or the burglary of diplomatic premises. Not surprisingly, Codd said he was against both. Asked whether he was a democrat, Codd replied: 'I am not familiar with these terms, I am afraid. You'll find my power over the English language not as great as you think.' Mr Justice Powell cut off the

Asked whether he was a democrat, Codd replied: 'I am not familiar with these terms, I am afraid. You'll find my power over the English language not as great as you think.'
line of questioning and added: 'I think you will find Mr Codd will certainly not engage in a reconnaissance patrol let alone a fighting patrol beyond the sand bags.' It was a neat summation of the defensive Codd style of answers.

Turnbull, still trying, asked whether Codd agreed with some of the recommendations of Mr Justice Hope for more ministerial statements on ASIO. Simos again objected, on the grounds that the personal views of Codd were irrelevant. The Judge allowed the question, with the comment: 'If that be so, it makes every other opinion he has offered on the subject irrelevant.' Turnbull produced *The Ties That Bind,* the Ball and Richelson book on the Anglo-Saxon security and intelligence agencies, which included a substantial section on Australia. Codd, the government's principal security adviser said that he had seen the book but had felt no particular reason to read it.

After being mild with Codd for a time, Turnbull led him into a trap and briskly shut the door. Paragraph 9b of Codd's affidavit had said that if Wright succeeded in Australia, former members of Australian security intelligence agencies might be encouraged to make like disclosures if they saw it could be done without penalty. Was this not 'utter codswallop?' asked Turnbull, thus unequivocally testing Codd's knowledge of the Australian Security and Intelligence Organization Act. 'No,' replied Codd. He was trapped.

The defence then asked what Cod knew about the Act. Sensing a problem, Codd became cautious. He knew 'a little' about it and he had read 'parts of it'. Turnbull handed up the Act, and drew attention to Section 18, which specifically prohibited any ASIO officer or ex-officer from communicating any information to any unauthorised person, subject to penalties. Codd had to admit then that any decision by Mr Justice Powell on Wright would make no difference at all to the Act. It was not only a matter of paragraph 9b of the affidavit being proved wrong in court, the argument about giving a free hand to disgruntled ex-officers had been used in the Canberra Security and Intelligence Committee, in Cabinet and also as a response to queries from backbenchers.

Codd, realising he was in trouble, raised the spectre of off-shore publication. This met with some mockery from Turnbull who questioned the extent to which ASIO memoirs might excite London and New York. Pressed on which foreign agencies would think the less of Australia if the book were published, Codd delivered a neat drop-kick at the law. 'What is being said [in the affidavit] is that there would be a perception that under the Australian legal system, and under Australian law, and through the Australian legal system, protection of sensitive information could be at risk.'

Few judges could have let such a put down of the law pass. Mr Justice Powell did not. Studiously polite, he asked 'You'll forgive me for saying so, but if that proposition is put in absolute terms, ASIO has not the slightest right to place any trust in MI5 because, in certain circumstances, sensitive information is not protected in the United Kingdom.' Turnbull took up the cue and led Codd through all the MI5 failures to protect information in England, ranging from Philby through to Bettaney. Codd tried to turn these failures to his advantage by constructing an argument that unless MI5 won its case in Australia, then ASIO would have to review its links with MI5, because MI5 had failed to protect its security of information. Mr Justice Powell, again prefacing his words with 'I am sorry,' bluntly said, 'a lot of this to me sounds like complete and utter moonshine.' In re-examination Simos gave Codd a platform to say something about Sir Roger Hollis and ASIO and Codd took it, saying that Hollis's connection with the foundation of ASIO was tenuous. He advised on organisation, but had not recruited anyone.

Codd was finished in time to catch a plane to Bangladesh where he had to attend a conference. As had Sir Robert Armstrong, Codd demonstrated that the public service high-flyer doesn't always translate well into the gladiatorial role of a fighter in court. Sir Robert might well have been angrier than Codd at being subject to the cross- examination but his control was much better. Codd's briefing appeared to have been poor, to have let paragraph 9b go through and then be trapped on the ASIO Act was a serious failure. What in particular was extraordinary was his admission that he, as principal adviser to the government, hadn't bothered to read *The Ties That Bind,* unquestionably the most thorough and definitive picture of the Anglo-Saxon security and intelligence community and which contained a great deal of previously unpublished information. Actually, listening to Codd, one heard clearly the voice of a member of that club; he saw its interest as primary.

The Secretary of the Prime Minister's Department was followed by the first witness for the defence, Gough Whitlam, Prime Minister of Australia from 1972 to 1975. However, before he could go into the box, the court had to hear Simos' objection. Whitlam, said Simos, could only be expressing his personal opinion as to what the Australian public interest required, because there was no body of specialised knowledge on these matters, a rather catch-22 argument. If the former Prime Minister were to be called he would, in the last analysis, said Simos, be debating issues, not giving evidence.

After ten minutes or so of this Mr Justice Powell was brisk. He probably could take judicial note of the fact that Whitlam had been Prime Minister for a period of some years and in that role was concerned with matters of national security. If, the Judge suggested, with 'the whole of his years of experience and his particlar experience as Prime Minister behind him . . .', Mr Whitlam were to say that '. . . the national security interests of the country would not be detrimentally affected by the disclosure of whatever material was in Mr Wright's manuscript', why is that entitled to less weight than the opinion of Mr Codd, who, if I may say with respect, appears to come to his office late, or for that matter, of Sir Robert Armstrong.' The Judge's rebuke concluded, Whitlam went into the witness box and affirmed rather than take an oath. The former Labor leader and Prime Minister then proceeded to put on a vintage Gough Whitlam performance, assured, relaxed and witty.

Asked if he had been the author of some historical works concerning his period in office, the ex-PM replied: 'Oh, not only historical,' and, after suitable dramatic pause, 'literary'. Asked if he had read Wright's book, Whitlam answered 'Yes,' in such world-weary tones that the listeners got the strong message that no rational man could understand what all the fuss was about. Codd, 'with his intense experience extending over nine months', got short shrift. Whitlam disagreed with the points made in his affidavit to the effect that the book could be damaging the activities of Australian security and intelligence services, especially in relation to terrorism. The only reference to terrorism in the manuscript related to what

Whitlam puzzlingly called 'freedom fighters'. Whitlam then made it clear that he was referring to the revelations that MI5 had considered the assassination of Grivas, the leader of the Greek underground movement in Cyprus in the 1950s, which had wanted union with mainland Greece.

Essentially Whitlam's evidence was a manifesto for the accountability of security services to the government. It was in the public interest that history should be written about secret intelligence services: 'I believe that it is essential governments and the people who elect governments should learn from history. Whether circumstances repeat themselves or not may be a subject for proverbs or maxims but there can be no doubt we should profit from experience in these matters.' Whitlam stressed ministerial responsibility again and again. Security and intelligence agencies should not do anything that they could not 'report' to the responsible minister. Whitlam outlined the changes that his government had laid down after being elected in 1972:

'Before that time ASIO had operated the same way as MI5. It would operate in breach of the law. It burgled premises adjacent to diplomatic premises. If it could it would burgle diplomatic premises.' It would bug diplomatic premises and neighbouring premises. It would watch selected migrant groups. It would watch certain writers. It would infiltrate some political parties.'

However, it was decided at the end of 1972 that ASIO should not undertake activities which couldn't be reported to the appropriate ministers in respect of migrants, trade unions, intellectuals, political parties. Whitlam made it clear that ASIO could only undertake activity where there was a real danger of politically-motivated violence and such exceptional activity should be reported to the minister. It was a world away from Sir Robert's justification for tapping the unionist's phone on the unqualified grounds that he was a communist. Whitlam was careful to point out that the Hope Royal Commission had firmed up the guidelines and that even after Labor was out of government from 1975 to 1983 the same principles were observed. Whitlam's evidence was a sober, temperate statement of the basic principle of accountability within a democratic society.

On the Massitter allegations of phone tapping of civil libertarians

Questioned on the Wilson allegations, Whitlam said: 'I would believe it a travesty of democracy if the Security Service was lending itself to undermining a government or the leader of a government.'

which, Turnbull reminded him, it had been admitted were true for the purposes of the case, Whitlam was very sharp: 'I think it monstrous a person should be paid for monitoring [Patricia Hewitt's] activities in civil liberties organisations in Britain.' Whitlam's ire was increased by his personal acquaintance with Miss Hewitt and a long-standing friendship with her mother. Asked if he felt she was a person to plot the violent overthrow of the British government, Whitlam allowed himself some characteristic irony: 'I have never felt myself at risk in her company.' Questioned on the Wilson allegations, Whitlam said: 'I would believe it a travesty of democracy if the Security Service was lending itself to undermining a government or the leader of a government.'

Simos' brief cross-examination of Whitlam was his most abrasive performance of the trial so far but still, as abrasiveness went, it was some distance behind Turnbull. The plaintiff's counsel set out to show that Whitlam's knowledge was dated and he could not be an authority. When Whitlam reverted to the Hewitt and Wilson cases, Simos became visibly angered and accused Whitlam of evading the question. But Simos was being talked down by a man who had learnt that skill on the rough and tumble floor of the House of Representatives. Mr Justice Powell intervened smoothly again and the former Prime Minister's evidence was over. His evidence was distinctly damaging to the UK government's attempt to claim that the contents of the book could be detrimental to either the United Kingdom or Australia.

The trial had to go on, even pending the almost certain appeal. With that argument over, Turnbull brought into the box William Herman Schaap, a lawyer from New York, to give evidence on the practice in the United States relating to the publication of writing by ex-intelligence officers. Schaap's curriculum vitae, outlined in his statement supplied to the court, was literally as long as his arm. Simos made a routine objection to Schaap's evidence, which was routinely set aside, and the American went into the box. Schaap had a rather firm officer-like presence – perhaps not surprising in a man

144

who for much of his life had been something of a scourge of the military (in 1972-76 he had specialised in military law, practising for the American Civil Liberties Union). As well as specialising in military law, he had also been involved in a number of federal courts in constitutional cases relating to the CIA and the legality or illegality under domestic and international law, of US actions in Central America. He had written and lectured extensively on his specialities at various universities. He was managing director of the Institute of Media Analysis, headquartered in New York, as well as a publishing company in Sheridan Square which published a range of books by ex-CIA agents. For good measure, he was director and co-editor of *Covert Action Information Bulletin,* a quarterly publication dealing with current operations of the CIA and western intelligence agencies. As a lawyer he had represented ex-CIA authors in legal actions and negotiations.

As befitted such a legal polymath, Schaap's evidence was concise but detailed. Speaking about books comparable with Wright's memoirs, he produced synopses of ten books by former intelligence agents which had been published following the normal process of submission to the CIA manuscript board of review. The first step was a submission, then there was the review, negotiation (in some cases), final clearance and publication. Schaap outlined the function of the board and brought out two significant points that Turnbull had not referred to. These were that authors could appeal from the board to the Deputy Director of the CIA who must give his decision within thirty days and that if the author was still unsatisfied he could go to a federal court. This was all light years away from the UK practice. Schaap had thoughtfully anticipated the possible argument that, whatever might be said about the CIA's internal operations, connections and liaisons with other intelligence agencies could not be discussed. He provided a number of examples where they had been. The American summed up:

'I have read those portions of the testimony and the affidavits of Sir Robert Armstrong which suggest the CIA would be extremely concerned at the publication of a book such as [Wright's], a conclusion I find untenable. The CIA, on its own, has approved the publication of books with information at least as intriguing as that in the book in issue herein and with

145

considerable, indeed, voluminous details about personnel, operations, technology and all aspects of intelligence work. The only restrictions which have been applied consistently to the release of information relate to the endangering of personnel still undercover and the exposure of operations still underway. Virtually all details have been released about countless old operations, and, as I have been informed the material in the book in issue herein is virtually all ten to twenty years old, I cannot see how, under the standards applied in the United States, such a book would be suppressed, in whole or in part.'

Turnbull's examination task was easy, after such a thorough build-up. In the course of it, Mr Justice Powell's errant eye caught one of the titles that had been submitted to the CIA board, *I Was Idi Amin's Basketball Czar.* Schaap said he had actually read the article and heard its author speak. 'He was a CIA agent in Uganda during the time Idi Amin was in power. His major problem was to keep General Amin happy. General Amin liked to play basketball. As the author says he was a very bad basketball player so the author as an experienced CIA officer was detailed the job of trying to improve his skills.' In the course of a long examination on published books, Schaap was able to tell a bizarre story about a memoir *Counter Coup* by Kermit Roosevelt, an American who had been involved in the Iranian coup in 1953 which had reinstalled the Shah. In the first edition of the book, Roosevelt had used 'Anglo-Iranian Oil Company' as a cover for British intelligence. When the company protested, the first edition of the book was pulped and British intelligence was substituted openly in the second. It made the point neatly that the US government allowed publication of a book giving an account of relations with a friendly intelligence agency. Schaap was also able to make the same point with Joseph Smith's *Portrait of a Cold War Warrior,* by an ex-CIA man who had talked about how, in the 1950s, the Australian Secret Intelligence Service had cooperated with the United States in carrying out anti-Sukarno operations.

Simos, speaking for the plaintiff, clearly didn't want to cross-examine Schaap, presumably on the grounds that it might be seen to give some status to the American argument. The plaintiff's counsel claimed that he would be unable to cross-examine, in any case, for two days because he had only received the Schaap statement that morning. After some jousting, Simos finally stated that he wouldn't be cross-examining Schaap at all.

It was another example of UK tactic or lack of them, that was baffling to observers. Schaap had come over very well in the box, he appeared as a thoughtful and reasonable man. But had the UK government wanted to knock him about a bit in the eyes of Mr Justice Powell, they need only have turned to the *Covert Action Information Bulletin's* current issue. The CAIB is pretty hardline, compared to the moderate Centre for National Security Studies in Washington, the mainstream liberal critic of the CIA intelligence services. It is not so much that the *CAIB* is Left in any narrow ideological sense, rather that the journal is such an unrelenting critic of the CIA as to deny the validity of its existence or, indeed, the existence of any such organisation. The issue currently available in Australia carried, under the joint by-line of Helen Ray and William Schaap, a page three article on the new United States ambassador to the UN, General Vernon Walters, headed 'Vernon Walters Crypto-Diplomat Terrorist'. It was a well-argued piece, setting out how Walters had been in a lot of trouble spots where there had been a lot of violence, but its tone was infinitely more militant than Mr Schaap in court. Given that the plaintiff had notice that Schaap was coming, they had plenty of time to prepare a set of questions to go after his credit. Was it just a case similar to no one in London bothering to get the CIA manuscript policy straight, or was there simply no expert in MI5 or MI6 who read the wide range of American anti-spook periodical literature?

Later that day, it was the defence's turn to back off from another confrontation. Turnbull announced the defence would not want to cross-examine an anonymous training officer who, allegedly, had been present when Wright signed his Official Secrets Act undertaking. About his affidavit, Turnbull said Wright would say: 'Never 'eard of 'im, don't know 'im, didn't train me, wouldn't have known what I was being trained about any'ow.' Wright sitting behind Turnbull grinned at the relayed Cockney. That over, the court adjourned until Thursday to await the setting of the timetable for the appeal.

In London, the briefers had been hard at work, bucketting the Australian judge on the documents issue. The *Daily Express* spoke of documents being 'highly secret and sensitive relating to national security'. The documents may have been secret but they did not relate to national security in any real sense of the word. They related to how the government reached its decisions on West's and Pincher's books and on the Massitter and Wright TV programmes. To pretend that this related to agents or operational techniques was deliberately misleading, the more so as the people feeding that line to the *Express* must have known that. As we know, the Judge had specifically ruled out, early on, any intention of discovery on operational techniques.

The other diversion of the week was the Greengrass gambit. The involvement of Paul Greengrass, the producer of the Granada TV show in 1984 which featured Peter Wright, was not clandestine. From the first day, he had sat in the court room, behind Turnbull, as part of the defence team. Greengrass had an almost unrivalled knowledge of the literature of the spy world, in particular, of public domain precedents which could upset the consistency case of the UK government. His presence as an expert was as valid as that of say, a structural engineer in a building case. For him to have breached the injunction on the contents of the book would have laid him open to penalties. Yet this week he was to be targeted.

The *Daily Express* on Wednesday, announced the bizarre discovery that Sir Robert's misleading the court was all Greengrass' fault. 'So far the plan has worked. It even forced Sir Robert to admit that he had misled the court.' Whoever had fed out this extraordinary bit of briefing showed a cavalier disregard for the facts of the court hearing. Whatever Greengrass might have heard in closed session about Wright's manuscript would have had nothing to do with Sir Robert's recollection or otherwise of the Attorney-General's role. The *Express* on the same day in an editorial attacked the 'flamboyant' Mr Justice Powell for letting secret information be blazoned forth to Greengrass. But the only secrets to which Greengrass would have become privy in closed session were the well-worn contents of the Wright manuscript which had been discussed at length in the London press for months. Quite simply Greengrass was a useful peg to attack the Judge and his decision on the

148

discovery of documents. The briefers influencing the *Express* were ignoring the fact that the Judge had said that the edited documents should only be shown to Wright and Turnbull, but then the disinformation over documents had so far muddied the waters in London that the facts in Sydney had long since become irrelevant.

The sustained press campaign against Greengrass, and its House of Commons parallel, surfaced in a brief passage before the court on Thursday morning preceding the Court of Appeals session upstairs.

Before Mr Justice Powell, the parties had agreed to an adjournment until Friday pending the Court of Appeal hearing. Before the court rose, Turnbull raised the question of the allegations made by a Conservative Member of Parliament accusing Greengrass of leaking material from closed sessions of the court to the Labour Party in England. Turnbull said the allegations appeared to be attributed to certain 'government sources' and 'ministers'. Turnbull denied the claims and appealed to the British government to either dissociate itself from the claims or to make them through their counsel in open court. Mr Justice Powell contented himself with a brief comment concluding: 'I propose to act on nothing unless it is said and done in this court and if Her Majesty's government does believe it has the evidence to take procedures against Mr Greengrass it is free to do so . . . ' Simos sat silent and the court adjourned.

The Appeals Court did grant leave to the UK government to appeal, over Turnbull's objections that the question of the documents was not of such importance to justify it, claiming that the appeal came disgracefully late in the day. Turnbull also stressed again that none of the documents related to operational matters. The Chief Justice and Mr Justice Kirby again sat on the bench and the third member this time was Mr Justice Glass. The Chief Justice offered a hearing on Thursday and Friday of the next week, but stressed that that did not mean a verdict. Turnbull was not at his best when he warned that his client was old and sick and could very well die in the witness box. The judges were visibly unimpressed. On the other side, the bench made it very clear to Simos that they would inspect the documents. The decision posed different problems for the two counsels. For Turnbull, it brought the prospect of a decision some time next year exacerbating the financial problems of his client, let alone the health difficulties. Simos, knowing the drift of recent Australian High Court cases, saw the odds were not good. There was scope for a compromise, but the question was whether or not the backseat drivers in London would allow it.

Mr Justice Glass caught the attention of some of the assembled journalists when, in referring to B1, the whale in the bay, he spoke of 'the synopsis'. This conveyed to shrewd listeners that the government had had the synopsis of *Their Trade is Treachery* in December, long before the previously-indicated February date, and in plenty of time for the fullest possible investigation and preparation of legal action.

Peter Wright came into the witness box at 2.20 in the afternoon after the appeal. For the first time since he had been in the court, he was visibly nervous and faintly flushed. The Judge politely told him that he, like Sir Robert, could ask for a break if fatigued. The witness's voice was deep, his pronunciation precise. The affidavit he had sworn that morning was produced, severely edited beforehand by the Judge in chambers, and Wright started to read the new version onto the record.

When he had joined 'The Service' in 1955, Wright had been paid by non-government cheque. In chapters two to four of the manuscript he had described the part-time relationship he had had with the Service while working with the Royal Naval Scientific Service and later Marconi. He'd been recruited into part-time work for MI6 by Frederick Brundrett, who had been the Director of the RNSS and later Deputy Scientific Adviser to the Ministry of Defence. Brundrett had been asked to find a scientific adviser to the Service by Sir Percy Sillitoe, the outsider policeman put in by Attlee. The unpaid, part-time job had come to take up more and more of Wright's spare time. As well, he sat on a committee set up to advise MI5 on scientific matters. This led to Wright being asked to write a planning programme for both MI5 and MI6.

He went on to tell the story of his success with the SATYR microphone and how he had come to join MI6 full-time.

Wright claimed that after he joined the Service, he had never been referred to any sort of confidentiality, other than the Official Secrets Act. He asserted that he had taken great care not to disclose anything 'which in my judgment as a professional intelligence officer might damage national security'.

150

Moving to details of the book, the first category was Techniques. All three pages in the affidavit were edited out except for:

'I have erred on the side of caution when writing about technology and I have not included in the book a number of more modern technological operations.'

Under the second heading, Operations, Wright was brief:

'The second area of material in my book consists of operations such as burglaries, the use of agents and covert interception. I have taken care only to discuss such non-technical operations during the period up to the mid-1960s. I am aware of a whole range of Operations which are much more current and which I have not revealed.'

Everything under Counter Espionage Investigations, the third section, was censored. The next heading, not numbered, was Wright's case against 'The Thatcher Statements in the Commons'. This, too, was heavily edited. Highlights of what was left included:

'The PM says that the information which led to Blunt's confession "was not usable as evidence on which to base a prosecution". This is now revealed as the evidence of Michael Straight who was an American who has published a book about it. Contrary to what Sir Robert has suggested, Straight stated that Blunt had recruited him as a spy for Russia, not simply as a member of the Communist Party. The PM's statement is false to the extent that it suggests the evidence was somehow inadmissible. The simple fact was that the law officers felt that in a conflict of testimony a man who was a knight and Surveyor of the Queens Pictures would be believed.

'I refer to the 26 March 1981 statement by Mrs Thatcher in the House of Commons [on Hollis]. This statement is substantially false and its errors must have been known to those in MI5 who prepared the brief for the Prime Minister. I shall deal with the statement a paragraph at a time:

'Mrs Thatcher says: "The extent of penetration was thoroughly investigated after the defection of Burgess and Maclean, as, indeed, the author of this book makes clear. The book contains no information of security significance that is new to the security authorities and some of the material is inaccurate or distorted. All the cases and individuals referred to

Wright: 'There was a lot of false material in Mrs Thatcher's replies and this is of my own knowledge, this is not hearsay because I was concerned with these cases closely.'
Turnbull: 'And the confidential part of your affidavit gives chapter and verse for your contentions, does it not?'
Wright: 'Yes.'

have been the subject of long and thorough investigation."
'It is simply not correct to say that the extent of penetration was thoroughly investigated.'

Wright's development of his case on the extent of penetration was edited out.

At that stage, Turnbull broke in to ask some clarificatory questions. He asked whether Wright, after having read carefully Mrs Thatcher's statements in 1979 and 1981 on Blunt and Hollis, had formed a view on whether or not they were true or false. Wright replied:

Wright: 'There was a lot of false material in Mrs Thatcher's replies and this is of my own knowledge, this is not hearsay because I was concerned with these cases closely.'

Turnbull: 'And the confidential part of your affidavit gives chapter and verse for your contentions, does it not?'

Wright: 'Yes.'

He went on:

'Mrs Thatcher says: "The case for investigating Sir Roger Hollis was based on certain leads that suggested, but did not prove, that there had been a Russian intelligence service agent at a relatively senior level in British counter-intelligence in the last years of the war. None of these leads identified Sir Roger Hollis, or pointed specifically or solely in his direction. Each of them could also be taken as pointing to Philby or Blunt. But Sir Roger Hollis was among those that fitted some of them, and he was therefore investigated." '

Two pages following this paragraph were also censored. Wright dealt then with some of Sir Robert's affidavit claims on the possible effect of the book, answering the allegations that informants and assistants could be threatened and that the practice of positive vetting was endangered with the straight-out assertion that 'the book is of historical interest only'. Wright also made a renewed offer for the blue-pencilling of the book.

On the effects the book may have on liaison with other services, Wright's partially-edited answer was:

'Information which is out in the public domain will not be prejudiced if it is released by me. Furthermore all of this information is out of date. More importantly perhaps, Britain and Australia's major intelligence partner, by a very long measure, is the United States . . . I have no doubt that if I were a former CIA officer I would have had no difficulty publishing my book. Therefore there is no prospect of the CIA or the other US agencies being offended by the publication of my book . . . Lastly the intelligence exchange with friendly services has survived a whole series of damaging high level penetrations, such as Philby, Blunt, Blake, Prime, Burgess etc. etc.'

Wright rubbished the claim that his writing about the tradecraft of dead letter boxes would be helpful to hostile agencies or terrorists by pointing out that the technique had been described by David Cornwell, in the Le Carre Smiley books as well as in the UK security commission reports on Prime and Bettaney.

On the identification of premises in his book, Wright said that although he was aware of dozens of secret locations used by British intelligence and friendly agencies, he had mentioned only a handful of buildings, all of which were well-known. He commented tartly that 'other friendly intelligence agencies like the CIA and ASIO do not maintain the absurd pretence that their intelligence agencies have no headquarters.' He repeated the offer made earlier by Turnbull to remove any names, nominated by the British government, from the book. On the so-called breakdown of trust within the Service that would follow the publication of a book like his, Wright said 'this was just an opinion of Sir Robert's.'

Wright returned to the attack on Sir Robert in discussing whether recruitment to the security service would be damaged by the publication of the book. '[Sir Robert] feels that it is in the Service's interest to appear good, competent and free from penetration even if it isn't.' On whether or not the study of old tradecraft and operational detail revealed in the book would assist enemies by allowing them to deduce more recent practice, Wright said: 'this is like saying you can detect the secrets of an advanced fighter plane by studying a Spitfire.' Looking at the question on revelations about internal organisational structure of MI5, Wright quite sensibly asked how his book differed from *The Ties That Bind,* Ball and Richelson's book which gave up-to-date charts.

When it came to the public interest for publication, the converted MI5 man was in favour of letting it all out. 'The present state of Britain is in part due to the penetration of the Establishment by the Russians and the subsequent cover-up.' Wright revived the thesis of how Russian intelligence officers cultivated politicians by getting them young and building them up. Turnbull, to try to establish that what his witness was saying wasn't just hearsay, sought to draw out that a former Director General, Furnivall-Jones, had told Wright about this personally. Simos objected and then Wright, who had lost any signs of nervousness, and was getting almost frisky, cut in with, 'I discussed the whole of this with him. I was the authority on this. I don't see why I shouldn't say so.' The Judge mildly rebuked Wright by pointing out that what could be said had been refereed beforehand in chambers and that he must stay within the rules. Returning to his statement, Wright went on to argue that the scale of penetration had to be understood to stop further penetration.

'The time has come for there to be an openness about the secret world, or at least the secret world of so long ago ... the consequences of Hollis being a spy are enormous. Not only does it mean that MI5 is probably still staffed by people with similar views to him, but it means that ASIO was established on terms with the advice of a Russian spy.'

The man who had lived in the secret world for so long had changed his mind on a number of issues. The next part of his statement, somewhat edited beforehand, read:

'I have referred to a great many acts by officers of MI5, including myself, which constituted breaches of the law.
[four lines censored]
'Our operations were officially authorised, illegal and deniable. I now believe this is the wrong way of doing things. I agree with the views of Mr Justice Hope and others who have said that intelligence services should not break the law. If they have to burgle premises they should do so with a legal warrant and not otherwise. In other words, Parliament should give MI5 the

legal tools to do its job. That way MI5 will be able to account openly to Ministers for what it does.

[fifteen lines censored]

'With so many spies, there is no hope of MI5 catching them all. The answer to Soviet penetration is greater public awareness of the problem. That is the object of my book.'

Wright then proceeded to the story of his relationship with Rothschild, a passage which was also heavily censored. Whatever reservations Wright had come to have about his other collaborator, Chapman Pincher, in the affair of *Their Trade is Treachery*, his loyalty to the third Baron was undiminished. Following his opening comments, the full page of his statement about the relationship with Rothschild was cut and the story only resumed with Wright's emigration to Tasmania in 1976. During the next few years they corresponded occasionally. Then there was a break until 1980 when Rothschild contacted him and said that he wanted Wright to write a list of his (Rothschild's) achievements in MI5 for possible publication. Wright went on to tell again the story of his meetings in London and Cambridge with Rothschild and Pincher and of his subsequent disillusionment with Pincher.

His disappointment persisted and, after the arrest of Bettaney in September 1983, became more acute. Wright told the story of the Granada interview and said that he had not been paid for his time. After the showing of the programme in July 1984 he had passed on, through Paul Greengrass, the producer of the TV show, his dossier to Sir Alister Kershaw, a Conservative MP who was Chairman of the Foreign Relations Committee of the House of Commons. Kershaw, without Wright's prior approval, passed the dossier on to Armstrong. Kershaw told Wright later that Thatcher had told him it was all old hat. Before ending his statement Wright came back to the question of money. He had received to date an advance of 18,000 pounds from Heinemann, but legal and accommodation costs would cut heavily into that figure. 'Once again my principal motivation for writing this book is not financial, rather it is to secure changes to MI5.'

Wright closed with a fine flourish: 'I finish with a quotation which is about a thousand years old. As Pope Gregory VII observed, (I only read the translation, not the Latin) ' "I have loved justice and hated

Wright closed with a fine flourish: 'I finish with a quotation which is about a thousand years old. As Pope Gregory VII observed, (I only read the translation, not the Latin) ' "I have loved justice and hated iniquity. Therefore I die an exile." '

iniquity. Therefore I die an exile." '

Dilexi iustitian et odi iniquitaten. Propeterea morior in exilio. The quote so enthuses Wright that he has it framed upon his wall at home in Cygnet in Tasmania. However, like many historical parallels it is more ambivalent than it appears. Gregory VII was the eleventh century pope who humiliated what amounted to the establishment of the time, the Holy Roman Emperor, Henry IV, whom he kept waiting in the snow at Canossa, before he would receive the Emperor's submission. However, some years later the Pope called on the Normans to help him defend Rome. Then, as now, mercenaries were awkward people to employ and they sacked the city, destroying much ancient architecture. The indignant inhabitants expelled the Normans and the Pope who had called them in and he retreated south to die amid the malaria-ridden swamps of Salerno. Justice hadn't quite been the issue.

Fleet Street reporting on Wright's evidence was straightforward enough, the alleged misleading of the Commons by Thatcher and the passionate clearance by Wright of Rothschild got as much attention as his more general allegations of Soviet penetration. Alongside the Sydney reports, the newspapers were carrying the Attorney General, Sir Michael Havers, as saying in the Commons that the possibility of prosecuting Pincher for inducing Wright to breach confidentiality was under consideration. The next day the *Daily Mail* rode out to put Wright in his place: '. . . one frail eccentric driven by the forces of his obsession . . . scandals of yesteryear . . . sad spectacle . . . delight the Kremlin . . . superannuated molecatchers should keep their rusty old traps shut' ending, with a considerable sleight of hand, to announce 'the man who is on trial for his political life is Neil Kinnock'. On the reverse side of the coin from the *Mail* that day's *Pravda* in Moscow said that the real reason for gagging 'the blabbermouth British James Bond' was fear that he would disclose his role in the Wilson affair.

Wright's cross-examination began next morning. Simos had

passed up cross-examining Schaap and, while aggressive, hadn't done all that well with Whitlam. His aim with Wright was to shake the witness's credibility by catching him out in some contradictions, the kind of standard attack Turnbull had employed so successfully against Armstrong. Simos started out on the question of confidentiality and gained an acknowledgement from Wright that, while at MI5, he had read something called the Security Notes. Simos left it at that. Sir Robert had been harshly dealt with over his answers to the interrogatories and now Simos sought to do the same with Wright over his Interrogatory 40(d) in which he had said he had lost Pincher's letters. Wright agreed that they had subsequently turned up and Simos made something of the fact that Wright had been slow to correct his answer. Mr Justice Powell commented that if that was the case the same could be said about the plaintiff.

Then Simos came to the centrepiece of his cross-examination, a neat ambush.

Simos: 'Mr Wright, would it be correct to say in relation to your contacts with Mr Pincher arising from your discussions with Lord Victor Rothschild that you were terrified of getting into trouble?'

Wright: 'No, I don't think that is true.'

Wright, now confident, wasn't going to be trapped into conceding confidentiality by admitting that he was in any way frightened. Turnbull sat mute: there was no possible legal objection to the line of questioning. Those journalists who had been at the press conference given by Wright on 25 November started to pay very close attention. Simos took Wright back to the question of confidentiality and was told: 'I am completely unaware of ever having been told during my thirty something years of anything "about confidentiality" ... I was completely unaware of the question of confidentiality until this case started ... '. Turnbull had what no counsel likes, a client in the box who had become a little too confident and was talking a little too much. A few more questions and Simos came back in, polite, even apologetic-sounding, with:

Simos: 'I just forget, I'm sorry, what you said precisely, but I think that you indicated that you had some apprehension when you were dealing with Mr Pincher.'

Wright: 'Apprehension is the wrong word ...'

Simos: 'I want to suggest you were terrified of getting into trouble.'

Wright: 'No.'

Simos: 'And if you yourself had said you were terrified of getting into trouble that would be untrue, would it?'

Wright: 'I would think so.'

Simos: 'Do you remember issuing a statement on 25 November which was handed to members of the press?'

Wright: '. . . I remember a statement being issued, but I don't remember what was in it . . .'

Simos: '. . . Do you remember these words appearing in it: "We had dinner with Pincher and discussed it, I was terrified of getting into trouble." '

The ambush had worked. When Simos said to the witness, 'So we have an inconsistency, do we not, Mr Wright?' the answer could only be 'Yes'. Having scored a very handy victory, Simos proceeded to get himself tangled up in the terms of the contract between Wright and Heinemann and its significance. Mr Justice Powell showed signs of boredom, but Simos resisted, saying: '. . . if the motive of the defendant was entirely altruistic, the situation would be different.' The Judge was not impressed. 'If all you wish to prove is, if I may be vulgar, that Mr Wright was in it to make a quid for himself, then tender the documents and that is the end of the question.'

Once again Simos' questions had the fingerprints of the London backseat drivers all over them, eager to make the point they had assiduously planted in some of the London press, the shock-horror disclosure that Wright would make money. Turnbull saw that too, although he drew an additional interpretation, that Heinemann might be in danger of being prosecuted in the UK. 'This is leading up to an endeavour to get some victims for persons like Mr Bailey [the Treasury Solicitor] to persecute in London.' After some bickering, Mr Justice Powell tried the balm of good humour, but it didn't work that well.

Mr Justice Powell: 'If this goes on I will have to send for Mr Mordey [a Sydney boxing promoter] who will stage the next world championship heavyweight contest. Since I am told there is a covenant in the lease here that says we are not allowed to have heavyweight contests here, the engagement will have to be somewhere else.'

Simos: 'One heavyweight and one lightweight, Your Honour.'

Mr Justice Powell: *'If this goes on I will have to send for Mr Mordey [a Sydney boxing promoter] who will stage the next world championship heavyweight contest. . . .*
Simos: *'One heavyweight and one lightweight, Your Honour.'*
Mr Justice Powell: *'That's your score for the day.'*

Mr Justice Powell: 'That's your score for the day.'

That wasn't the end of the blow-up, there was a three-sided haggle for about a quarter of an hour and, even then, when the cross-examination settled down, Simos testily got into a clash with Wright. The Judge applied humour again: '. . . Please do not get into an argument with Mr Simos. He is a fearsome sight when he gets angry.'

When Turnbull came to re-examination, his way of dealing with the embarrassment over 'terrified' was to stress how the statement had to be done in a hurry, a try, but not altogether convincing. He drew out more from the witness on what he had meant by a deniable operation and his experience of them. Wright said that in his service life he had been involved in many deniable operations, 'certainly tens, probably hundreds' and reaffirmed his belief that the Pincher/Rothschild operation had been a deniable operation. Asked to define a deniable operation, Wright was concise: 'It is an operation which the authorities that had mounted it will disown if anything goes wrong.'

The court went into closed session for about an hour for Wright to be questioned on his manuscript and then that was an end of the last witness. Proceedings moved into a housekeeping mode, with Turnbull putting in another six books, while Simos made his customary objections and then the court adjourned till 2 p.m. so that a film of the Cathy Massitter interview could be shown. The film showed her performing very well, coming across as balanced and thoughtful. Earlier Turnbull had hoped to call her as a witness, but the expense of getting her from England would have been too great. Still for his purposes the TV interview was probably more effective.

As the sitting in Sydney was drawing to a close, the Commons on 15 December debated a motion from the indefatigable Dale Campbell-Savours, who called for a judicial enquiry into the Wilson allegations; all party discussions on reform of the Offical Secrets Act and consistency in the application of the existing law. His speech showed that Campbell-Savours had certainly been talking to someone who had read the Wright manuscript, because he was specific about the number – thirty – of MI5 officers included in operations against Wilson. This drew a response from Merlyn Rees, the former Labour Home Secretary, who admitted that when he held that portfolio in 1977 the Prime Minister, James Callaghan, had cleared the Security Service, but now posed the question for the government, 'Tell me not what was investigated then – I accepted that in good faith – but that Wright's allegations were investigated then. If they were not, surely they should be looked at afresh, and I, at least, was fooled at that time. I want the matter cleared up.' Another Labour member, Tam Dalyell, foreshadowed that in the new year after the conclusion of the court case in Australia, he would be moving to establish the existing Security Commission as a Tribunal of Inquiry into the affair. The government might have thought that the debate would be easily dealt with on party lines, but two Conservative backbenchers showed they were concerned and one said he would like a judicial enquiry, that the matter had not been cleared up. It was this same Tory backbencher, Jonathan Aitken, who had made the comment that it seemed 'almost inconceivable' that an operation of the scale described by Wright could have been carried out on a freelance basis.

While the debate was talked out the message was clear, the topic of the Wilson allegations would be back in the new year, even if the Labour leadership was not that keen.

Next day, Wednesday, when the court resumed there were a few more housekeeping chores, but the question people were waiting for was whether there had been a compromise on the discovery of documents issue. Unless a deal could be made, the Court of Appeal would sit on Thursday and Friday to hear the UK government's application with the almost certain result of a reserved judgment which would not be delivered until February or even March next year. So pressure had been on for an agreement, and when Simos asked for another three-quarters of an hour for further discussion, Mr Justice Powell queried: 'Do you need a judicial baseball mitt to beat each other around the head?' Simos said he hoped not. They were back a little later and Simos announced an agreement.

160

The highlights of the agreement on the documents were:

'1. *A Matter of Trust*. The British Security Service became aware that Mr West was writing the book and believed that it contained information provided to him by former officers of MI5 and/or another intelligence organisation by the 23rd of September 1982.

The British Security Service had the original manuscript by the 23rd of September 1982.

The material deleted included previously inhibited material as to names of officers of intelligence agencies, references to operations and investigations of the Security Service and references to sources within the Security Serivce.

2. *Their Trade is Treachery*. Synopsis Attached and Given to the Defence.

The security intelligence agencies received the synopsis on or a little before 15 December 1980. The letter dated 15 December 1980 from a security organisation to the Security Service indicates that the writer had been informed that Chapman Pincher intended to publish, probably February or March 1981, a book about the Security Service, a synopsis of which was enclosed.

It was generally agreed in the security and intelligence services that there would be no point in trying to encourage specific deletions or changes to the text, but no reasons are expressed for this view.

The security and intelligence services first became aware of the book on or a little before 15 December. The manuscript was first read in February 1981 when it appeared that much of the information in it had come from former members of the security and intelligence services. By 12 March 1981 several sources had been identified, but it was stated in writing by an officer of the Service to Sir Robert Armstrong that the Service was a long way from obtaining hard useable evidence on sources and it was stated orally to Sir Robert Armstrong that the advance copy was obtained on conditions which made it impossible to take any action about it, which view was later recorded.

3. *Too Secret Too Long*.

So far as documents disclosed the Security Service first knew on 19 July 1984 of the report in *The Times* as to the forthcoming book. On 3rd September 1984 the Security Service was informed that Chapman Pincher was claiming that he had received material from former MI5 officers. On 26 October 1984 the Security Service had a copy of the book. The documents do not state reasons for not seeking an injunction, but state the view that the central argument is much the same as in *Their Trade is Treachery* about whether Hollis was a spy, filled out with additional detailed comment.

4. Peter Wright TV Interview

The Security Service had information by 4 May 1984 that there were plans for a 'World in Action' programme in which Wright was assisting and might take part. The Security Service had information by 3 July 1984 that Granada TV intended to show an interview with Wright in which Wright would re-open the Hollis case and, in effect, present the case against him and so advised the Treasury Solicitor in a letter of that date. Following a report in *The Times* 16 July 1984, the day of the broadcast, the likelihood that Wright had breached the Official Secrets Act was noted . . . [That day] the possibility of asking for a preview of the programme and seeking to restrain publication, if necessary by means of injunction, was discussed on the telephone between the Treasury Solicitor's department and the Security Service. The view was expressed that, if a preview was refused going for an injunction would undoubtedly be a hard fight and if a preview was agreed the government would be put in the position of appearing to have approved it, whether or not they asked for cuts.'

The Judge's order for the discovery of the documents was rescinded by consent so the Court of Appeal could go into its Christmas vacation. Turnbull said after discussion he would not require Sir Robert to return to Australia providing no point was taken against him for failing to do so. He couldn't resist the apposite comment that there were 'some fairly startling differences between what is in the documents and what Sir Robert had said,' a curtain raiser for what he would say in his closing submissions next week. Certainly the government's claim to consistency had another few nails in the coffin, to use the Judge's colourful phrase. The UK government had given ground to limit the discovery and to ensure that Sir Robert would not have to sample British Airways food again, or Turnbull's cross-examination, but they had paid the price. It was agreed that closing submissions would open late on Monday morning.

On Monday morning, before Simos could open his final submission, Turnbull produced his client as an expert on typewriters to deal with B1, that synopsis of *Their Trade is Treachery,* that he had obtained last week. Wright was cheerfully confident that the synopsis had been typed on Pincher's typewriter and cited in particular, the regularity in the letters d and e with other correspondence he had received from Pincher. Simos tried to put down his experience but Wright, very chipper, clearly won on points. It was his last appearance in the box. If it went to the Appeals Court they would not be wanting witnesses.

So Simos got his final submission under way a little late and opened, predictably, on the question of contracts, drawing on a range of cases and authorities that went back for a hundred years, including Sir Edward Carson, and Rufus Isaacs, along with the Supreme Court of Ceylon. There was, however, a fallback position. Simos put it to the court that independent of contract there was a developing equitable doctrine of confidentiality which could be applied in the case. He went briskly and confidently in the earlier parts of his argument. When Simos came to the question of authorisation and in particular the case of *Their Trade is Treachery* the Judge became active. As he put it: 'I haven't the faintest doubt you had Pincher dead to rights.' He was referring to the UK's potential case against *Their Trade is Treachery.* Simos under fire twisted and turned. His argument finally came to the point that, even if the government had not acted efficiently, that didn't alter the basic principle. When Simos struggled to bring in the Australian public interest, he encountered the Judge's assessment of Codd's evidence: 'With great respect to Mr Codd, I don't think much of his evidence.'

The Judge displayed his reading of history, sometimes to the slight confusion of Simos. A reference to the time of Sir Francis Walsingham (the Elizabethan bureaucrat, accounted the founder of Britain's Secret Service) drew from Simos: 'Your Honour has the advantage of me again.' At one stage, Mr Justice Powell wondered out loud how many times Sir Winston Churchill had broken the Official Secrets Act during the thirties when he spoke out against German re-armament. Simos, missing the historical time, affirmed that he was sure Churchill had been authorised in everything he had said. As was to be expected, Simos made a lot of Wright's admission that he was terrified. Still his dealing with Wright and his personality was punctiliously courteous, nothing like the language of treachery, breach of solemn oath, etc., so common in London and certainly much milder than Turnbull's treatment of Sir Robert. When Simos sat down after two days on his feet, anyone in the court room could sense that the odds were certainly running against him.

Perhaps the longest citation made by Malcolm Turnbull, with his typical capacity for surprise, in his closing address came not from a legal text, but from Thucydides *The Peloponnesian War* written between 410-400 BC. Turnbull used the quote deftly to ridicule Sir Robert's obstinate adherence to the proposition that insider histories were always more authoritative than outsider histories. Within the quote he gave emphasis to how Thucydides dealt with varying sources in writing his history:

'. . . the endeavour to ascertain those facts was a laborious task, because those who were eye witnesses about several events did not give the same reports about the same things, but reports vary according to their championship of one side or the other, or according to their recollections.'

That, Turnbull argued, was how history was written: which was the more authoritative – Hitler's *Mein Kampf* or Alan Bullock's *Study in Tyranny*. Not that there weren't plenty of legal citations in the closing address.

Predictably he dealt harshly with Sir Robert:

'Sir Robert's evidence and his demeanour shows him to be a man with no regard for the truth, rather a man determined to say whatever he felt would advance the government's case, regardless of its truth or falsity. His evidence is worthless.'

Turnbull returned several times to the *Commonwealth v. Fairfax* case where Mr Justice Mason had spoken so strongly on the public interest in the disclosure, and added a barb: 'There has been an unfortunate tendency for English judges to accept any statement from the government as determinative so long as it is claimed to relate to national security.' Turnbull used the concessions the UK government had made on documents heavily in his case on *Their Trade is Treachery*. The collaborative relationship between Wright and Pincher, if there was any vestige left, would be shattered finally by Turnbull's attack on the author. He reminded the court that the synopsis of the book had been given to MI6 on or before 15 December 1980 and went on: 'The message of the synopsis was that the book would not damage the intelligence services and would only embarrass the civil services, who of course are the traditional foes of the intelligence community. This synopsis was not stolen. It was plainly written by Pincher, on his own typewriter. Its circulation would have been very limited: Pincher himself, Rothschild possibly, Pincher's lawyer possibly, Pincher's publisher probably. In other words the synopsis was not stolen and it is hard to see how it could have been, given its necessarily limited circulation: it must have been given to MI6 by someone who had a right to have it, that is to say someone with a direct interest in getting the book published.'

Turnbull was able to pose fifteen leading questions on the inconsistency of the government in allowing *Their Trade is Treachery* to be published, all strengthened by the disclosures made about the documents. He may not have got all he wanted from the UK government, but he could well feel that he got enough for his purposes. The fifteen questions were:

• Why would Lord Rothschild with all his connections, wealth and respectability suggest such an unlawful enterprise to Wright and then procure the writer and act as a channel for the royalties?

• Why did Rothschild fly Wright to England, if all he needed was the list of achievements? Wright could have done that in Tasmania and sent it back with the courier.

• Why would someone close to Pincher provide the synopsis (of *Their Trade is Treachery*) to MI6, when if the government was opposed that would be certain to draw an injunction?

• Why would the synopsis so provided be so concerned with assuring its reader that the book would not damage the intelligence services? A synopsis for a publisher would presumably be more devoted to emphasising the sensational features of the book, rather than its political responsibility.

• There was plainly a good cause of action to get an injunction on the basis of the synopsis, why didn't the government act?

• Pincher was a friendly journalist. Why not at least try to talk him round, at least get him to cut some material out?

• Why did someone close to Pincher provide the page proofs to MI6: if the government was opposed that surely would draw a hostile response?

• Why didn't the government seek an injunction after it got the page proofs?

• Why did the government receive and then accept such ludicrous legal advice?

• Why did the government not seek the advice of the Attorney General or some other senior lawyer? According to Sir Robert this sort of matter is in the Attorney's area of responsibility.

• Why did Sir Robert give false testimony about the Attorney's role in the affair and why did the Attorney allow him so to do for so long after he must have known what Sir Robert was saying about him?

• Why did Pincher draw a very different conclusion in his book from that favoured by Wright? Pincher's conclusion was precisely what the government wanted to hear: no current penetration problem, no need for an inquiry.

• Why were the synopsis and page proofs sent to MI6, then headed by Pincher's lunching companion, Sir Arthur Franks? The logical place to send it first was to MI5 to which it was sent by MI6.

• Why did Pincher give twenty-one months' warning of *Too Secret Too Long* to Sir Arthur Franks? Why did Franks report this straightaway to Sir Robert Armstrong?

• Why did the government do nothing to attempt to track down the source? It was only a matter of making routine enquiries about Pincher's movements and having the police interview the local suspected informants and then Wright would be narrowed down very quickly as the principal informant. It was an effective case for the Lilliputians stitching up Gulliver.

ACTION TO PLUG SPY LEAKS

Tory MPs seek Kinnock's return

...tem leaks on secur ... matters...

Judge in MI5 case

...of 'mumbo jumbo' over me...

...ish Government is acc...

...py case judge... ...rders Britain ...o show papers

demands papers

Richard Norton-Taylor ...ydney

Australian court ye... ...dered the Bri...

...political mileage from the MI5 row

John Hunt reports on Opposition plans to make political mileage from a Prime Minister

Labour sleuths plot to catch a Prime Minister

Whitehall was today or...red to make available to Mr ...eter Wright and his lawyers ...dited versions of secret docu...ments inspected at the week...end by the judge in the MI5 ...book case.

From Stephen Taylor, Sydney
consultations to ascertain whether there would be an application for leave to appeal.

The papers relate to meet... ings and corr...

claim that all the papers were covered by public interest immunity said: "I would sen... ously question even, in the... United Kingdom...

...ered to pro... ...dence that MI5 had ...the publication ...the se...

...dity was that of Australia, and ...not that of Britain. He ha...t concluded that there would be no detriment to Australia...

"Having considered the... these matters in question... conclude...

Parliament
Thatcher attack 11
Sydney hearing 11
Frank Johnson 20

West, and television pro- grammes in which Mr Wright and Miss Cathy M... another...

Armstrong disgraced his country, MP say

Armstrong, Secretary had disgraced his ...n ...st case, Mr ...Work...

"He has disgraced his country and earned the justifiable con- tempt of Australia; and done irreparable damage to the his- toric relationship between our two peoples", he said.
..."What has happened: to the values?" (Conservative ...ter) "Or was I brought... ...) in a myth?"

John Cole The MI5 affair

Allason's relationship with MI5 and MI6 was far more interesting. In the front of his book there was reference to a ...ere setting out the whole plan ...re of MI5 until 1965. ...he get his information? ...all that material ...ublic domain. ...saying that is ...law stands at ...formation ...available ...ere no ...tailed inquiry ...into the alleg... ...satisfied the ...grounds for ...in the com... ...ality of... ...for instit... He ha... ...at no ...service ...agent... ...of ...som... ...elec... ...Do...

Two tales from two cities

Grand opera in a Sydney courthouse

Is the MI5 case another Westland? Has the Government found its last banana skin in this clash between Bri- tain's ludicrous love affair with secrecy and Australian love of pommie-baiting? Have people in high places lost their marbles? Is ...ent in a gale o...

...the ultimate KGB plot to destabilise ou...

earned some commentators' praise as a Rolls- Royce performance. That always seemed a misjudgment. His ducking and dodging, and ernment's refusal to allow key Civil Service witnesses even to appear merely demons- trated what a toothless tiger the Westminster select committee system still is—compared, for example, with what has fallen beleaguered Reagan in W... Hill in w...

More earthbound observers of the political scene can only hope that if any future British Prime Minister suspects he is being spied upon by servants of the Crown, he will not have to rely on American senators or Cl... chiefs for information. A ...might be to inf...

'National Security' – at what price? 3

Mr Justice Powell, who presided over the trial in Sydney. A lawyer who
admired the Privy Council and most things English, he was bizarrely accused of being
a Pom-basher.
Photo: Associated Press

Much of the language used in writing about espionage, counter-intelligence, national security, or treason cries out for a George Orwell. Jargon abounds: there are dazzling leaps from affirmation to conclusion; elisions; brazen contradictions; innuendoes; hints; dogmatic assertions and outright lies are the normal currency of discussion. All this is true of the great MI5 molehunt. The most telling comment during the trial on the world of the Fluency Committee, and by extension, their journalistic collaborators, came from a man whom no one could call a left-winger: Miles Copeland, former CIA head of station in London, whose frank book *The Real Spy World* published in 1978 after he left the agency would have been grounds for garrotting if he had been an MI5 man. Writing in *The Times* Copeland, speaking of the Fluency Committee report, extracts of which had been passed on to the CIA when he was head of station, described it as 'on a par with that of the information which former MI5 agent Peter Wright seems to have leaked to Chapman Pincher, the journalist, full of connotive words, judgmental phrases, dramatic leaps to conclusions, and mountains made of molehills.' Like corrupt political language, which as Orwell acutely points out, cancels out human beings, so too does the language of spook paranoia. Its users are often afflicted with a morbid fascination with the words 'treason' and 'treachery'. A very

171

influential writer in creating this climate has been Rebecca West, with her *The Meaning of Treason,* first published in 1949, revised several times and most recently reprinted in 1984. There is an underlying shrillness, edging towards vituperation, in her treatment of the very different individuals in her book, who range from 'Lord Haw-Haw' William Joyce, through Klaus Fuchs, to people like Molody, otherwise known as Lonsdale, the professional Russian intelligence officer, and on to the Profumo Affair.

As she tells it, Rebecca West listened to Lord Haw-Haw during the war when he broadcast from Nazi Germany to England. From this stems her rage with traitors, mixed up with a swag of snobbery. To Rebecca West, treason is essentially singular and, logically then, a matter of black and white. There are no graduations of motive. Treason, like Sir Robert Armstrong's confidentiality, admits of no degree.

Against this rigidity of view, it has to be seen that there are very different kinds of treason, with different motives: money, envy, hatred, idealism, naivety and fear. One English writer, John Lear, with an intelligence background (spooks seem to be going in for thrillers) put it very accurately and acutely in *Death in Leningrad*, published in 1985.

'He or she adhered firmly to that naive, self-righteous, overcredulous and downright bloody silly school of journalism that pretends to analyse and explain treachery. And does so, oblivious to the fact there must, as Anna Karenina said of "kinds of love", be just as many kinds of treachery as there are heads, minds and hearts.'

Miss West would have none of that. She wouldn't be able to see that, for Blunt (believing that the survival of the Soviet Union was at risk), there was nothing morally wrong in passing on material obtained from Leo Long, who in turn obtained it from the codebreakers, on the German order of battle. It is no solution to scream traitor at Blunt for his action. There is the moral dilemma involved. Because Miss West is sophisticated her prejudices appear reasonable. Sometimes, however, she does go over the edge and certainly when it comes to homosexuals. On Vassall this sentence serves as an example: 'But because of him the public imagination was haunted by the vision of the slender figure in sweater and tight

Rebecca West is reprinted again and again because her moralising generalisations about the nature of treason continue to find a market. . . . Formed in this intellectual tradition, to 'Spycatcher' types and their journalistic cheerleaders, extremism in pursuit of treason is no vice.

jeans who lurks in the shadow of the wall, just outside the circle of the lamplight, whisks down the steps of the tube station lavatory, and with a backward glance under long lashes offers pleasure and danger.' Rebecca West is reprinted again and again because her moralising generalisations about the nature of treason continue to find a market. Her contempt and 'rage' come close to hatred of the scapegoat, the position she has assigned the traitor. Formed in this intellectual tradition, to 'Spycatcher' types and their journalistic cheerleaders, extremism in pursuit of treason is no vice.

This is where the language of the spook world, the style of argument of Peter Wright, assumes importance. The search for certainty, for a science, as it were, of counter-espionage permeates the arguments against Sir Roger Hollis. The jargon of the world of the training schools of spies is an even more convoluted form, rarely exposed to the public. Wright, in court in Sydney, however, gave an explanation of the 'collateral verification theory', evidently to anticipate how his old colleagues might use it against him. It assumes that 'the hostile intelligence service has received information from a spy or defector concerning MI5. That information must be information relating to events occurring in the period when I was in MI5, otherwise my book would provide no collateral verification at all. The theory goes that the defector spy has told the hostile service, for example, facts A, B, C, D and E. Facts B to E may still be sensitive and potentially damaging if leaked. Fact A is, in the service, old hat, but once it is confirmed by my book it causes the hostile services to believe B to E.'

Why should this have to be dressed up as a 'theory' when it is a matter of simple common sense, that if one person supports another person on one point, while it doesn't necessarily confirm all the others, it does make them more plausible. What it certainly doesn't do, in any plain meaning of the word, is 'verify'. The difficulty of disentangling 'collateral verification' into common sense applies equally to the circumstantial evidence accumulated against someone

173

like Hollis. While Wright and the other anonymous Fluency/K7 people have got the message across to writers like Pincher, they have to admit there is no smoking pistol in most of their cases and that their evidence is circumstantial. But where the cases come to be written up the emphasis has very quickly changed to 'evidence' and the qualifying adjective 'circumstantial' has a way of disappearing.

The central problem with circumstantial evidence is that it is all a matter of interpretation and, in a court, the credibility of the person doing the interpreting can be tested. The hypothesis can be looked at, excluded or perhaps accepted after the battle of cross-examination. When we come to Arthur Martin, Stephen de Mowbray and Peter Wright, it has to be said that the credibility of interpreters who believe in Golitsin is distinctly flawed. One might wearily assume that in early 1987 Golliwog has been telling people that Gorbachev's release of Sakharov confirms his point that Sakharov is not genuine. The CIA people who spoke of flat earth theories were right. The capacity of the hard core of the Fluency/K7 group to stand back and judge objectively the events they have taken part in, the investigations they have taken part in, is called into question by the fact that both Aitken and Pincher were led into writing major factual errors about what the Trend report actually said. However, of course, in recent years the general reader hasn't known of that touching belief in Golitsin or how Aitken was given a distinctly wrong steer in 1980.

Each bit of circumstantial evidence also has to be weighed into probability and possibility, and here again judgment is crucial. The problem is that when a long extended hypothesis is constructed about Hollis, each step becomes self-validating. Occam's Razor, which laid down that hypotheses should not be multiplied endlessly, seems unknown in the world of the Fluency Committee. The difficulty is that for any critic of, say, the Hollis theory, it almost requires a book to examine the credibility of each and every one of the links in the chain of argument. It has been tried: Philip Knightley in the *Sunday Times* took apart Pincher's elaborate thesis about the 'link' between Hollis and the Soviet agent Sonia Kuczynski, who had been in Shanghai when Hollis was there in the early thirties and who was at Oxford during the war when Hollis was working at a decentralised MI5 office nearby. An example of the argument in this part of the case put by Pincher was the way he dealt with the fact that, in 1948 when some MI5 officers came to interview Sonia, she remained 'totally relaxed in what should have been a highly dangerous situation' and went on to say it 'certainly pointed to her having been forewarned of the visit by someone.' It doesn't, of course 'certainly' do anything: an alternative explanation could be that Sonia was an exceptionally cool, level-headed person, or perhaps that she understood the English legal system well enough to know that it required proof of illegal activities.

The sentence exemplifies the problems of dealing with a string of such assertions. However, it is possible to test the credibility of the assertions against Hollis and another spy discovered by the Fluency Committee, Colonel C.H. (Dick) Ellis, by examining in some detail the allegations passed on to Pincher about both of them in relation to Australia. For both men, the claims about events in Australia form a crucial part of the Fluency/K7 case against them. On examination the material is riddled with so many errors as to make it risible were it not for the fact that men's reputations, and even their freedom, might have been at stake.

Dick Ellis was one of those Australians who in World War One preferred to join the British Army (many never returned). He was an officer in the Middlesex Regiment (known as the Diehards), which was sent into Siberia in 1918 and ended up protecting the last White Russian ruler of Siberia, Admiral Kolchak, not only from the Bolsheviks but also from his fractious supporters. When they withdrew Kolchak was executed by the Reds. The experience made the young officer an expert on communism. Between the wars he worked in Europe for MI6 under cover as a journalist. The case against him in the refined version in *Too Secret Too Long* says that after retiring from MI6 in late 1953 he went back to Australia and signed a contract with the Australian Security Intelligence Service, the equivalent of MI6, learned of Petrov's impending defection, resigned and fled back to England to warn the Russians through Philby. The case can be broken down into the following five parts:

1. He resigned after only two months to return to England, saying he wanted to be remarried. A later investigation showed that he didn't marry the woman he said he would.

Doesn't prove anything. Coming back to your birthplace after thirty years could easily have not worked out and Ellis could have invented an excuse so as not hurt his new friends in Australia.

2. He was told soon after arrival, by the Director General of ASIO, Colonel Spry, that the Petrovs were going to defect and then decided to return. Hearing that, Spry 'asked [him] to brief MI5 and MI6 on the latest situation regarding Petrov as this seemed to be the most secure way of achieving that.'

Spry denies that he was the first who told Ellis about the Petrovs. He does recall a meeting when Ellis came along with the Director General of ASIS, Alfred Brooks, to offer help in any interrogation of Petrov. What Pincher hadn't been told is that Spry was in fact very hostile to ASIS, and especially to Brooks personally, so he saw the effort as a takeover bid. There was in any case no need to use Ellis as a messenger, because there was an MI5 liaison officer resident in ASIO who communicated with London, and further an MI5 liaison team was already being planned to help in the handling of Petrov.

3. At the stage ASIO briefed Ellis 'it was expected Petrov would defect in April and Ellis arrived back in Britain in March.'

Spry erred in his memory on the timing of the meeting with Ellis and Brooks, which he now thinks was after the defection. In fact, it was long before the defection because the Immigration Department records show that Ellis left Australia on 6 January, and the boat arrived at Tilbury six weeks later. The records of ASIO show that it was on 9 January, three days after Ellis left the country, that for the first time Petrov mentioned April as a possible date for his defection. So there is no way that Ellis could have taken the April date back to England for the Russians.

4. On his return to England, Ellis defied instructions that he should not see Philby. Later, in his book, *My Silent War* Philby refers to having received a message 'through the most ingenious of routes . . . from my Soviet friends.' Pincher writes that the Fluency Committee inferred from this that Ellis had not only warned Philby about the coming defection which would incriminate them both, but also put him in touch with the Russians.

Breaking the ban on talking to Philby doesn't prove evil intent. Many of his old friends in MI6, even if wrongly, believed Philby to be a victim of McCarthyism. As for being the messenger who restored Philby's links with the Soviets, *Conspiracy of Silence* establishes

Golitsin says that two courier guards were dispatched and failed to reach Sydney by only a few hours; there is an extra touch on how the guards were reprimanded for their delay ... the two guards left Rome for Australia on 11 April, some eight days after Petrov defected and five days after the embassy discovered his defection and arrived in Sydney on 15 April.

that the channel was Blunt. As Blunt confessed in detail how it was done on the tapes, it is odd that Wright did not disabuse Pincher of his belief.

5. Ellis, about the same time, passed the news of the defection to the Soviets. Golitsin says that two courier guards were dispatched and failed to reach Sydney by only a few hours; there is an extra touch on how the guards were reprimanded for their delay.

First, there were almost six weeks after Ellis' arrival in London, surely enough time to arrange guards efficiently. The 'few hours' is simply wrong. ASIO records show the two guards left Rome for Australia on 11 April, some eight days after Petrov defected and five days after the embassy discovered his defection and arrived in Sydney on 15 April.

So the case against Ellis over Petrov doesn't stand up. The Soviets are supposed to have been able to blackmail Ellis into spying for them when they discovered in 1945 he had been a spy for Germany. During most of the war, Ellis had been number 2 to William Stephenson, the latter known by the code name Intrepid, and who was head of the British Security Commission (BSC) in New York, a mix of a secret service agency, lobby, and purchasing, vital for Britain's war effort. It was also a conduit for defence science exchange. Ellis, as number 2, was, like his boss, cleared to the highest level. He knew about the successful codebreaks at Bletchley and Operation Double-Cross, which successfully turned almost all Nazi agents in England. If Ellis were a Nazi spy it would have been a disaster for England and the United States. There is not a shred of evidence in the extensive captured archives to show they knew of the success of these operations. What there is in the German records is the claim that Ellis was a source of some material in 1939 in Paris. Ellis was working for MI6 specialising in the White Russian emigre community, a bear-pit of double, triple and even quadruple agents.

One of Ellis' agents was a White Russian brother-in-law, who also worked for the Germans. Ellis traded with him, giving something to get something, and seems to have pocketed some money. The operational world of running agents is more complex than the desk analysts comprehend. Of course he 'confessed', although the leaker showed exasperation that they didn't get him to confess to spying during the war and for the Russians. On this flimsy foundation of play in double-agentry among the emigres of Paris, a vast structure has been built to make poor Ellis one of the spies of the century. Dick Goldsmith White, who discussed the matter with Ellis after his 'confession', has told friends that Ellis should have kept London better informed of his tricks and not pocketed the cash. White accepts his later denials.

Turning to Hollis, the first Australian count in the Fluency indictment stems from his visit in 1948 as part of the UK pressure on the Australian government to establish an independent counter espionage organisation like MI5. Pincher asserts that 'The KGB traffic to and from Australia was almost unique at that time in that it could be deciphered easily and quickly . . . ' The deciphering of the KGB messages out of Canberra was not routine, like the other operations in the UK and USA. It was erratic and painstaking, a scrap here, a scrap there. One man involved in it described it to me as 'like pushing a hand-mower over a long-overgrown golf course looking for a few stray lost golf balls.'

Far from relating to the current period, the breakthroughs in traffic picked up in 1948 went back to late 1945 and early 1946. Shortly after Hollis returned to the United Kingdom, the KGB changed their code pads. So Pincher says, 'Yet another coincidence in the list becoming too long for credence.' However, as David C. Martin disclosed in *Wilderness of Mirrors*, an employee of the US code breaking service, the Armed Forces Agency, William Weisband, is now known to have sold to the Russians in 1948 the information that some of their older codes were being cracked. This naturally enough would have stimulated an immediate change in code pad procedure. The case is based on an error and doesn't take into account the alternative explanation published years ago by Martin.

The essential part of the case against Hollis for the fifties is that every operation against the Russians mounted by MI5 and known to him failed. As Peter Wright put it in the Granada interview: 'All the operations against the Russians, whether they were double agent or technical operations had failed and could be shown to have failed fairly soon after they were started.'

There were two Australian cases which Hollis knew about which did not fail. Sir Charles Spry in late 1986 explicitly cleared Hollis by stating that he knew about the defection of Vladimir Petrov in 1954. Spry said, 'Hollis knew about Petrov several months before Petrov defected. If Hollis had been working for the Russians, to have let the defection take place would have been unthinkable.' In *Too Secret Too Long,* dealing with Hollis, Pincher repeats the story that Ellis was the person who briefed Hollis after his return, which is refuted by the travel dates as well as by Spry's declaration. Pincher goes on to repeat the diplomatic courier story. As one writer, Robert Manne, in his recently published book *The Petrov Affair* says:

'There is actually not one part of Pincher's analysis of the role of Hollis in the Petrov defection that can withstand close scrutiny. As we have seen the Soviet diplomatic couriers who Pincher believes were sent to Australia to seize Petrov actually left Rome airport on 11 April, eight days after Petrov defected and five days after the Soviet embassy in Canberra had become alarmed about his disappearance.'

So the circumstantial evidence which proves that the Russians knew about Petrov's defection collapses. It is very odd that the Fluency Committee was unable to obtain this evidence. They could have had access to the ASIO files which would have shown the date when Petrov mentioned April for the first time, the Immigration Department records showing when Ellis left and the couriers arrived, and the ASIO files on the couriers' air movements. Finally, in London, surely they would have had the reports of the liaison officer in Melbourne. Why didn't the Fluency/K7 groups carry out these searches? Manne now, as a writer and historian, has, after thirty years, access to those ASIO files, after weeding, as does any Australian researcher, whereas in England similar files are closed forever.

Manne's testimony against Pincher gains more force because he is an avowed neo-conservative and tends usually to be rather respectful towards Pincher. *The Petrov Affair* was published after the trial, which was lucky for the UK government, because it would have provided devastating cross-examination material for Turnbull. The former head of ASIO, Sir Charles Spry, was interviewed extensively and is quoted directly. On Sir Robert's and Codd's logic, MI5 should mistrust ASIO because it has not preserved confidentiality. The book also has many quotations from ASIO files about the techniques of handling agents, dealing with defectors, as well as bugging cars and safe-houses.

No one should try and mount the argument that in 1954 the Russians, having received information about the impending defection either from Hollis and/or Ellis, would have been prepared to sacrifice Petrov. Although he had been an inept spy in Australia and had only stale information about espionage there, Petrov had a great deal to tell western intelligence agencies about names, practices, and ciphers. Further, Mrs Petrov had worked in the thirties and forties with the codebreakers in Moscow. Peter Wright and his colleagues who see as sinister the failure of all MI5 attempts to successfully attract defectors should read Robert Manne's book closely; with its extensive use of documents, it makes clear what an extraordinarily difficult task it is to cultivate a defector successfully. The reality is that the overwhelming majority of Russian defectors or spies are 'walk-ins', who come over without any cultivation. There is a CIA anecdote from Langley, Virginia which illustrates the point. In the wake of the ex-CIA man Philip Agee's disclosure of many names and the shooting of a CIA man in Athens, a meeting at headquarters was agonising over the fact that CIA heads of station were being identified. Harry Rositzke, who has written a sophisticated and level-headed book on the KGB, *The Eyes of Russia,* cut in with the comment: 'we should have neon signs on the roof of a head of station's house. The only good ones we ever get are the walk-ins.'

A second Australian case while Hollis was still Director General is always overlooked by his detractors. In February 1963 the Australian government expelled the Soviet second secretary, Ivan Skripov, for espionage after he had been trapped by a woman Russian speaker, loaned by MI6. Hollis was aware of the operation in plenty of time to have informed the Russians.

To analyse and refute just a few of the confident assertions passed

To analyse and refute just a few of the confident assertions passed on to Pincher by his informants has taken hundred of words as well as some effort digging through books, press cuttings and archives.

on to Pincher by his informants has taken hundred of words as well as some effort digging through books, press cuttings and archives. The result is to destroy a significant part of the Pincher informants' case against Hollis and Ellis. However, it is, of course, not possible for the average reader to find their way through the thickets of assertions without research. Once they are published, they become the raw material for recycling in a hundred feature articles. Hollis and Ellis are dead and can't defend themselves. Their families and friends lack the time or the skills to do so and, in any case, can only confront the proxies of the real accusers who have been able to be both judge and jury in secret and broadcast their findings without responsibility.

There is an overwhelming public interest argument for the publication of Wright's manuscript which wasn't canvassed amidst the legal technicalities of the arguments during the trial. *Spycatcher* should be on sale so that the arguments and thought processes of those behind Pincher could be brought into the open for scrutiny. To adapt the UK government's defence of insider/outsider we have a right to see how the insiders think. Secrecy, with its absence of scrutiny of the evidence, has given a bogus status to the material peddled to journalists. However, one of the disconcerting things about discussion, especially in England on the trial, was that the dispute was seen as though it was all about preserving secrecy, which was seen to be vital to something called national security. The telescope was turned around. Sometimes the arguments tended to get muddled up with something like football team barracking, as with one contributor to the *Sunday Telegraph* who wrote:

> 'Sir Robert's problems are cultural in origin. Many of the values and assumptions that make up his beloved Whitehall culture are simply not shared in Australia and above all that is true of the British Civil Service's devotion to official secrecy.'

This piece of pretentious pomposity aptly uses the word 'devotion', usually associated with religion, to describe this Whitehall feeling about secrecy. The judgments of the High Court in Australia which call this 'culture' into question do not derive from something exotic in the Antipodean climate, they come out of a long Anglo-Saxon struggle for the freedom of the public to know. It was no coincidence that one of the judges could cite the fate of James II. Unhappily in England national security seems to have reached the status in some minds of a voodoo incantation which, if invoked in an affidavit, should be unquestioned. That a Cabinet Secretary who has sworn an affidavit could actually be cross-examined seemed, to some commentators, to be the height of bad taste. James II had the same kind of problem when he thought about his critics. Turnbull, in cross-examining toughly, was doing no more than fulfilling an English tradition rather older than Whitehall secrecy, that the lawyer is supposed to do the best for his client whether he is the Yorkshire Ripper or an obstinate old man who wants to publish a book.

Looking at some of the commentators in London it was difficult to believe that they were writing about the same case. Sir William Rees-Mogg certainly was not:

'I do not know why so many Australians have chips on their shoulders; Gallipoli seems to me to be a long time ago, and Botany Bay an even more remote piece of history, yet the atmosphere of the court seems to be seething with class resentment, as though Powell and Turnbull were citizen 'sans-culottes' relishing sending M. le Comte de Armstrong to the guillotine.'

'Seething with class resentment' from the cheery Anglophile Mr Justice Powell, full of nostalgia for the Privy Council and the would-be Liberal party candidate and millionaire, Malcolm Turnbull. What did Sir William Rees-Mogg expect Turnbull to do with Sir Robert, kiss him?

If national security, as implicity defined by Sir Robert in his affidavit, was a way of seeking to avoid any fundamental issues being raised, then, when it passed into the political realm in December, it became even more removed from the rational arguments about public interest, taking place in the court room in Sydney. When the case opened, the government was facing another month before the House of Commons rose and the certainty of

Opposition attack about the conduct of the case. Campbell-Savours was ready to stir from the backbench and the leader, Neil Kinnock, scented a chance to embarrass Mrs Thatcher. Within a few weeks, all was changed, and it was Kinnock who was on the defensive. As a professionally executed piece of political manoeuvring, it had to be admired. Macchiavelli would have given good marks and Bobby Kennedy might have admired the brutality of it. When in doubt, create conspiracy – and that is what the government media minders very effectively did.

Turnbull in his effort to force the government into retreat had talked to a great number of people, including, it transpired, people from Kinnock's office, and on one occasion, Kinnock himself. It was an error of judgment on Kinnock's part to do this in a climate where newspapers could seriously suggest that Wright should be in prison. Accused, Kinnock made the error of putting out a six page defence, breaching the sound political rule that when you are on the defensive, be very short. The briefing of the press was, even by Whitehall standards, pretty rough. Jim Coe, the Prime Minister's deputy press secretary, suggested that Kinnock was unfit to be Prime Minister. The Home Office was specialising in anti-Powell and anti-Turnbull background. The Greengrass shock-horror scandal was also a Home Office plant. How the government got the information about Turnbull's phone calls was an interesting question, and some MPs raised the cry of phone tapping, though there is some reason to believe that Peter Wright had been ringing up Lord Rothschild to tell him of Turnbull's manoeuvrings. Wright was no doubt still thinking that the powerful Lord Rothschild was a useful conduit for frightening the government. For good measure, Pincher exposed the fact that Turnbull had spoken to him.

With the trial dragging to a close someone in the Labour leadership sounded the retreat. On 15 December *The Times* carried an obviously inspired story which began: 'Labour's front bench will not be making a big effort to pursue further allegations that MI5 plotted to oust the Prime Minister Mr Harold Wilson in 1974.' Whether or not the leadership can hold the troops back after Mr Justice Powell's judgment may be another question.

The Zircon spy satellite affair in early 1987 showed that Kinnock was prepared to form up behind the national security banner. The

183

Special Branch were sent out to raid a BBC studio looking for the tapes of a show, scripted by Duncan Campbell, which among other things was going to tell people that the UK was going to have its own spy satellite, like big brother. To anyone who has read any of the mountain of American literature on spy satellites or even *The Ties That Bind,* the affair is ludicrously out of all proportion, but it was the ritual invocation of national security again. Listening to Mrs Thatcher speak in the Commons on both the MI5 trial and Zircon, a listener has to come to the view that, while some of those who beat the drum in December might well have been cynical, the Prime Minister believes in a Platonic ideal of national security, an ideal that has never been violated by critical thought. This passion for national security chimes in with the dislike that she has come to feel for Wright, reciprocating his. Again the message comes from the background briefers who harp on how strongly she feels about Wright making money from his memoirs.

This brandishing of national security as an untouchable means that, although the Commons can be told of internal, unspecified reforms at MI5, there can be no scrutiny like the Royal Commissions in Australia and Canada. The briskness with which Sir Robert rejected in Sydney the idea of such an inquiry speaks for itself. The underlying theme of the whole Wright trial and the legal arguments is the question of what are the limits and under what directions internal security services should operate. Sir Robert's easy acceptance in Sydney of the mere fact that being a communist justifies having your telephone tapped and his casual attitude towards the similar tapping of civil libertarians manifested a mandarin unconcern for such a question.

The appearance of the Council for Civil Liberties as a subversive organisation is not new in the milieu of the secret world. ASIO borrowed its earlier organisation and operational procedures from MI5 and like MI5 has a close relationship with the police Special Branches. In 1978 a Supreme Court judge in South Australia, Mr Justice White, reported on his enquiry into their state's Special Branch. He found that it had kept a file on the local Council for Civil Liberties for many years and commented: 'Not everyone will agree with all the aims of the Council. Nonetheless it is absurd to treat the Council and its members as if they are security risks.' If big brother

The price of some security measures might well be too high. When peripheral security risks have been driven out by over-zealous security measures, the second state of the nation may be worse than its first.

ASIO told the South Australian Special Branch decades ago that they should keep files on the Council for Civil Liberties, it's not unreasonable to assume that ASIO learnt the lesson in the earlier days from big brother MI5. Mr Justice White's report had some wise things to say about the limitations on a security service in the monitoring of political ideas in a free society:

'The dangers to freedom of thought and political action inherent in the exercise are so grave, that any counteractivity, including collection of information, should be conducted – if at all – at the highest level of intelligence, with the most exquisite delicacy, and with constant vigilance that any 'security' benefit derived from such security activity is not achieved at the expense of such freedoms. The price of some security measures might well be too high. When peripheral security risks have been driven out by over-zealous security measures, the second state of the nation may be worse than its first.'

The second state of the nation may be worse than the first — advice any security service or government should heed. Hollis' comments to Arthur Martin about a Gestapo recognised the dangers of the abuse of power by security services. Unhappily Peter Wright and his colleagues don't seem to comprehend that kind of argument. An inquiry in England, like the Royal Commissions of Canada or Australia, which stimulated some genuine debate and discussion about the role of the security service could do nothing but good. Such an inquiry should open the way for accountability and oversight to and by parliament. Dr Christopher Andrew, another one of those brushed aside by Sir Robert in Sydney, wrote towards the end of the trial: 'Over the last decade the United States, Canada, West Germany and most of our NATO allies (as well as several non-NATO powers such as Israel) have set up intelligence committees which meet in secret.' Dr Andrew could have added Australia, which with bi-partisan support passed legislation while the trial was going on to set up an oversight committee. Australia has also recently redefined subversion to make it clear that ASIO should only be

185

involved if there is violence or a reasonable prospect of violence from any political ideology. As well an outside Inspector General has been established to check ASIO periodically.

After Peter Wright's book has been published, wherever and whenever that may be, after the last of the point-scoring on national security has petered out, the issues of principle for England on how a security service should operate in a free society and what checks and balances can work will remain. If such questions were addressed, then some good may have come from the old spy's revenge. The fifteen questions wove a web that would be almost impossible for the British government to escape. The defendants had gone in as the Lilliputians against Gulliver, but Turnbull had stitched up the case very well. The London back room boys, with all the power and resources of the United Kingdom government hoped for victory, perhaps they had probably forgotten that on Swift's geography Lilliput was located somewhere in South Australia.

Mr Justice Powell was rostered as duty Judge for the January part of the legal vacation, which did nothing to speed up production of his verdict. As far as the court was concerned, *Attorney General of the UK vs Heinemann and Another* was just another case on the list. So on the first day of the new term in February the Judge was back on the bench. His case was on that borderline of the law which calls for the wisdom of Solomon, what to do when doctors want to give a blood transfusion to a baby who is the child of Jehovah's Witness parents whose religion forbids such transfusions. (The baby was made a ward of the state.) The Judge plugged on with his judgment and by mid-February the final date of 13 March was set.

On that morning Court 8-D was more crowded than at any time during the trial, indeed more crowded than it is ever likely to be again before the building is demolished, with edgy deadline-conscious journalists from the Australian media, now more aware of the case than three months ago, as well as the Fleet Street contingent who had returned en masse, crammed into any seat and sitting on the floor and standing against the walls. A few of the courtroom regulars managed to get in, but most of them were too late and ended up outside. Copies of the judgment were stacked in piles around the Judge's Associate, Patricia Voight, who had fielded the phone calls of an over-anxious press for months. Neither Sir

Robert Armstrong nor the London legal team returned. The United Kingdom High Commissioner, Sir Francis Leehy, came up from Melbourne and Theo Simos was back at the bar table. Peter Wright was in hospital in Hobart with stress and diabetic complications, which led to some false reports of a heart attack. Malcolm Turnbull was there, not particularly cocky. Indeed something of the personal commitment he had got himself into showed up in the worried comments he had been making the previous week about what a loss would do to Peter Wright.

Mr Justice Powell came through the door on time, made some preliminary remarks to the effect that he wouldn't read the judgment because of its length and for the same reason the media would have to pay $13 for a copy, although to smooth things this was left to their honour to pay up later, a rare tribute to journalistic honesty. That done, the Judge proceeded to announce his formal orders. By the sixth word of the first order, it was over for the British government: '1. Order that the proceedings be dismissed.' As usual, another order gave the British a stay for twenty-eight days to file appeal and fight again. Costs were awarded to the defendants and for good measure, as is common in equity cases, the defendant could apply to a court officer, the Master in Equity, for damages suffered by reason of the delay. Then the Judge and the court were on their feet, everyone bowed, he retired and as far as the Equity Division of the Supreme Court of New South Wales was concerned that was an end to the case.

The judgment ran to 279 pages of text, with seven pages of appendices, about 85,000 words. It was a sober and restrained document without the humour and asides with which the Judge had enlivened the hearing. It was a judgment written for posterity, legal posterity and any appeal courts. Mr Justice Powell quoted from some eighty-four cases. Some of them were distinctly exotic. The problems of establishing a contractual public service relationship in Ceylon needed some Privy Council references on the status of Roman-Dutch law. The only jokiness found anywhere came when the Judge ventured into literary criticism of the manuscript. When Wright wrote of technical matters it was in layman's language, which could hardly help hostile technicians, however when he came to non-technical matters, like counter-espionage operations he did so, as Mr Justice Powell observed, 'in a style which seems more appropriate to the *Boys Own Paper* or *Biggles Flying Omnibus* rather than to an arid scholarly work'. The judgment contained an extended narrative repeating much of the circumstances of Wright's working life with MI5 as well as the mole controversies over the years. The greyness of the text was broken up with reproductions of various exhibits. Chapman Pincher's synopsis of *Their Trade is Treachery*, done in December 1980, was reproduced and any reader could scrutinise the quirks of the typewriter keys to check on Peter Wright's evidence. They could also read in full Jonathan Aitken's letter to Mrs Thatcher, as well as a range of press cuttings.

The Judge's comments on the personalities involved were studied and formal, it was the UK government that got the most severe criticism and the Judge indicated again and again that he was general with his criticism because he did not know who had actually made the decisions in Britain. As to Sir Robert Armstrong, the Judge was a third of the way through before he posed the question of 'the view I have formed of the acceptability, or otherwise, of Sir Robert Armstrong as a witness' and answered it 'much of his evidence on matters of importance must be treated with considerable reserve'.

He went on to point to two other matters about Sir Robert:

'The first of such matters is that it is, in my view, clear that, as to many of the matters as to which Sir Robert Armstrong gave evidence, he has no personal knowledge whatsoever, but is reliant upon information conveyed to him – the possibility, therefore, that any evidence which he has given on such evidence is, at least, likely to be affected by error is sufficiently demonstrated by the retraction which he was obliged to make in respect of the evidence which he first gave as to the failure of the British Government to take proceedings in respect of the pending publication of *Their Trade is Treachery*.'

The second point made by the Judge about Sir Robert's evidence was that although he might have been the Prime Minister's principal adviser on security and intelligence matters he had,

'no personal knowledge or expertise in matters of security or intelligence, and, in particular, as to operational matters in those areas, and, second, that any information he might give, or opinions which he might offer, is, or are, derived from others.'

The judgment outlined at length the relationship between Wright, Lord Rothschild and Pincher in late 1980 with a comment that 'while in the circumstances which existed at the time Lord Rothschild's letter to Mr Wright, although a little out of the ordinary, may attract no real comment, there is, to say the least, much about the events which followed it, which I find decidedly curious'. But the Judge rejected Turnbull's submission that the failure of the British government to stop the publication of *Their Trade is Treachery* was part of a conspiracy to let the story of Sir Roger Hollis come out into the open through the pen of a 'safely conservative' journalist, and so he implicitly also rejected Wright's belief that he had been involved in a 'deniable operation'. Mr Justice Powell did say that because the explanations offered by the British government were unsatisfactory it was perhaps tempting to accept the Turnbull conspiracy thesis, but he would not do so.

Still, it was *Their Trade is Treachery* primarily that brought the English case tumbling down. All the hours of cross-examination that Turnbull put in on the book paid off handsomely. (Also there was reason for gratitude to those moles in Whitehall who had passed on information to help Wright.) Given the publication of the allegation that Sir Roger Hollis was a spy would damage the security service, Mr Justice Powell said that he could 'but describe it as incredible' that nothing was done to stop publication. *Their Trade is Treachery* was the foundation, but as well the Judge listed other books of Pincher's and West's, together with the Wright and Massitter TV programmes and a range of magazine and newspaper articles. On *Conspiracy of Silence*, published during the trial, the Judge said that the British government's passivity in confining itself merely to reminding certain former officers who had been quoted of their obligations, appeared 'to make a mockery of what Sir Robert Armstrong has asserted' to be government policy. Summing up the argument that UK policy required the services to seem to be leakproof, Mr Justice Powell was tough:

'Over the last five years, at least, former officers, including at least one former Director-General, Sir Dick Goldsmith White, have felt free to disclose confidential information received by them while in the Service, and have done so without any action being taken against them, and, further, far from there appearing to be, even if not being, "leakproof", it must have been apparent to anyone who had cause to consider the matter, that, as a result of the acquiescence, or inaction, of the British Government, the Service has, for years, leaked like a sieve.'

The government, by its inaction, had surrendered its claim to confidentiality so it could not be said that it would suffer any detriment by the publication of Wright's book. There was no consistent policy, despite Sir Robert's claims. The Judge dealt briskly with the insider/outsider distinction on which Simos had lavished so much attention. Against what had been allowed to be published in so many places, the Judge said that the notion that republication at the hands of an insider could cause detriment was 'decidedly hollow'. Another decisive argument against detriment was that the material in the manuscript was not likely to hurt the United Kingdom because it was so old, in most cases twenty years old. The Judge referred to the CIA practice of providing clearances for old material. Running as a thread through the discussion of detriment and national security were the Australian High Court cases on the limits of the definition of national security and right of courts to scrutinise submissions from governments.

Once he had reached the conclusion of 'no detriment', the Judge said that it was strictly unnecessary to deal with the other arguments from the defence and the plaintiff although he would make some brief comments. On public interest the Judge signalled that he might have taken a rather restrictive view. While impropriety by an organisation which had relations with ASIO and ASIS arguably should be exposed, Mr Justice Powell added the rider: 'I can see no reason, why, if they had still been confidential, the Australian public interest would require the general operations of the Service to be exposed.'

The Australian bureaucrat, Michael Codd, who had been dealt with so briskly in the box was dismissed with the description of his evidence as 'a rather tortuous process of reasoning'. On Whitlam's evidence the Judge summarised his arguments without comment and when it came to Schaap and his testimony on CIA practice Mr Justice Powell described his testimony as 'detailed, and abundantly supportive'. Peter Wright's affidavit was briefly described and the

Judge chose not to make any comment on the author as a witness. While restrained on named individuals, the Judge delivered a very strong rebuke to the Whitehall backseat drivers, starting from the way in which they had mounted their belated public interest immunity argument, which revealed:

'. . . yet further instances of the British government's apparent unwillingness to abide by the decision of the Court, and yet another instance of the British government's apparent wish perpetually to change its ground in search of some obscure tactical advantage which only it could perceive. Lest it be thought that this comment is overly critical of the British government, I would but say that its apparent unwillingness to abide by the Judgment of the Court, and its constant changes of ground, do not reflect the type of attitude, or the approach to the conduct of proceedings, which one is accustomed to meet, and, indeed one has come to expect, from governments and governmental authorities which have been, or are, litigants in this Court."

The actual organisation MI5 largely escaped criticism. What part its members had played in the decision the Judge so harshly criticised was unknown. However earlier on in the narrative the Judge did allow himself to comment on the fact that the form that Wright had signed on the Official Secrets Act when he joined MI5 in 1955 was itself classified:

'(I pause, here, to observe that the fact that it seems to have been thought necessary officially to classify as "Confidential" what is clearly a pro-forma document in common use and which, in any event, does little more than reproduce some of the provisions of a public Act of the Parliament of the United Kingdom, seems symptomatic of that obsession for secrecy – some might call it paranoia – which appears to inflict (*sic*) members of the bureaucracy wherever they might be found throughout the world.)'

Lastly, hidden away in the judgment was a paragraph which would have mightily annoyed Whitehall and the government itself. Although rumours had been rife and there had been claims in the House of Commons that the manuscript contained allegations of a conspiracy by MI5 officers against Harold Wilson in 1974, because the direct reporting of contents of the book was effectively banned in the United Kingdom by injunctions there had been no authoritative confirmation.

References to the book's material on the plot had been made in Wright's statement to the court early in December, but by agreement they were not read in open court.

However Mr Justice Powell cited the relevant paragraph dealing with Wright's time as personal assistant to Sir Michael Hanley, the Director-General of MI5. 'In my book, I deal only very superficially with my period as Hanley's consultant as many of these matters may still be current. The only incidents with which I deal in any detail are, firstly, the plot to destabilise the Wilson government, and secondly Lord Trend's inquiry . . .' This paragraph made it very difficult for the government to evade the question of just what did happen in MI5 in 1974. Wright's statement had him claiming to deal 'in detail' with the plot; in my opinion it is hardly possible to have 'detail' about something that is just talk.

The UK government had twenty-eight days in which to lodge an appeal, however it could not appeal on questions of fact, but only on the questions of law in the Judge's verdict or his conduct of the case. This meant that there would be no canvassing of details again, no witnesses, just legal argument. An appeal to the first recourse, the Appeals Court of New South Wales, could perhaps come up in May with a judgment in June, then if a second recourse was needed by either side they could come before the High Court in perhaps July/August, with a final verdict a month later. Judicial timetables are notoriously open to dislocation, in any case the High Court not uncommonly announces a decision at the conclusion of the hearing and publishes its reasons later. Heinemann would need a month to get the book out and into the shops, so Australia might see *Spycatcher* in time for the Christmas market. However the English injunction would still hold unless lifted, so *Spycatcher* would in England achieve the status of the 'dirty book from Paris' of yesteryear, a prohibited import under the counter, alongside titles like the *History of Flagellation* and *Spanking of Mistresses*. That Friday, the day of judgment in Sydney, the judge retired for lunch at the Intercontinental Hotel, the Fleet Street morning people scattered in a frenzy with less than an hour to get their stories through to London, Malcolm Turnbull held an impromptu press conference, Lucy Turnbull was again written up as the daughter of an Establishment QC. and, there being a lull in the news about the ambitions of Joh Bjelke Petersen to become prime minister, the trial got onto the Australian front pages.

In Hobart in a room on the fifth floor of St John of God Hospital the old man got the news. His wife and the nurses kept most callers to the sick man at bay. That afternoon one journalist got through and after the politenesses about health asked the question, What did he think of the verdict? Peter Wright laughed and laughed and laughed.

FOR THE BEST IN PAPERBACKS, LOOK FOR THE

In every corner of the world, on every subject under the sun, Penguins represent quality and variety – the very best in publishing today.

For complete information about books available from Penguin and how to order them, write to us at the appropriate address below. Please note that for copyright reasons the selection of books varies from country to country.

In the United Kingdom: For a complete list of books available from Penguin in the U.K., please write to *Dept EP, Penguin Books Ltd, Harmondsworth, Middlesex, UB7 0DA*

In the United States: For a complete list of books available from Penguin in the U.S., please write to *Dept BA, Viking Penguin, 299 Murray Hill Parkway, East Rutherford, New Jersey 07073*

In Canada: For a complete list of books available from Penguin in Canada, please write to *Penguin Books Canada Limited, 2801 John Street, Markham, Ontario L3R 1B4*

In Australia: For a complete list of books available from Penguin in Australia, please write to the *Marketing Department, Penguin Books Australia Ltd, P.O. Box 257, Ringwood, Victoria 3134*

In New Zealand: For a complete list of books available from Penguin in New Zealand, please write to the *Marketing Department, Penguin Books (N.Z.) Ltd, Private Bag, Takapuna, Auckland 9*

In India: For a complete list of books available from Penguin in India, please write to *Penguin Overseas Ltd, 706 Eros Apartments, 56 Nehru Place, New Delhi 110019*

FOR THE BEST IN PAPERBACKS, LOOK FOR THE

A CHOICE OF PENGUINS

Adieux: A Farewell to Sartre   Simone de Beauvoir

A devastatingly frank account of the last years of Sartre's life, and his death, by the woman who for more than half a century shared that life. 'A true labour of love, there is about it a touching sadness, a mingling of the personal with the impersonal and timeless which Sartre himself would surely have liked and understood' – *Listener*

Business Wargames   James Barrie

How did BMW overtake Mercedes? Why did Laker crash? How did McDonalds grab the hamburger market? Drawing on the tragic mistakes and brilliant victories of military history, this remarkable book draws countless fascinating parallels with case histories from industry world-wide.

Metamagical Themas   Douglas R. Hofstadter

This astonishing sequel to the best-selling, Pulitzer Prize-winning *Gödel, Escher, Bach* swarms with 'extraordinary ideas, brilliant fables, deep philosophical questions and Carrollian word play' – Martin Gardner

Into the Heart of Borneo   Redmond O'Hanlon

'Perceptive, hilarious and at the same time a serious natural-history journey into one of the last remaining unspoilt paradises' – *New Statesman*. 'Consistently exciting, often funny and erudite without ever being overwhelming' – *Punch*

A Better Class of Person   John Osborne

The playwright's autobiography, 1929–56. 'Splendidly enjoyable' – John Mortimer. 'One of the best, richest and most bitterly truthful autobiographies that I have ever read' – Melvyn Bragg

The Secrets of a Woman's Heart   Hilary Spurling

The later life of Ivy Compton-Burnett, 1920–69. 'A biographical triumph . . . elegant, stylish, witty, tender, immensely acute – dazzles and exhilarates . . . a great achievement' – Kay Dick in the *Literary Review*. 'One of the most important literary biographies of the century' – *New Statesman*

FOR THE BEST IN PAPERBACKS, LOOK FOR THE

A CHOICE OF PENGUINS

An African Winter   Preston King   With an Introduction by Richard Leakey

This powerful and impassioned book offers a unique assessment of the interlocking factors which result in the famines of Africa and argues that there *are* solutions and we *can* learn from the mistakes of the past.

Jean Rhys: Letters 1931–66
Edited by Francis Wyndham and Diana Melly

'Eloquent and invaluable . . . her life emerges, and with it a portrait of an unexpectedly indomitable figure' – Marina Warner in the *Sunday Times*

Among the Russians   Colin Thubron

One man's solitary journey by car across Russia provides an enthralling and revealing account of the habits and idiosyncrasies of a fascinating people. 'He sees things with the freshness of an innocent and the erudition of a scholar' – *Daily Telegraph*

The Amateur Naturalist   Gerald Durrell with Lee Durrell

'Delight . . . on every page . . . packed with authoritative writing, learning without pomposity . . . it represents a real bargain' – *The Times Educational Supplement*. 'What treats are in store for the average British household' – *Books and Bookmen*

The Democratic Economy   Geoff Hodgson

Today, the political arena is divided as seldom before. In this exciting and original study, Geoff Hodgson carefully examines the claims of the rival doctrines and exposes some crucial flaws.

They Went to Portugal   Rose Macaulay

An exotic and entertaining account of travellers to Portugal from the pirate-crusaders, through poets, aesthetes and ambassadors, to the new wave of romantic travellers. A wonderful mixture of literature, history and adventure, by one of our most stylish and seductive writers.

FOR THE BEST IN PAPERBACKS, LOOK FOR THE

A CHOICE OF PENGUINS

The Book Quiz Book   Joseph Connolly

Who was literature's performing flea . . .? Who wrote 'Live Now, Pay Later . . .'? Keats and Cartland, Balzac and Braine, Coleridge conundrums, Eliot enigmas, Tolstoy teasers . . . all in this brilliant quiz book. You will be on the shelf without it . . .

Voyage through the Antarctic   Richard Adams and Ronald Lockley

Here is the true, authentic Antarctic of today, brought vividly to life by Richard Adams, author of *Watership Down*, and Ronald Lockley, the world-famous naturalist. 'A good adventure story, with a lot of information and a deal of enthusiasm for Antarctica and its animals' – *Nature*

Getting to Know the General   Graham Greene

'In August 1981 my bag was packed for my fifth visit to Panama when the news came to me over the telephone of the death of General Omar Torrijos Herrera, my friend and host . . .' 'Vigorous, deeply felt, at times funny, and for Greene surprisingly frank' – *Sunday Times*

Television Today and Tomorrow: Wall to Wall Dallas?
Christopher Dunkley

Virtually every British home has a television, nearly half now have two sets or more, and we are promised that before the end of the century there will be a vast expansion of television delivered via cable and satellite. How did television come to be so central to our lives? Is British television really the best in the world, as politicians like to assert?

Arabian Sands   Wilfred Thesiger

'In the tradition of Burton, Doughty, Lawrence, Philby and Thomas, it is, very likely, the book about Arabia to end all books about Arabia' – *Daily Telegraph*

When the Wind Blows   Raymond Briggs

'A visual parable against nuclear war: all the more chilling for being in the form of a strip cartoon' – *Sunday Times*. 'The most eloquent anti-Bomb statement you are likely to read' – *Daily Mail*

FOR THE BEST IN PAPERBACKS, LOOK FOR THE 🐧

A CHOICE OF PENGUINS AND PELICANS

The Second World War (6 volumes)   Winston S. Churchill

The definitive history of the cataclysm which swept the world for the second time in thirty years.

1917: The Russian Revolutions and the Origins of Present-Day Communism
Leonard Schapiro

A superb narrative history of one of the greatest episodes in modern history by one of our greatest historians.

Imperial Spain 1496–1716   J. H. Elliot

A brilliant modern study of the sudden rise of a barren and isolated country to be the greatest power on earth, and of its equally sudden decline. 'Outstandingly good' – *Daily Telegraph*

Joan of Arc: The Image of Female Heroism   Marina Warner

'A profound book, about human history in general and the place of women in it' – Christopher Hill

Man and the Natural World: Changing Attitudes in England 1500–1800
Keith Thomas

'A delight to read and a pleasure to own' – Auberon Waugh in the *Sunday Telegraph*

The Making of the English Working Class   E. P. Thompson

Probably the most imaginative – and the most famous – post-war work of English social history.

FOR THE BEST IN PAPERBACKS, LOOK FOR THE

A CHOICE OF PENGUINS AND PELICANS

The French Revolution   Christopher Hibbert

'One of the best accounts of the Revolution that I know . . . Mr Hibbert is outstanding' – J. H. Plumb in the *Sunday Telegraph*

The Germans   Gordon A. Craig

An intimate study of a complex and fascinating nation by 'one of the ablest and most distinguished American historians of modern Germany' – Hugh Trevor-Roper

Ireland: A Positive Proposal   Kevin Boyle and Tom Hadden

A timely and realistic book on Northern Ireland which explains the historical context – and offers a practical and coherent set of proposals which could actually work.

A History of Venice   John Julius Norwich

'Lord Norwich has loved and understood Venice as well as any other Englishman has ever done' – Peter Levi in the *Sunday Times*

Montaillou: Cathars and Catholics in a French Village 1294–1324
Emmanuel Le Roy Ladurie

'A classic adventure in eavesdropping across time' – Michael Ratcliffe in *The Times*

Star Wars   E. P. Thompson and others

Is Star Wars a serious defence strategy or just a science fiction fantasy? This major book sets out all the arguments and makes an unanswerable case *against* Star Wars.

FOR THE BEST IN PAPERBACKS, LOOK FOR THE 🐧

A CHOICE OF PENGUINS AND PELICANS

The Apartheid Handbook   Roger Omond

This book provides the essential hard information about how apartheid actually works from day to day and fills in the details behind the headlines.

The World Turned Upside Down   Christopher Hill

This classic study of radical ideas during the English Revolution 'will stand as a notable monument to . . . one of the finest historians of the present age' – *The Times Literary Supplement*

Islam in the World   Malise Ruthven

'His exposition of "the Qurenic world view" is the most convincing, and the most appealing, that I have read' – Edward Mortimer in *The Times*

The Knight, the Lady and the Priest   Georges Duby

'A very fine book' (Philippe Aries) that traces back to its medieval origin one of our most important institutions, modern marriage.

A Social History of England   New Edition   Asa Briggs

'A treasure house of scholarly knowledge . . . beautifully written and full of the author's love of his country, its people and its landscape' – John Keegan in the *Sunday Times*, Books of the Year

The Second World War   A. J. P. Taylor

A brilliant and detailed illustrated history, enlivened by all Professor Taylor's customary iconoclasm and wit.